LEADERSHIP SKILLS FOR EVERY MANAGER

LEADERSHIP SKILLS

SKILLS

FOR EVERY

MANAGER

New Techniques to Improve
Organisational Effectiveness

JIM CLEMMER & ART McNEIL

PIATKUS

This edition first published in
Great Britain in 1990 by
Judy Piatkus (Publishers) Ltd of
5 Windmill Street, London W1

First paperback edition published 1991

First published in Canada as *The V.I.P. Strategy*

British Library Cataloguing in Publication Data

Clemmer, Jim
  Leadership skills for every manager.
  1. Management.   Leadership
  I. Title   II. McNeil, Art
  658.4'092

  ISBN 0–86188–963–0
      0–7499–1024–0 (PB)

Printed and bound in Great Britain by
Mackays of Chatham PLC, Chatham, Kent

Contents

Acknowledgements

"If I have been able to see further than others, it is because I have stood on the shoulders of giants."

— Sir Isaac Newton

Achieve Clients: Your eagerness to find ever better ways to develop leadership skills has been a constant source of inspiration and instruction to us. Your openness to share your experiences and explore new approaches with Achieve and other Clients has made us all stronger leaders.

Fellow Achievers: We hope your patience and understanding in this "temporary project" (2½ years wasn't really *that* long was it?) will be rewarded in this collection of our experiences and learnings. We thank every Achiever for their contributions, especially those who typed, proofed, evaluated and/or encouraged us through the countless (it just seemed endless) manuscript revisions.

Achieve Associates: We appreciate your ideas and suggestions, as well as consulting experiences. Special thanks to Zenger-Miller, Inc. You had the faith to join with us, the patience to see us through those darker "investment years" and the belief in our vision of the future. We especially appreciate the outstanding leadership development programs and their constant revisions that allow us to stay with you on the leading edge of performance improvement.

Thank you **Robert Appel** for your creativity and "wordsmithing." You skillfully sifted out the nuggets and kept us on track.

And thank you especially, **Heather Clemmer and Judy McNeil**, our personal performance coaches. Your family leadership is a source of inspiration, strength and balance.

Jim Clemmer
Art McNeil

INTRODUCTION

In the fall of 1987, as we were completing this book, we knew something was afoot. By the time the original edition was published in the spring of 1988, the murmurs had become a dull roar. During the next 6 to 12 months, a full-blown, noisy revolution was under way.

The issue is service quality, which has become critical to the future of both public and private sector organizations. Customers, taxpayers, consumers, and patients are fed up with shoddy service and aren't taking it anymore.

The service quality revolution began with all of us who consume products, buy services, and pay taxes. Building on our brewing discontent, print and broadcast media have further incited the revolt. A recent *Time* magazine cover article was entitled, "Puleeze! Will Somebody Help Me!" A major newspaper ran a feature article typical of many appearing across North America. Loaded with all too common examples of bad service, it was headlined, "Disappearance of Service with a Smile." Consumer reporting, a growing media specialty, has turned more attention to after-sales service, bureaucratic entanglements, and services that don't.

Our best managers have always considered service quality to be a critical success factor. Others are just awakening to the revolution. A recent Gallop Poll of 615 CEOs shows that more than 50 percent consider service quality to be the single most important issue their organizations face. Many executives are now feeling the heat from disgruntled customers directly. Others are being burned by foreign and domestic competitors using service quality as a powerful competitive weapon. Aggressive world-class companies are gaining a strategic edge by improving customer service. American Express is typical of this emerging group. Their CEO, James D. Robinson, III says, "Customer service is our patent protection. Our goal simply stated is to be the best in the service industry."

The service quality revolution can be either an exciting opportunity or a serious threat—that's up to you and your management team. You can take it or leave it, but it won't leave you alone.

There are payoffs and penalties from the rapid shifts in service quality levels and expectations. If your organization takes effective action to improve its service quality, the payoffs are substantial. If you fail to act, the penalties will be severe.

For companies looking to improve profitability and growth, service quality improvement provides an unparalleled, almost unbelievable, multiplier effect. Executives who lose sleep over a couple of market share points and sweat blood to produce a few percent more profit are often astounded by the lucrative payoffs of improved service quality. According to *Fortune* magazine, "In a gargantuan historical study, the Strategic Planning Institute (affiliated with Harvard University) has analyzed the performance of some 2,600 businesses over 15 years. Awkwardly named The Profit Impact of Market Strategy, or PIMS, this research shows that financial performance is tied directly to the perceived quality of a company's goods and services. By almost any measure—market share, return on investment, asset turnover—businesses that offer higher quality come out on top. Among the most powerful tools for shaping perceptions of overall quality, the PIMS study finds, is customer service." In fact, the PIMS study discovered that high-service companies have a return on sales *twelve times greater* than low-service companies.

There are at least three reasons why failing to substantially drive up your organization's service quality levels will cripple and quite possibly kill you. First, by not grabbing market share and dominating your industry through high service quality, you are not capitalizing on the single greatest source of revenue growth available today.

Second, you will miss out on the substantial cost savings and efficiencies that high service quality carries with it. Contrary to most management notions, high-quality producers are usually low-cost producers as well. That's because their Cost of Quality (COQ) is much lower than most. Whether in the factory, office, or field, high service quality organizations do it right the first time, and consistently out-perform their lesser competitors. And they take those savings and revenue gains straight to the bottom line.

Third, by failing to improve service quality, you have decided to erode your customer base. It's only a matter of time until your customers find someone else who coddles them better than you do. As you read this, your customers are talking about you. The

Washington-based firm, Technical Assistance Research Program (TARP) found that your unhappy customers are saying unflattering things about your organization to anywhere from eight to twenty of their friends and associates. Worse yet, most of these disgruntled rumormongers are talking behind your back. TARP found that up to 90 percent of your unhappy customers don't complain to you. They simply disappear—and then get even. TARP also found that "word-of-mouth" is the dominant buying influence today, despite all your expensive marketing and sales efforts. They conclude that it costs most companies *five times* more to get new customers than to delight and retain their existing ones. An insurance Client of ours found their ratio is seven to one.

But what of "captive" customers who are served by public institutions, monopolies (such as many utilities) or internal staff support groups? "Captive" internal customers can quit in a variety of ways. They might go to outside suppliers, do the job themselves, or bring in consultants. Their dissatisfaction can also be manifested through chronic conflicts, disagreements, and apathy or disdain with their internal supplier(s).

The public sector is especially vulnerable today. Exploding technologies, unpredictable economic changes, and the "global village" heralded by falling national barriers and world-class competition is causing wrenching change. At the same time, the public's insatiable demand for more programs and services continues to spiral upward. This clashes squarely with skyrocketing deficits and a strong sense that taxes have reached their upper limits. The situation is compounded even further by slipping pride and morale inside most public sector organizations. Employees' work ethic is shifting. Among other things, they feel constrained and unappreciated. As a result, many public servants are highly frustrated and uncommitted to their jobs.

Service quality improvement is providing a low-risk, sure way out of this public sector quagmire. Effective service quality improvement reduces operating costs. The improved levels of service, at less cost, greatly enhances public image and support. The process creates a context for enthusiasm and teamwork that employees, politicians, and management can support. Public sector organizations who improve service quality have higher levels of morale and quality of work life. They also can do more with less.

Since writing this book, The Achieve Group has

developed an improvement process for organizations called the Service Quality System, which incorporates many of the leadership elements, skills, and development steps you will find outlined in this book.

In Chapter One we describe the changes buffeting every organization today. These changes caused organizations to look first at improving productivity. In the early eighties, North America began to realize that the rest of the industrialized world, especially Japan, was moving ahead on more than the productivity formula of low cost and high output. And so, product quality became the rallying cry for many beleaguered manufacturing companies. A plethora of books (*Quality Is Free, In Search of Excellence*, etc.) and magazine articles lead the charge. The resulting gains in product quality and organizational results have been impressive.

The third stage of our improvement evolution has clearly become service quality. And to stay in the game on all three fronts (productivity, product quality and service), your organization needs a fourth renewal factor woven throughout this book—innovation.

Even more than productivity and product quality, service quality improvement is a people issue. That brings it squarely into the leadership arena. To us, leadership means a set of actions for dealing with people-related issues.

Achieve recently developed a process that helps frontline service teams to develop internal and external customer service strategies. We call it the Enhanced Service Process™ (ESP) because of a simple model that defines what "service" means. (See diagram)

Enhanced service quality means frontline employees are going above and beyond the call of duty and their customers' expectations. That only happens voluntarily. You can't manage, legislate, mechanize, or command your organization into the "third ring." You can only lead your people there. As we describe in Chapter Two, that means you have to capture their hearts as well as their hands and heads. You must have their emotional commitment and energy.

Creating corporate energy and commitment begins with a compelling vision and set of values. Frontline employees will voluntarily provide enhanced service when they are drawn to, and excited by, the direction the organization is headed. A strong

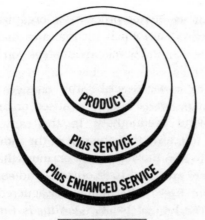

PRODUCT
Customer Appeal
based on meeting requirements

PRODUCT Plus SERVICE
Customer Satisfaction
based on meeting expectations

PRODUCT Plus ENHANCED SERVICE
Customer Delight
based on exceeding expectations

sense of purpose provides a motivating context that aligns day-to-day behavior for exceptional performance. This is reinforced by clear core values, which are central to improving productivity, quality, and service.

Developing a nurturing environment that fosters enhanced service quality requires high people skills throughout the organization. These leadership skills form the foundation for productivity, quality, or service improvement efforts. At the heart of this book are the four sets of leadership skills that have helped hundreds of organizations achieve exceptional performance: Personal, Coaching, Team, and Cultural leadership. Our experience shows that when these skills are weak, efforts to improve service quality will slowly die.

Now here's the rub: knowing what to do and doing it are two very different things. Clearly the best way to get rich is to make a lot of money; the surest way to cure insomnia is to get a lot of sleep; or the way to reduce weight is to exercise more and eat less. While awareness, understanding, knowledge, and even inspiration are critical to improving performance, these alone won't do it. It's of little use to aim high if your gun isn't loaded.

Many managers are aware of the need for new approaches. They understand what high performance looks like. They know they must connect the hands, heads, and hearts of people in their organizations. Astute managers know that leadership skills need improvement throughout the organization. They know *what* needs to be done but struggle with *how*. How do they load the gun?

The root of the improvement problem is execution. Organizations struggling to redesign themselves in the image of today's highest performers often fall into the "implementation-assumptions trap": they assume that if they simply install new structures, policies, slogans, technology, management systems, products/services, or improvement programs (such as quality teams, statistical process control, or "just-in-time") they will improve performance. Often the implementation assumption is further compounded by confusing education with training, inspiration with habits, intentions with behavior, knowledge with skills, and project results with cultural change.

Our last chapters deal with this leadership content (what) *vs.* process (how) dilemma. Chapter Twelve outlines the critical steps to implementing leadership skill development programs that have proven successful numerous times. Whether building leadership skills for productivity, quality, or service improvement, the approaches outlined are vital for improving personal and organizational performance. But like any plan, it's only as good as your action.

May you be one of the service quality revolution's victors rather than a victim.

Jim Clemmer
Art McNeil

CHAPTER ONE

World of Change, World of Challenge

"All is flux, nothing stays still."

—Heraclitus (540–480 BC)

As we move through the electronic age—the "global village" as Marshall McLuhan called it—the effects of change become dramatically different, more potent, and, if not handled correctly, potentially more devastating than ever before.

An unusual virus that paralyzes the immune system crops up in Africa, and within months its impact is felt around the globe. A smokestack on the east coast of America emits contaminants into the air, and in central Canada, entire lakes turn acidic and fish die. A technician in an obscure Russian city slips up for just a moment and triggers a nuclear episode that will affect our global food chain for generations to come.

Change cannot be ignored. And it cannot be avoided.

Any way you slice it, "the future arrives sooner than it used to." Futurist John Naisbitt, in his bestseller *Megatrends*, says that society is moving in a totally new direction. The Industrial Age is giving way to the Information Age in which knowledge is a primary commodity. Technology is here to stay, but it now has to share the spotlight with something Naisbitt calls "high touch"—a more human dimension of the inhuman world of "high-tech." (Look at the drive toward "user-friendly" software in the computer industry, and at how new assembly technologies are allowing producers to develop goods more personalized —friendlier—to individual markets.)

5

The Times, They Are A-Changin'

Time magazine's 1983 man of the year was a computer. A senior executive at a major telecommunication-equipment manufacturer begins his presentation of the "factory of the future" with a dark slide—the lights are off because the factory contains only robots. AT&T believe that information is now more important than gold—and they offer a high-security underground vault to store it! More than 50 percent of all the published professional research journals have emerged in the last fifteen years. A home computer purchased for just a few hundred dollars today will process more information in less time than a multimillion-dollar mainframe of just fifteen years ago. More than 90 percent of the greatest scientists who ever lived are alive now. And General Electric has speculated that a newly recruited professional engineer's knowledge will be largely obsolete within five years.

"Look abroad through Nature's range,
Nature's mighty law is change."

—Robert Burns

BOOMERS ON PARADE

The baby boomers are here, and they are a force to be reckoned with. Fully 48 percent of the workforce in North America was born between 1946 and 1964. The "senior boomers" (those now in their mid-thirties) will soon be running our companies and ultimately our countries.

Baby-boomers' attitudes toward the work ethic and so-called quality of life veer strongly from the traditional. Boomers tend to spurn discipline for permissiveness, reject authority figures, insist on immediate gratification, and seek participation in decision making. They also shy away from promotions they feel will disrupt family life or leisure time. A 1957 AT&T study found that 50 percent of middle managers wanted promotions. Today the number is less than a third. A 1980 study asked the question, "Are work and pleasure the same?" In the fifty to sixty age group, one in five said yes. In the under forty group, one in ten said yes.

6

There can be no doubt: the boomers are a force to be reckoned with. They will comprise over half the electorate by 1988. Some 63 percent of entrepreneurs are under age forty-five. Their political affiliations are loose, almost non-existent. They espouse maximal liberties and minimal government control. They are more tolerant of non-conformity and believe in equal opportunity. Generally, they are less receptive to the idea of "top-down" command flow.

Do People Still Want to Work?

Researcher Daniel Yankelovich found in a 1983 survey of 845 American jobholders that 52 percent adhered strongly to the work ethic: "I have an inner need to do the very best job possible, regardless of pay." Studies by the Public Agenda Foundation show that workers often give more to their jobs than their bosses expect of them and yet are giving less to the job than they could. The U.S. Chamber of Commerce noted that nearly nine out of ten workers said it is personally important to them to work hard and do their best. Three out of four workers in a Connecticut Mutual Life Insurance Company study said they frequently feel a sense of dedication to their work. And the last word on the subject probably goes to Perry Pascarella, Executive Editor of *Industry Week*, who blames poor work performance on the "extreme mismatch" between what people want from work and what they get from it.

"This new attitude towards effort and work as an aim in itself may be assumed to be the most important psychological change which has happened to man since the end of the Middle Ages."

—Erich Fromm

The boomers are not a curse; quite the contrary, they are a resource waiting to be cultivated, a harvest of human potential waiting to be picked. But before this can be accomplished, a new look has to be taken at what the boomers are asking for—and how to make them believe that they are getting it. The consequences of ignoring their demands can be severe for management. (Recently, after a corporate acquisition, the Kraft company offered promotions and transfers to California to 350 employees. More than two-thirds declined.)

Popular futurist (*Future Shock*, *The Third Wave*) Alvin Toffler, like the boomers, is a great believer in the worth of human capital. "The long-term employee's claim to retraining ought to be treated as the legal equivalent of a supplier's claim for payment of a debt," he states. "I find it repulsive that the president of a failing company demands wage cuts from the union but increases his own salary . . . . For every dollar we put into new machines, several dollars will have to be invested in human capital, in training."

WITH THE "NEW" WORKER—A NEW KIND OF WORK

In the late fifties, for the first time, white-collar workers began to outnumber blue-collar workers—and work was never the same again.

Indeed, by the year two thousand, traditional manual blue-collar workers could be only a tiny minority of the workforce. They may experience the same plight as has befallen the farmer: less than forty years ago, between one-quarter and one-third of the population of the developed countries (Britain being the exception) were still on the farm. Today, in no major nation except the U.S.S.R. is the farming population greater than 10 percent of the whole —and the percentage is shrinking rapidly (to less than 4 percent in the U.S. currently).

We have moved to an employee society. Eighty to 90 percent of national income is paid out as wages and salaries in developed countries. Management may not yet understand it, but employees are becoming the main owners and the decisive source of capital. (Some 25 percent of all publicly traded stock is estimated to be in the hands of organized labor. Could it be that the "bosses" labor wails so bitterly about will shortly turn out to be themselves?)

Many high-performing organizations now farm out routine tasks to computers and instead cultivate the non-routine aspects of their employees' work. Researcher and author Charles Garfield suggests that, if "agriculture" is the cultivation of land, and "aquaculture" the cultivation of the sea, then "cogniculture" applies to this new kind of mental farming. Whatever name you tag on to this new phenomenon, it seems to be here to stay.

"He that will not apply new remedies must expect new evils."

—Francis Bacon

Since this is considered to be the new Information Age, it follows that such an age should produce a new type of worker: the information or knowledge specialist. These new "gold-collar" workers are generally engaged in complex problem solving instead of ordinary bureaucratic routine. They offer their employers imagination and original thought but at a price: they are not nearly as docile as the workers they replace. Often knowing more than the managers who supervise them, they place a high value on getting along with their co-workers and are difficult, if not impossible, to manipulate. Their respect for authority is conditional —based on proven expertise or actual results, not on a job title or size of office. They offer loyalty, but expect recognition and opportunities for participation in return.

But these new workers bring with them new expectations. Moonlighting is rampant among gold-collar workers; many develop alternate sources of income to maintain their lifestyle, yet perceive no moral conflict in doing so. Gold-collar workers see themselves as their own best investment—and their willingness to spend generously on health, creature comforts, and education reflects these values.

THE NEW GLOBAL ECONOMY

"We desire a more closely integrated world economy in which competition is no longer confined by regional or national boundaries."

—Nobuo Matsunaga, Japanese ambassador to the United States

The rise of international competition and its threat to the North American economy is not a temporary problem, nor can it be wished away, forgotten like a bad dream or tariffed out of existence. Well-worn though it is, the example of Japan is still worth citing. The Japanese, after the Second World War, had no bureaucratic or philosophical barriers to break down. The war had left them with a clean slate. The entire nation shared a single vision: achievement. Pundits have not overlooked the irony inherent in the method the Japanese chose to reach these goals: American management consultants like W. Edwards Deming spent a great deal of time in post-war Japan preaching a message North America had ignored: put quality first and everything else will follow.

"Today's commodity can quickly become tomorrow's buggy whip."

Markets sometimes enlarge even when we don't wish them to. This may be the explanation for much of the grief North American suppliers are now experiencing. Overnight (or so it seems) their neighborhood market became a world market, as new suppliers slipped in and stocked local shelves with foreign products, and buyers liked the variety. National economies also no longer exist in isolation. They have meshed to form a world-wide economy that is interdependant. That was demonstrated by the concerted effort of the G-7 countries to lower interest rates in October 1987. To compete, businesses must be made to understand that their competition is not just across the street, but also across the ocean, on the other side of the globe.

Furthermore, the accepted role models for economic success may no longer hold. Alvin Toffler cites Germany as an example of "high-tech" at the expense of "high-touch": "Today Germany has the highest unemployment rate in 30 years. . . . [It] did little to create a viable Third Wave sector. It's weak in biotechnology. It has a rigid over-specialized educational system that discourages innovation, creativity and entrepreneurism. By pushing large scale centralized technology, it fostered the impression that future technology must, of necessity, be big, centralized, and inhuman."

Third Wave problems really need Third Wave solutions. The old reliable business "Band-Aid"—throw money at it and it will go away—simply won't wash in a society caught in our whirlwind of change. Alvin Toffler is emphatic that no single approach can suffice: "Today's crisis is not a crisis of redistribution but a crisis of 'restructure,' . . . the breakdown of the old Second Wave industrial era economy and the emergence of a new Third Wave economy. And Second Wave remedies . . . can only intensify the crisis."

North American industry is starting to get the message. Many assembled products—from airplanes and tractors to office desks and computers — are made in batches. Seventy-five percent of all machined parts today can be produced in batches of fifty or fewer on a cost-effective basis. If it is determined that the product mix has to be changed in mid-stream, flexible manufacturing systems can handle that as well. Different products can be made on the same line at will. A new term has been coined just for this phenomenon: "economies of scope."

"We are indeed in the early stages of a major technological transformation, one that is far more sweeping than the most ecstatic of the 'futurologists' yet realize, greater even than Megatrends *or* Future Shock."

—Peter Drucker

Flexible manufacturing has been dubbed the "ultimate" entrepreneurial system. It will allow fast-thinking manufacturers to move swiftly into brand-new fields and to leave them just as swiftly if need be — all at the expense of less-agile older producers. Many companies may even find themselves blind-sided by competitors they never knew existed.

But the transition to flexible systems will be slow and painful for some organizations. Many older companies could be classified as "barrier-reefed," with one tired technology piled on top of another. The less-innovative managers content themselves with trying to chip slowly away at direct labor costs without looking at better ways to organize the workforce or investigating the new technologies that might make the direct labor costs less of a burden. They are on the road to ruin.

Fortune magazine suggests: "Flexible manufacturing allows John Deere to build a tractor at least twice as fast as before. And now the company claims it can compete not only against other big manufacturers but also against 'short liners' that make only one farm implement in higher volumes."

The need for more flexibility has sounded the death knell for the assembly line as we know it. Would Henry Ford have approved? Probably, yes. The Ford Motor Company recently put $3 billion into the development of its Taurus/Sable assembly process, so that it embodied flexibility and shared responsibility at all stages. The result is a vehicle that leads the industry in both styling and technology. Although it's hard to conceive of this car as the legacy of a man who originally offered cars of only one colour, we should

11

be quick to note that the new model is one of the biggest successes in the company's history.

FINALLY — THE "NEW" CONSUMER

Markets today are becoming extremely segmented. There is a surfeit of general cookbooks in the market right now. But books on "cooking with tofu" or "using a wok" regularly translate into big dollars because they reach a highly specialized market. Complete "demassification" is not here yet, but it is definitely coming.

The "me" society is still with us, only now it's the "us" society. Organizations ignore at their peril the signals their members are sending. The new consumers are a highly informed group willing to go to great lengths to attain a perceived reward. Their ability to make value judgments about products is a source of constant bewilderment to marketing whizzes. These new consumers will choose a "no-name" brand of soap to save a few pennies because those few cents saved are judged to compensate adequately for the lack of a name brand on the package. Yet, with equal aplomb, they will pay about double the normal price for soap advertised as "containing cold cream " or other exotic pampering ingredients. There is logic here — but it is a new logic, a new pattern.

And so change, the eternal constant, becomes ever more violent and dislocating. Consider the following lament: "The world is too big for us. Try as you will, you get behind the race in spite of yourself. Science empties its discoveries on you so fast you stagger beneath them . . . . The political world witnesses new scenes so rapidly you are out of breath trying to keep up . . . . Everything is high pressure . . . ." Sound familiar? That comment appeared in the *Atlantic Journal* in 1837!

"Yesterday's home runs won't win tomorrow's ballgames."

—Babe Ruth

So what's the bottom line? Where does this "third wave" lead? Can the futurists really be certain about what is coming? Not at all. It has been argued, for example, that a futurist in the 1920s would have been totally shocked by the market collapse since, at the time, there were so few clues pointing to its arrival. James

"Not-So-Crystal" Balls

The stock market turmoil of October 1987 reminded the world how difficult and deadly predictions can be. Too often, in fact, today's knowledge, today's technology, and today's point-of-view act as blinders to further obscure our view of what is to come.

"Everything that can be invented has been invented."
—Charles Duell, Director U.S. Patent Office, 1899

"Heavier than air flying machines are impossible."
—Lord Kelvin, 1895

"There is no likelihood that man can ever tap the power of the atom."
—Robert Millikan, Nobel prizewinner, physics, 1923

"The Americans have need of the telephone—but we do not. We have plenty of office boys."
—Sir William Preece, chief engineer, British Post Office, 1876

In planning for the future, let's remember that most economists can't describe a place they've never been:

"An extrapolation of the trends of the 1880s would show today's cities buried under horse manure."
—Norman MacRae, English writer

"Forecasting is very difficult—especially if it's about the future. He who lives by the crystal ball soon learns to eat ground glass."
—Edgar Fiedler, from *Why Things Go Wrong* by Laurence J. Peter

Dick Bolles, author of the career-management bestseller *What Colour Is Your Parachute?*, ponders what may be the ultimate solution: *"The best we can do [concerning the future] is organize ourselves and our knowledge or picture of what we are looking for in such a way that we will be prepared to take advantage of whatever may come along—by accident, luck, circumstance, serendipity, fate, Providence, or an Act of God."*

O'Toole, a UCLA professor, has speculated that even Toffler may have missed the boat: his predictions for the seventies completely missed one of the major social developments of that decade: the Women's Movement!

There are only two certainties: there will be a future. It will be different from the present.

"The only certainty is nothing is certain."

—Pliny the Elder

Ways of Dealing with the Future

—Try to Ignore It
—Try to Predict It
—Try to Control It
—Try to Respond to It

Our experience shows us that the first three ways just will not work. That's why 3Mers all over Canada are working vigorously to
    RESPOND TO THE FUTURE
—Sign in offices of 3M Canada, London, Ontario

HARNESSING CHANGE

There is nothing particularly sinister about change, any more than there is malice in a snowstorm or anger in a windy day. Change simply is. Because the pace of change is reaching hurricane force, because advances in technology are greater, organizations have a wonderful opportunity to harness those forces. Change is like winds at sea. A good sailor can utilize a gale to cover great distances in a short amount of time. Others too often find their ship becalmed after the storm or smashed against the rocks in a lonely corner of the ocean.

"Life can only be understood backwards; but it must be lived forwards."

—Sören Kierkegaard

The Mennen company extracted considerable profits from the firm and socked them away safely in a bank. It took no risks, in-

14

troduced no new products, and made no investment in plant or equipment. The strategy was initially successful: high interest from the money markets brought in a higher return than would have been earned in the short term from the comparatively expensive process of developing and marketing new products. In the long run, however, the company suffered. Today, Skin Bracer — once the market leader — controls only 3 percent of its market.

New Rules, New Game, New Threats . . .
Great Opportunities

Tom Peters is getting desperate. As we've worked with him over the last few years, we've noticed a growing sense of urgency. He feels that the keys to organizational excellence outlined in *In Search of Excellence* and *A Passion for Excellence* are no longer "nice to do" but are becoming too little too late. In his latest book, *Thriving on Chaos: Handbook for a Management Revolution*, he warns of the dire consequences or incredible payoffs of our rapidly changing world:

—"There are no excellent companies . . . IBM is declared dead in 1979, the best of the best in 1982, and dead again in 1986. People Express is the model 'new look' firm, then flops twenty-four months later."

—"The only excellent firms are those that are rapidly evolving."

—"Nothing is predictable . . . multiply them [changing forces and trends], then add in the fact that most are in their infancy, and you end up with a forecaster's nightmare . . . no firm can take anything in its market for granted."

—"Our competitive situation is dire. The time for 10 percent staff cuts and 20 percent quality improvements is past. Such changes are not good enough."

—"Violent and accelerating change, now commonplace, will become the grist of the opportunistic winner's mill. The losers will view such confusion as a 'problem' to be 'dealt' with."

—"Today, loving change, tumult, even chaos is a prerequisite for survival, let alone success."

"It costs a lot to build bad products."

—Norman R. Augustine

The constant changes of our world quickly make obsolete the rules of the business game. What was once superior is today rejected. Fierce competition, new technology, demanding consumers, shifting work values, economic upheaval, and the sheer volume and pace of change itself have dramatically altered the factors leading to high performance, if not survival.

As we've worked with organizations bent on mastering or exploiting change for their growth and improvement, we've noticed a few recurring themes or key issues. It's becoming clearer that these are the issues that effective organizations will use to thrive in our chaotic world. And failure to meet these challenges will kill or seriously cripple less responsive organizations. *The four key, interwoven issues are: quality, service, innovation, and productivity.*

QUALITY

Quality, according to the American Society for Quality Control, is "a systematic approach to the search for excellence."

Surveys undertaken by the Strategic Planning Institute (a research organization affiliated with Harvard University) identified "relative *perceived* product quality" as the single most important factor in an organization's long-term profitability: "Changes in relative quality," according to the researchers, "have a far more potent effect on market share than do changes in price."

In doing the original research for *In Search of Excellence*, Tom Peters and Bob Waterman found that, of some seventy high-performing organizations, sixty-five differentiated themselves from their peers not by lower costs and higher prices, but on the basis of highest quality. The relationship between quality and bottom-line profit is becoming increasingly evident.

Dunkin' Donuts, known for its outstanding coffee, has twenty-three pages of specifications listing what it requires in a coffee bean. Its rules state that beans are to be used within ten days of their delivery. Otherwise, they are returned. The coffee can be served for only eighteen minutes after brewing; then it must be thrown out and a fresh batch used. And the coffee must brew at a temperature of between 196 and 198 degrees Fahrenheit. In 1984, the company sold more than 350 million cups of coffee.

Quality means not only giving the customer more but also figuring out what it is she wants in the first place. Quality means getting close to the customer. It is one thing to say that your organization is quality oriented or customer driven — and quite another to make it happen.

SERVICE

Consultant and professional speaker Joel Weldon says: "Elephants don't bite; it's the mosquitoes and black flies that get you. The little things do you in." That, in a nutshell, is what service is all about. Consumers *expect* the goods they buy to work. But what really catches their eye is the *way* goods are sold and serviced, the *manner* in which they (the customers) are treated, the *environment* that the organization creates.

A recent survey to assess the reasons that people leave one car dealer for another found that only 14 percent left because of complaints about the product, while 68 percent switched because of the "indifference shown to them by a dealer's service persons."

In other words, while are there obvious benefits to providing better service than the customer expects, providing inferior service will lead the customer to "penalize" the business not only by taking his own business elsewhere but also by telling others about the problem. They don't get mad, they get even. On average, more people will receive word-of-mouth reports about bad or ineffective service from a dissatisfied customer than will hear about effective service from that same customer!

Most dissatisfied customers let their discontent smolder *silently*. In one study the following reasons for "not complaining" turned up: "It's not worth the hassle"; "I don't know where or how to complain"; "I don't believe anything will come of it."

In *Service America: Doing Business in the New Economy*, Karl Albrecht and Ron Zemke point to service as the area that gives the most potent competitive edge: "When two or more companies are competing in roughly the same market, for the business of the same customer, [service is] the only way any of these companies can gain a competitive edge. Even in industries that manufacture hard goods, service is an increasingly important discriminator in an era of cheap technologies, mature industries, indistinguishable products, and slim competitive edges. . . . It would behoove every organization to identify and manage its 'service' package."

Albrecht and Zemke note that simply providing what the customer already expects is no longer sufficient. For example, customers expect hospitals to be clean, so a clean hospital is not perceived as providing any extra measure of service.

"It's a funny thing about life, if you refuse to accept anything but the very best you very often get it."

—William Somerset Maugham

And the bottom line, the authors argue, is the inevitable "moment of service truth": "Some moments of truth are more telling than others . . . the moment when a customer first sets foot inside the hotel; when the service manager at the repair shop presents the bill; when the physician's receptionist greets the patient, they strengthen the image of the establishment in the customer's mind. If handled clumsily, they create apprehension, animosity, and negative expectations."

The authors add their voices to a growing chorus: customer service depends on an expanded notion of customer/supplier relationships. Dissatisfied customers are the harbingers of an organization in peril. For this reason, everyone within the organization must be focused on serving customers, both internal and external. (Albrecht and Zemke pose the interesting question: "If you have a 'customer service' department, what's the *rest* of the organization up to?")

In the change-driven eighties and nineties, organizations are discovering that traditional notions of service as "something you do for the customer" will no longer suffice. Harvard Business School professor Theodore Levitt states bluntly: "There are no such things as service industries. There are only industries whose service components are greater or less than those of other industries. Everybody is in service."

Beyond Service?

An interesting issue can be raised: when one provides service for customers, is that service for the ultimate benefit of the customer—or the organization? In other words, who is servicing whom? Proctor & Gamble maintains a toll-free 800 number for all of its eighty-plus products. It deals with more than 750,000 phone calls and customer enquiries a year. But to what end? Are informed customers the only goal? Hardly. P&G quickly learned that such "service" systems are literally a two-way street: information the company gleaned from sifting through customer problems time and again gave the company the "edge" it needed to spot a new market niche and then fill it quickly. To give just one example, a successful line of cold-water detergents was developed in response to P&G's awareness that consumers were using less hot water in an attempt to save energy.

Service is not readily quantifiable or observable. It's the little things: like the lawyer who promises to return all his calls on the same day or the car oil-change service that gives clients a complimentary newspaper to read while they're waiting for a free bay. Service is an attitude, a commitment, a drive to make the customer feel not just special but more special than the competitor does.

Service is more than just delivering a quality product today. Service is keeping that product working next week, or next year, and letting the customer know that if there are problems, help is only a phone call away. One of the great paradoxes in modern business is that organizations spend so much money looking for new customers and so little servicing the ones they already have. Tom Peters maintains that the name of the game is to take those people who are already your customers and grow them into larger customers. Ron Zemke and Karl Albrecht say: "Will service be as important a part of our economic tomorrow as it is today? No, it will be more important."

INNOVATION

After studying a number of selected companies over many years, Rosabeth Moss Kanter, author of *The Change Masters: Innovation and Productivity in the American Corporation*, defines innovation as "the process of bringing any new, problem-solving idea into use; [it] is the generation, acceptance and implementation of new ideas, processes, products, or services. It can thus occur in any part of a corporation, and it can involve creative use as well as original invention."

"Anybody can cut the prices, but it takes brains to make a better article."

—Philip D. Armour

Innovation is not something you inject into an organization like vitamins; rather it arises from the general attitude of the organization's *employees*. Kanter says it "needs people capable of adapting as circumstances change because they already have a broader base of skills." Innovation is the key to increased service, quality, and productivity. It is absolutely vital to building a flexible organization that can respond swiftly to wrenching shifts in external or internal conditions.

Blazing New Trails

"If you want to succeed," John D. Rockefeller, Sr., commented, "you should strike out on new paths rather than travel the worn paths of accepted success."

A groundbreaking two-year study of high-performing midsized companies for the American Business Center found that some 74 percent "got their start with an innovative product, service or way of doing business." Further, some 84 percent characterized themselves as "frequent innovators," and all survey respondents felt that, on average, more than 25 percent of their sales came from products that simply didn't exist five years ago. Collectively, the high performers felt that their own companies accounted for 40 to 60 percent of all the major innovations in their respective industries.

As the ferment of change intensifies, organizations that cannot continually innovate will no longer have the luxury of playing catch-up. They must either lead, run with the pack, or go the way of the dodo bird. The home video field is a good example. New products and designs arrive on the shelves almost monthly, yet consumer demand remains healthy. To cope, the new organization needs not only more sophisticated technologies but also a faster decision-making process—and a means of implementing those decisions once made. The keys to survival are less bureaucracy, more accuracy, and higher commitment. A telecommunications company recently found that to compete effectively in the international market it had to reduce the length of its product-development cycle, conception through delivery, from twenty-four months to six.

"Creativity in a business organization cannot be ordered like breakfast at the Waldorf; instead it must be stimulated, motivated, induced."

—Roy Ash

Many organizations don't understand innovation. Sure, they talk about it. They even say it's something they want more of. But innovation is like a rainbow: it doesn't happen because you want it, it happens because the conditions are right to make it happen. The organization that desires innovation (and most are quick to include themselves in this number) must provide an environment that nurtures and encourages it. The right combination of elements — and people — must be in place.

Innovation can be as elusive as a butterfly; you can see it, but you just can't catch it. The "father of modern management," Peter Drucker, makes the point that, until the mid-nineteenth century, innovation was looked upon as the occasional flash of genius, the product of a "half-romantic, half-ridiculous figure, tinkering away in a lonely garret." Today innovation is an entirely different animal. According to Drucker, it has become "a systematic purposeful activity which is planned and organized with a high predictability both of the results aimed at and likely to be achieved . . . . [The modern organization] has to learn to practice systematic innovation."

RESEARCH AND DEVELOPMENT DOES NOT ALWAYS EQUAL INNOVATION

A common pitfall is the delegation of innovation to the R & D department. Many well-intentioned organizations talk the language of innovation while singing the song of bureaucracy. Throwing money at R & D is not enough. Innovation must be introduced into the day-to-day business of the organization, into the process of performance. Developing a better product, service, or system is one thing. Successfully putting it to use in the market is another matter entirely.

21

The Accelerating Pace of Innovation

Clearly, in a world where everyone is trying to innovate, the speed at which innovation takes place becomes critical. Rosabeth Moss Kanter has more than once accused domestic industry of "almost literally handing a market over" to foreign competition by failing to respond quickly. The Japanese invasion of the small-car market in the seventies is an example that amply illustrates the point. Product change and improvement must occur quickly if organizations are to maintain a competitive edge in their industry. The moral? Constantly increase your rate of innovation — or else!

Here are some recent examples of the accelerating pace of innovation:

—The new Xerox 9900 copier took three years to develop. This is down sharply from the five years needed for an earlier similar model.

—When John Scully became chairman of Apple in 1984, he set a goal to reduce their product-development time to one year from three and a half.

—To counter a threat from Yamaha in the Japanese motorcycle market, Honda introduced thirty new models within a six-month period.

The pace of innovation can be more important than innovation itself. Compaq Computer came out of nowhere to challenge IBM in certain segments of the microcomputer market. Compaq claims its product-development time of nine months gives it an edge over IBM's thirteen-month cycle. Witness the way Compaq scooped IBM in 1986 with the introduction of the first mass-market computer based on the mighty Intel "386" chip—a feat it took IBM an extra year to match. More dramatic is the lesson learned by the Phillips company in the home video field. Their v2000 video-disc player was technically excellent but came in only one model and was late getting to market. Licking its wounds, Phillips carefully prepared itself for the CD-player craze by putting an entire series of flexibly designed units on the market, in most cases ahead of the competition. Today it claims as its own more than 20 percent of that lucrative market.

Gordon Forward, president of Chapparal Steel, one of the few world-class domestic steel companies in terms of innovation, profitability, and productivity, makes the point: "[Those] companies all put in vice-presidents of research. [They] built important-looking research centers, places with 2,000 people in a spanking new facility out in Connecticut or somewhere, with fountains and lawns and little parks—those places were lovely, really nice. But the first time I went into one of them I thought I was entering Forest Lawn. After you spend some time there you realize you are in Forest Lawn. Not because there are no good ideas there, but because the good ideas are dying there all the time."

"A research laboratory is not simply a building that contains apparatus for conducting experiments. I contend that it is a state of mind."

—Charles F. Kettering

In much the same way that putting a feeder on the back lawn will attract feathered friends, creating an atmosphere that encourages innovation and then giving power to the people with the skills to achieve the desired results is the key to successful innovation.

In performance-seeking organizations, innovation is more than a missing piece of the excellence puzzle, it is also a way of finding other pieces; innovation is an approach to business, a philosophy of getting things done that, by its nature, gets to where it wants to go in spite of anything that gets in its way. Innovation and "volunteerism" go hand-in-hand—the latter describes an organizational atmosphere in which people don't just do work, they *relish* their work and are constantly on the lookout for ways to improve. Innovation requires a way of looking at the world in which problems become opportunities to improve.

PRODUCTIVITY

Improved productivity is often a byproduct of improvements in service, quality, or innovation. Robert Ranftl, corporate director of managerial productivity for Hughes Aircraft company, defines productivity as the "ratio of valuable output to input, i.e.: the efficiency and effectiveness with which available resources

23

—personnel, machines, materials, capital, facilities, energy and time—are utilized to achieve a valuable output."

But does increased productivity necessarily lead to increased profitability, quality, or excellence? It perhaps should, but doesn't always. This "productivity paradox," as Harvard business-administration professor Wickham Skinner calls it, happens because many business folk have trouble distinguishing between efficiency and effectiveness; in their zeal to enhance the former, they often sacrifice the latter: "not only is the productivity approach to manufacturing management not enough . . . it hurts as much as it helps. It is an instinctive response that absorbs managers' minds and diverts them from more effective manufacturing approaches."

In the early eighties North America's hopes for reclaiming its competitive edge focused on a panacea from Japan called "quality circles". Rather than take the time to prepare people for change, a packaged QC system was dumped into many organizations. Most were not culturally ready for a collaborative style of operation. At first, there were improvements to the bottom line, but eventually a lack of management commitment and the subsequent employee distrust caused many QC programs to fail. North America's attempt at a quick efficiency fix with a made-in-Japan program left many companies with severe morale problems that negatively affected performance.

"The surest foundation of a manufacturing concern is quality. After that, and a long way after, comes cost."

—Andrew Carnegie

The American Society for Quality Control brings us this thoughtful caution about getting too carried away with productivity. "Quality used to be an American tradition. Trouble was, we thought we could get better products and services through short cuts in the recipe, by emphasizing productivity, often at the expense of quality. Today . . . *many corporations are discovering that quality drives the productivity machine.*"

But if it is really quality that drives productivity, is it not possible that there are interrelationships between the other "strategic issues" as well? Might not innovation and service go hand in hand?

The "Dark" Side of Productivity Improvement

John Goodman, president of the Washington, D.C. firm, Technical Assistance Research Programs, has seen both sides of productivity: the good and the not so good. According to Goodman, there are pitfalls galore in improvement for its own sake without a plan to take the skills of performance and integrate them into the culture of the organization.

1. "Cutting out fat" could negatively affect service. It could even harm cash flow or profitability. One utility company reduced staff but found it could no longer handle basic customer queries. The problem was further compounded when customers withheld payments (thereby inflating receivables) while waiting for the responses they were no longer getting.

2. As one organization discovered to its horror, improving efficiency by reducing the time allowed for the recording of telephone orders results in a situation where errors actually increase because orders are no longer repeated back to the customer.

3. Job specialization too often creates an "it's not my job" syndrome. This is especially frustrating because customers soon learn to demand to talk to someone who can resolve their specific complaint.

4. Automation has its risks as well as its rewards. Automatic tellers, for example, have an accepted downtime of 3 percent, meaning that theoretically one could be inoperative for ten hours on a Sunday when it is needed most!

SO WHAT ELSE IS NEW?

We've examined how dramatically our world has changed in the last few years and how organizations are responding.

Some of the key changes impacting organizations are:

- increasing complexity of technology;
- information overload;
- shifting values of a younger workforce;
- globalization of markets with fierce competition;

- unpredictability of economic trends;
- rapid growth of white/gold-collar jobs;
- rise of flexible manufacturing
- new independence and diversity of consumers

Our list of key trends is but a sample of the many changes rushing to reshape our world. Energy supplies and prices, Third World debt, political shifts, and military conflicts are among a number of other variables affecting change.

Those organizations that are mastering change and improving performance are doing so by dramatically improving their products' quality, increasing customer service, boosting productivity, and improving their innovativeness and ability to adapt to change. While we've looked at each one of these key issues individually, they are not separate. Productivity, quality, or service cannot improve without innovation. Improving quality also increases productivity and generally enhances customer service. A narrow focus on productivity can easily kill service and innovation.

So what? To this point we've said nothing that hasn't already been well dissected, documented, and discussed by countless researchers, writers, academics, and consultants. We've stated what's fast becoming common knowledge: the world is rapidly changing, and organizations must reach new performance levels or be swept aside by these powerful currents. It's common sense, a "blinding flash of the obvious."

"All worthwhile men have good thoughts, good ideas and good intentions, but precious few of them ever translate those into actions."
                                                            – John Hancock Field

The trap snaring a growing number of organizations is that *common sense doesn't automatically become common practice.* There is a vast gulf between knowing what needs to be done and actually doing it. As Peter Drucker so aptly puts it: "Having a good idea is one thing, implementing it is another." He has found that "the reason firms have excellent ideas in them yet perform poorly is that the people who have ideas can't get them implemented."

That jibes with our experience. Having begun our consulting practice in the "strategic planning era" of the seventies, we quickly experienced the "implementation problem" with clients. Brilliant plans and strategies stalled. Customers and employees didn't behave as they were expected to. It became increasingly clear that the organization's environment or culture, as well as the skill levels of management and employees, often blocked progress.

In 1983, we began work with Tom Peters and the California consulting firm, Zenger-Miller, Inc., to implement an executive action process based on the excellence research of Peters and Waterman. Later we worked with clients and 3M's Quality Management Service on specific quality or service improvement efforts. Again, implementation became a key issue. Organizations had the technology (computers, manufacturing processes), management systems (statistical process control, team structures), and a high degree of motivation and understanding of what needed to be done. While some have done well, many efforts spurted and died. Quality teams lost energy; customer-service slogans rang hollow; creativity dried up. "Managing by wandering around" wandered off. The intentions were right, but the follow-through, the implementation, was wrong.

The most common and consistent cause of the "implementation problem" is proving to be *lack of leadership skills* throughout the organization. The words *leadership* and *skill* mean different things to different people. In the next few chapters, we'll define specifically what we've come to mean by *leadership*. We'll examine its key elements in some depth.

The key to changing the leadership elements or conditions that exist (consciously or not) in all organizations lie in the skill levels of all organizational members. We'll look at the four basic sets or clusters of leadership skills that determine an organization's performance levels. Finally, we'll outline how other individuals and organizations have improved or developed those skills and the payoffs from doing so.

"With regard to excellence, it is not enough to know but we must try to have and use it."

—Aristotle

CHAPTER TWO

The Performance Triangle: Technology, Management and Leadership

"Fine art is that in which the hand, the head, and the heart of man go together."

—John Ruskin

Most managers understand that a taut, well-run organizational machine requires a balance between technology, management, and leadership. What is not often appreciated is how difficult it is to achieve just the right blend of the three. Getting these diverse elements in the correct proportion is a tricky balancing act.

North American organizations are for the most part well supported by at least two "faces" of the performance triangle: they have combined the latest in technology with disciplined management systems. These organizations are, at best, stable. They are also mediocre. As the carnival barker said, "Two out of three don't count." As society and the economy change, two-faceted organizations just can't keep up. They move as fast as they can to stay where they are. As productivity and performance gradually erode, these companies' technomanagers search for technological miracles and tighter management control.

TECHNOLOGY: ONLY THE FIRST STEP . . .

Technology is centered in the field of science, which can be defined as "the study or knowledge of the laws and products of nature; particularly and collectively, physics, chemistry, biology, astronomy, geology, and related subjects." Technology could more easily be defined as *what* the organization does or provides (GM makes cars) and *how* it does it (robotics).

Technology is both primary and secondary. The primary technology of an organization is the product, service, or expertise that it produces. Secondary technology is what is needed to produce the primary one. (An organization's primary technology, for example, may focus on computers, plywood, meat, or even thumbtacks. In the service sector, primary technology might be accommodation, information, or food preparation. Secondary technologies encompass such things as robots, communication hardware, engineering, and so on.)

Technology can be further subdivided into "industrial" and "intellectual" technologies. Office-automation specialists Kathleen Curley and Philip Pyburn assert that intellectual technology is aimed at "expanding the power of the human brain." "Unlike industrial technologies," they say, "where the principal constraint on the use of the equipment is physical, intellectual technologies are primarily limited by the user's imagination."

MANAGEMENT

Management has been explained in many ways. Harvard Business School professor Theodore Levitt defines management as "the rational assessment of a situation and the systematic selection of goals and purposes; the systematic development of strategies to achieve these goals; the marshalling of the required resources, the rational design, organization, direction and control of the activities required to attain the selected procedures."

"Method is like packing things in a box; a good packer will get in half as much again as a bad one."
— Robert Cecil

Management's primary job is to make the technologies work. This is accomplished through systems: financial, production, service, and administration. Management by its nature seeks optimum efficiency of its technologies through easily controlled structures and chains of command. Decisions concerning resource allocation are based on logical, quantitative, and statistical analysis. Management prefers to deal with facts only — that's the scientific way. (Their motto becomes: "To err is human — to prevent the reoccurrence of error is science.")

LEADERSHIP

"Too many people who know all about financial values know nothing about human values."

—Roy L. Smith

Leadership is that part of the organization that concerns itself with people. It is the human dimension. It is difficult to find a definition that is more precise. The late Gordon Lippitt, professor at George Brown University, after studying the subject for years, concluded: "Leadership is the worst defined, least understood, personal attribute sometimes possessed by human beings."

William Prentice, president and vice-chairman of Bryant and Stratton Business Institute, says: "Leadership is usually not studied at all. Popularity, power, showmanship, and wisdom in long range planning are studied instead. . . . *Leadership is the accomplishment of a goal through the direction of human assistants.* The person who successfully marshalls human collaborators to achieve particular ends is a leader. A great leader is one who can do so day after day and year after year in a wide variety of circumstances . . . . The leader's unique achievement is a human and social one which stems from understanding fellow workers and the relationship of their individual goals to the group goal that must be carried out."

"Wars may be fought with weapons, but they are won by men. It is the spirit of the men who follow and of the man who leads that gains the victory."

—General George S. Patton

Where management and technology are focused on things, leadership concerns itself with people. Which people? People who buy or use the organization's technologies; people who produce, support, or control the technological processes; people who supply the new technologies; and people who coordinate other people. Leadership seeks to orchestrate the dynamics of people working with people. Leadership recognizes that people may sometimes be irrational, emotional, uncontrollable, and even unpredictable. Leadership develops an inspirational context using vision and

Understanding the Critical Three

TECHNOLOGY

FOCUS	– equipment, expertise, products
PREDICTABILITY	– high (based on science)
CONTROL MECHANISMS	– physical laws
TRACKING RESULTS	– high (measurable output)
FINANCIAL THRUST	– scientific breakthroughs
KEY ELEMENTS	– manufacturing, delivery, services
KEY WORDS	– research, facts, precision

MANAGEMENT

FOCUS	– administrative systems
PREDICTABILITY	– medium (based on probabilities)
CONTROL MECHANISMS	– legal and accounting principles
TRACKING RESULTS	– medium (measurable process)
FINANCIAL THRUST	– cost containment
KEY ELEMENTS	– budgets, rules, plans, and controls
KEY WORDS	– efficiency, objectives, structure

LEADERSHIP

FOCUS	– people
PREDICTABILITY	– low (an art form)
CONTROL MECHANISMS	– emotional commitments
TRACKING RESULTS	– low (perceptions and attitudes)
FINANCIAL THRUST	– revenue enhancement (value added)
KEY ELEMENTS	– vision, values, environment, and behavior
KEY WORDS	– feelings, motivation, pride

values to create a sense of purpose and commitment. Leadership, properly deployed, integrates people as teams. The teams have purposes, and those purposes will in turn bring about new vision.

Leadership can be as complex or as simple as the people who utilize it—and the people who are exposed to it. Leadership, by its nature, deals with the best and worst of the human animal—and gets results *anyway*.

Most people confuse leadership with a position or role—a leader is usually thought of as the head of all or part of an organization. But the people in charge are likely to be more administrators, managers, technologists, or bosses rather than true leaders. Leadership is reflected in the ability to initiate action and move others to a shared goal. This is "persuasion", not position power. Its product is the will to win, the desire to belong.

Technology and management are critical elements. But if you want to capitalize on them, you need a firm foundation. You need leadership.

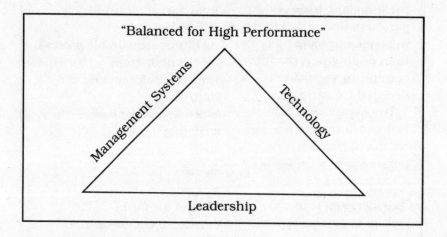

"Balanced for High Performance"

Management Systems

Technology

Leadership

THE NEED FOR BALANCE

Which is more important: technology, management, or leadership? That is like asking whether air, water or food is more important to life. All are critical. Organizations that have demonstrated consistent high performance show that technology, management and leadership are needed, and that the three need to be balanced.

A "Technology Tilt" Can Kill a Business!

The owner of a small distribution firm was considered to be a brilliant expert in his field. He had successfully managed the worldwide shipping and distribution of parts for a giant multinational equipment manufacturer. In 1981 he began his own business. Initially, things went well. His old employer even became a client. As expansion took place, the need for a computer system became clear. Because of his fascination with technology, the owner became obsessed with finding just the "right" system. He and his assistant began to log eighteen-hour days testing and refining the new computer system. His people skills began to decline. He was seen by employees to be overbearing, disrespectful, and insensitive. A hard-working and aggressive assistant developed suggestions to streamline the firm's messy accounting process, but the owner vetoed the idea because he felt that the assistant was overstepping her authority. The sales department floundered because the owner was more interested in developing existing products for the clients he already had than finding new products or new customers. The company became unresponsive to client needs, and eventually the firm declared bankruptcy.

The owner, a technological wizard, lacked the leadership skills to form a team and to allow that team to make the company grow. His product worked, but his enterprise failed because it was unbalanced.

Consider our "triangle of performance" (page 32). The triangle is just as secure on any one of its faces as it is on the other. Its three sides combined provide greater support than one or two alone. *An organization that correctly balances technology, management, and leadership can support greater achievement.*

Letting the triangle lean off-center will bring instability and organizational paralysis. This imbalance often comes about in four ways: the creation of a technology-tilted organization; a sideways drift into the madness of management; a failure to move beyond the limits of leadership; and — most commonly — a wrong turn into the oil-and-water brew of technomanagement.

TILTED TOWARD TECHNOLOGY

"Computers are useless. They can only give you answers."

—Pablo Picasso

Organizations tilted toward technology are driven by architects, academics, scientists, dentists, craftsmen, and other experts. Too often the key to success is seen to be the breakthrough product or service that will make the world beat a path to the organization's door. The specialists or technocrats assume that their knowledge of a narrow subject is not only critical but essential to the organization. The main goal of this type of business is to be "on the leading edge" of its field.

Robert Cole, a research associate at the Center for Japanese Studies at the University of Michigan and author of *Work, Mobility and Participation: A Comparative Study of American and Japanese Industry*, says: "The boosters of the new technology sometimes fail to consider the impediments to effective decision-making that complex information systems can erect when their output creates information overload and finely honed models that are far removed from reality." Cole goes on to cite studies that "question conventional wisdom concerning computers and productivity." One study of forty firms concluded that "there is no direct and simple co-relation between managerial productivity and information technology."

Organizations that are "tilted" toward technology include those that are electronic/machinistic in structure, as well as those that rely on an information base—such as medical and law practices. As the professionals in these organizations work to perfect the technical capacity of their profession, management systems and the human element often slip out of balance.

All too often a technology-tilted business suffers from a benign neglect of management system and structure, most particularly a lack of attention to the "human" dimension. Productivity as well as the ongoing coordination of primary and supporting technologies is usually poor. The organization almost always suffers from morale and motivation problems. Employees who do not consider themselves part of the organization's "technological elite" become disenchanted, and performance reflects their discontent.

In a manufacturing organization that was technology tilted, a salesperson was overheard trying to soothe an important customer irritated by the plant manager's rudeness. Her explanation had a familiar ring to it: "He's a brilliant engineer and has dramatically increased productivity. If it's any consolation to you, he treats people here worse than he treated you."

Technology-centered people demand the same order and efficiency in life that they create in their computer programs. Things out of order violate the rules and challenge their routines. Predictability becomes an obsession.

By promoting technical experts to management without paying attention to whether they have the leadership skills necessary to do the job, many organizations unwittingly tilt toward technology. The finest ingredients and the latest Moulinex alone won't produce a gourmet meal—for that you need a talented chef.

ON TO "MANAGEMENT MADNESS"

An organization "driven by management" is one dominated by accountants, lawyers, MBAs, consultants, and efficiency experts. Here the key to improved performance is seen as designing a superior planning-and-control system, one that contains costs and at the same time optimizes the use of technological assets. Top managers strive to get the facts or numbers through objective analysis and to make rational decisions.

"Anyone can hold the helm when the sea is calm."

—Publilius Syrus

In *A Passion for Excellence*, Tom Peters and Nancy Austin explain how this obsession with management came about. "We have lived in a house of cards. It was, in fact, pretty difficult for management to mess up an American corporation during the twenty-five years immediately following World War II . . . . From 1946 until the early sixties, we opened the spigots full bore, just to meet the domestic demand." With an expanding economy and strong consumer demand, North American managers concentrated on efficiency and maximizing profit from the seemingly endless sale of products and services their organizations produced. As technical specialists and entrepreneurs developed new products and services, the need for a more organized and systematic management of emerging technologies became obvious. The larger and more complex the organization became, the greater the need for orderly planning and control. Business schools rushed in to help corporations manage their growing operations more efficiently. Many smaller organizations tried to follow this lead.

The Dark Side of Cost Efficiency

An efficiency expert reports on hearing a symphony at the Royal Festival Hall in London:

For considerable periods, the four oboe players had nothing to do. The number should be reduced and the work spread more evenly over the whole of the concert, thus eliminating peaks of activity.

All the twelve violins were playing identical notes; this seems unnecessary duplication. The staff of this section should be drastically cut. If a larger volume of sound is required, it could be obtained by electronic apparatus.

Much effort was absorbed in the playing of demi-semi-quavers; this seems to be an unnecessary refinement. It is recommended that all notes should be rounded up to the nearest semi-quaver. If this was done, it would be possible to use trainees and lower-grade operatives more extensively.

There seems to be too much repetition of some musical passages. Scores should be drastically pruned. No useful purpose is served by repeating on the horns a passage that has already been handled by the strings. It is estimated that if all redundant passages were eliminated, the whole concert time of two hours would be reduced to twenty minutes and there would be no need for an intermission.

The conductor agrees generally with these recommendations but expressed the opinion that there might be some falling off in box-office receipts. In that unlikely event it should be possible to close sections of the auditorium entirely, with a consequential saving of overhead expenses, lighting, attendance, etc. If the worst came to the worst, the whole thing could be abandoned and the public could go to the Albert Hall instead.

"Our life is frittered away by detail . . . simplify, simplify!!"

—Henry David Thoreau

In their headlong rush to "professional management" many organizations began choking on the medicine that made them so healthy. They fell into the trap of the headache sufferer who believed that if two painkillers were good, twelve must be six times better. Unworkable long-range plans became commonplace. (*Fortune* magazine reported that in 1981 roughly half of the Fortune 1000 were using some form of long-range or strategic goal-setting mechanism.) They lost their sense of balance. To patch things up, they added new systems and techniques to shore up the ones that weren't performing. Management went out of control. Organizations became overly planned, segmented, and depersonalized.

MANAGEMENT MADNESS IN ACTION

"Auditors go in after the war and bayonet the wounded."

In the seventies, much of the power in organizations was in the hands of the financial and planning staff groups. These specialists laid out intricate long-term plans and strategies and attempted to take the guesswork out of doing business. Planners applied complicated formulas to make life as predictable and controllable

---

Management Gets the Employee Relations It Deserves

Instead of blaming workers for unions, management should take a look in the mirror. Management most often gets the employee relations it deserves.

Recently in a large manufacturing plant, the workers presented management with a list of their problems and asked management to do something about them. After much delaying and avoiding, a meeting was set up. When the meeting came to order, the company president stood up and said, "We are not sure exactly what your beefs are, but let me remind you that if you are not happy you can always quit." Within a month, the plant was unionized.

---

as possible. The not-surprising result was that organizations committed to double-decker management suffered economic and financial whiplash in the change-driven eighties. The survivors pay heed to a lesson well learned: their planning groups are still around, but numbers are substantially reduced and their input, though valued, is no longer considered gospel.

Typically, in management-driven organizations, uncaring, un-committed people are pushed by management to increase the output of outdated technologies. In a downturn, managers may scramble to reorganize a shrinking pie through "down-sizing"—and so treat the symptom but not the disease. Em-ployees who are not part of the bureaucratic elite feel alienated and distant. Their motivation is further diminished as they real-ize that a rapidly changing world is leaving the organization behind.

In this environment, the distinction between people and machines, people and product, people and technology, is blurred and indistinct. A general manager once described his own duties as follows: "I am responsible for the progressive discipline of line staff by following the Union Contract and our Employee Policy Guide; preparation, updating, and modifying of Commercial Activity Report and transmitting same to Corporate Office month-ly; generally, handling of all difficult situations with utmost diplo-macy and tact . . . ." The obvious question arises: who—or what!—is being managed here?

A management-driven organization will in no time accumulate a bureaucracy. The inevitable need for reports, statistics, and plans virtually guarantees that managers will want permission in triplicate before investing in a new pencil sharpener or changing a burnt-out lightbulb. The need to be perceived to be doing the right thing soon becomes more important than actually doing it. Tom Peters maintains that any time more than five people get together they become a hopeless bureaucracy. (Senator Lawton Chiles of Florida discovered that among the 4,987 forms used by the federal government was one that would be sent to city officials after a nuclear attack to find out how many citizens had survived. "The implication," said Chiles, "is that even if nothing else survives a nuclear blast, bureaucracy will rise from the ashes.")

"Reporting facts is the refuge of those who have no imagination."

—Luc De Clapiers, Marquis de Vauvenargues

In a management-driven organization, management assumes that designs that work well on paper should work well in the real world. Teamwork is conspicuous only by its absence. Engineers "hand off" design plans to the production department, who then depend on the purchasing departments for raw materials, on shipping/receiving for inventory control, and on the quality department to (they hope) catch production defects. Problems are attacked by seeking out the "defective" department or person. Somewhere in the cycle, management reasons, is a broken part waiting to be fixed—there has to be, that's the way the system works. Rarely, however, is management itself examined for its own role in declining innovation, service, quality, or productivity.

Organizations that operate in this way become highly formalized. Power and control belong to those few who run the system. Organizations where management has gone mad become more concerned with *how* work is carried out than with *what* is accomplished. The result is an organization in which relationships are impersonal and distant. Executives become master manipulators, lumping together finances, production, and human resources. People become faceless pieces on the business gameboard to be moved about according to exceedingly rational but spiritless strategies.

Overmanaged organizations often confuse activity with accomplishment and efficiency with effectiveness. Too many managers become "paper entrepreneurs" who generate profits through clever manipulation of rules and numbers. An example is the new executive who took over a water-treatment subsidiary where sales had been growing but profits lagging. He boldly slashed marketing, sales, training, and other budgets. By "belt tightening" and "fat trimming," profits increased dramatically. The executive ultimately earned a promotion to corporate headquarters but left in his wake a weakened management team and a successor who wasn't able to keep all the balls in the air at the same time. Within three years revenues had plummeted. He had won the battle, but the organization lost the war.

"Logic.n. The art of thinking and reasoning in strict accordance with the limitations of the human misunderstanding."

—Ambrose Bierce, *The Devil's Dictionary*

SYMPTOMS OF MANAGEMENT MADNESS

One outcome of management madness is the choking of the innovative process. Long-range planning, it is wryly suggested, is based on the notion that tomorrow will look more or less like yesterday. Oil executives, predicting that the world price of crude would continue to climb, committed their companies to projects beyond their economic means. When world prices dropped, these long-range plans were thrown out, followed closely by the "mad-management" analysts who had written them.

A decrease in employee commitment is another indication that management madness has taken hold. The scenario is all too familiar: management sets up control systems to keep employees from stealing, slowing down, goofing off, or coming in late. Employees respond by looking for ways to beat the system, and management countermoves by trying to plug the loopholes.

Another symptom of the management-imbalanced organization is that, instead of looking upon themselves as players on the same team, employees start to look upon themselves as players on different teams. ("Tom? You'll find him over in quality control. He never comes to visit us!") Just as a football team would have a performance problem if half the players ran one way while the other half ran the other, organizations with a "we/they gap" have a serious obstacle to overcome.

The blame for the we/they gaps lies at the door of management. It is management that sets the tone, the pace, the direction, and the methods. Managers are the ones who ran wild with "management by objectives," gearing this system to machines rather than to human beings. Managers put in place the rules, committees, and structures that sustain the life of today's bureaucratic monster. Managers are the ones who regularly confuse activity with accomplishment—both in their own jobs and in the jobs of others.

Although too much management can hamper an organization, the right kind of management is essential. Without good management systems, organizations severely handicap their technology. The greatest mousetrap in the world will not be profitable without an organized production system, distribution method, order-taking system, and invoicing structure. *Management needs technology and technology needs management.* And, together, they both need the third face of the triangle — leadership.

THE LIMITS OF LEADERSHIP

An organization that focuses only on its customers and employees is just as unbalanced as those driven exclusively by management systems or technology.

A leadership-dominated organization is driven by its salespeople, public-relations specialists, and marketing gurus — people who are traditionally viewed as relying on charisma, persuasion skills, and generous amounts of positive thinking and glad-handing. Such an organization keeps employees, suppliers, and customers in a continual state of hype and must constantly inspire its people to pedal faster in the gales of technological change and increased competition.

"Don't just learn the tricks of the trade, learn the trade."

Typically, such leadership-driven organizations are smaller in size than management- or technology-driven companies and are often found in creative, "people-oriented" industries like advertising, direct sales, or consulting. Such organizations are usually trapped in a high-energy leadership treadmill powered by "mad motivators." These people feed on the nirvana of positive thinking, and those "you-can-do-anything" books, tapes, and seminars. The message is that enthusiasm, optimism, and PMA (positive mental attitude) will lead the true believer to the fountain of eternal happiness, the holy grail, or success.

Such energy is powerful for getting people or ideas moving, but it isn't enough for the long haul. As sales increase, owners and managers of these organizations often expand too rapidly or spend too much on plush offices, expensive cars, or big homes. They starve their organizations of cash, keep unprofitable operations running long after the patient has died, and find out about huge losses only when it's too late. Many are small businesses using yesterday's technology and "shoe-box" accounting. (That is, they throw money in the shoe box as sales come and take money out of the shoe box to pay bills. When there is a surplus, they put it in their pocket.)

In the highly charged atmosphere of unbalanced leadership, emotions are on a roller-coaster ride that never ends. The resultant stress burns out many employees and causes inestimable damage to their personal lives. Turnover is high. Although the leaders may have the best of intentions, the smoke-and-mirrors facade that creates the illusion of glitter and wealth eventually gives way and reveals a hollow truth within.

The leadership-dominated organization must constantly inspire employees to seek new heights even if its workers are not yet acclimatized to the old. Ironically, leadership-driven organizations are often warm and exciting places to be. They tend to attract high flyers who bask in the glamor and glitter of recognition programs, hype, and hoopla.

Leadership is not the sole key to high performance. If unsupported by proper technology and effective management, even the most skilled leaders will fail.

TECHNOMANAGEMENT: A MORE SOPHISTICATED IMBALANCE

As we have just seen, many organizations become unbalanced by placing undue emphasis on one of the three sides of the triangle. But it is also possible to create a lopsided organization by focusing heavily on two sides of the triangle to the exclusion of the third. In fact, the majority of today's organizations tend to get by on a foundation that takes the latest in high-tech and combines it with sophisticated management systems. We call this more common approach "technomanagement."

Emphasis on management and technology to the exclusion of leadership may, in the short run, lead to successes. Over the long haul, however, serious problems will surface. Innovation in such organizations declines, while service, quality, and productivity are maintained, if at all, at greater and greater expense. These companies never operate at their true potential and have to work harder and harder just to keep up.

Such organizations are filled to bursting with autocratic managers and supervisors, endless conclaves of bureaucrats, and iron-fisted technocrats. Technomanagers tend to put new faces on old problems, much like rearranging deck chairs on the *Titanic.*

"Technology . . . the knack of so arranging the world that we don't have to experience it." —Max Frisch

Technomanaged organizations are run by things (computers, systems, and techniques), not people. The renowned psycho-analyst and philosopher, Erich Fromm offers this disturbing insight on such a value system: "The tendency to install technical progress as the highest value is linked up with a deep emotional attachment to the mechanical, to all that is non-alive, to all that is man-made. This attraction to the non-alive which is in its more extreme form an attraction to death and decay (necrophilia) leads to . . . indifference towards life instead of reverence for life . . . . They want to control life because they are afraid of its uncontrolled spontaneity."

No manager would publicly proclaim that the organization's machines or systems were in control. Indeed, most managers speak convincingly of their belief that people are their "most important resource" or that "the customer is king." On closer inspection, however, the daily actions of executives, managers, and supervisors reveal a different picture.

The main focus (and weakness) of a technomanaged organization is that everyone connected with the business is viewed as an asset in need of maximization. All resources, financial or human, become a blur of numbers and statistics to be planned, directed, coordinated, and controlled. Like puppeteers, these managers seek to make their breathing, flesh-and-blood assets dance to their tune. Technomanagers act as if people are faceless objects to be controlled or coerced into serving management systems and technology.

"Too many managers see human beings as resources with skin wrapped around them."

Low Returns from High-Priced Technomanagement

A robot in every pot? That's the future techno-experts see for the organization. Technomanagers tend to favour the mechanical solution over the human one. They prefer things to people. There is, however, lots of evidence that their way doesn't work. Consider the following examples:

—Stephen Roach, a senior economist at Morgan Stanley, reckons that white-collar output stands today just about where it was in the 1960s. In fact, this lack of increase in productivity explains why, in Roach's opinion, cutbacks in technosystems are now being considered across the board in many organizations. It reflects, he says, "a growing dissatisfaction with high tech's productivity payback."

—An MIT study looked at the auto industry in the 1960s and concluded that one reason Toyota was able to outdistance Nissan was that Toyota concentrated on managing workers while Nissan poured money into robots and computers. The study concluded that the advantage Toyota gained from its people-oriented approach was so great that it was *still* outproducing its rival, Nissan (in terms of vehicles per employee per year), some twenty years later.

—International Data Systems estimates that approximately $10 billion has been spent so far on inventory-management systems, but only 25 percent of these systems have achieved the objectives set at the time of installation.

—A study comparing flexible manufacturing systems installed in Japan to those installed in the United States suggested that the U.S. systems showed an astonishing lack of flexibility. "Researchers also found that U.S. systems took 2.5 to 3 years and 25,000 man-hours from conception to full operation. Japanese systems, on the other hand, took only 1.25 to 1.75 years and 6,000 man-hours to implement. The conclusion? Management makes the difference."

—In the view of Tom Peters: "We are misusing automation. Americans still see it as a tool to reduce the need for labor, not as a tool to aid labor in adding value to the product. In consequence, efforts to staff our plants with robots are not working."

Technomanagers—By Their Actions Ye Shall Know Them

The surrender of an organization to systems and technology seldom happens deliberately. The process takes place slowly and invisibly. Parents don't notice the daily growth of their children; the result is obvious only when someone or something draws it to their attention.

Business and people become separated. Technomanagers justify insensitive or inhuman practices on the basis of "the real world." They urge employees to act " like professionals," but their use of the word *professional* gives it a disturbing meaning. To be considered "professional," a manager must let the system take precedence over often messy and sloppy human relationships. Directives are impersonally aimed at whoever happens to be responsible for a task's execution; the fact that the effective leadership and mobilization of people demands participation and commitment is forgotten. Technomanagers act as if 90 percent of their job is to make thoughtful decisions and plans. *Implementation is viewed as a troublesome detail.* If the workers don't comply, technomanagers replace them, or buy another company that is already doing what they want done.

The overall thrust of technomanagers is to replace uncontrollable and unpredictable people with predictable and controllable machines and procedures. But such systems often don't perform as well off the drawing board as they do on it.

Symptoms of a technomanagement-dominated organization include:

– the frequent use of consultants to produce reports and make recommendations;

– the belief that computers alone can solve productivity problems;

– the assumption that all employees learn at the same rate and are motivated by the same things;

– an emphasis on organization and structure rather than on the acquisition of skills;

– the gathering of suggestions by impersonal systems rather than by the personal activity of skilled managers;

– a tendency for supervisors to hover over employees looking for errors—"snoopervision."

"As I grow older, I pay less attention to what men say. I just watch what they do."

—Andrew Carnegie

Bureaucracy, a threat in any organization, thrives in a techno-management-driven one. (As one observer commented: "Any organization with five hundred or more people can find enough work to occupy itself for one year without any contact with the outside world.") An innate need for absolute authority leads many technomanagers to establish a rigid chain of command. In his classic article "Asinine Attitudes toward Motivation," Harry Levinson says: "Such bureaucratic structures are based on a military model that assumes complete control of the organization by those at the top. In a pure form, it is a rigid hierarchy, complete with job descriptions and fixed measurable objectives."

The "Failure" of "Successful" Technomanagement

One of the more instructive business stories of the 1980s has been the slippage of General Motors in an industry it had dominated for decades. GM is a good example of the long-term failure of technomanagement. The company put management and technology on a pedestal, above its people and customers. In *My Years with General Motors*, Alfred Sloan laid out the company's original operating precepts. Significantly, these were still the company's *raison d'être* as it entered the turbulent 1970s:

1. GM is in the business of making money, not cars.
2. Styling is more important than quality to buyers who, after all, are going to trade up every year.
3. Foreign competitors will never gain more than 15 percent of the domestic market.
4. Energy will always be cheap and abundant.
5. Workers do not have an important impact on productivity or product quality.
6. Consumer, environmental, and other social concerns are unimportant to the public.
7. Strict centralized financial controls are the key to good administration.

The imbalance within a technomanagement-dominated organization doesn't stop with bureaucrats. There is another important group that contributes its fair share to the imbalance — the autocratic bosses. These people are insensitive to the feelings of others. They see the system as supreme and live in a world of numbers and gadgets. They are as blind to human emotion as some people are to color.

Autocratic bosses often miss emotional cues that influence behavior. Their response to low employee performance is to "kick butt and take names." They talk of people as "resources" or "subordinates" (and themselves "superiors"). To control motivation they use techniques that work on the family dog. Seeing themselves as the all-knowing masters, autocratic bosses use rewards, punishments, and commands to bring employees to heel. This carrot-and-stick approach, often railed at by senior technomanagers, is the norm. Such bosses search endlessly for "hot buttons" to manipulate employees.

"Warning to all Personnel: *Firings will continue until morale improves.*"

The inevitable outcome of all this is a reduction in employee pride, commitment, and motivation — which, ultimately, lowers innovation, quality, service, and productivity. One employee reportedly said of an autocratic boss: "When he dies, I want his heart — because it has never been used."

Tom Janz of the University of Calgary found a correlation between organizations that controlled employees through the use of power, as well as rules and regulations, and unionization. He concluded: "the higher the employees rate the power scale, the more receptive they are to union organizing drives." In other words, the more management pushes (instead of pulling through leadership) the more employees feel a need to unite and push back.

"*Had the employers of the past generation dealt fairly with men, there would have been no trade unions.*"

                                              —Stanley Baldwin, 1931

Where Systems Rule, Service and Innovation Die

Good systems maximize technology and greatly strengthen the hand of organizational members to improve perform-ance. These systems serve and support. On the other hand, like weeds gone wild, overbearing systems will stifle and choke innovation and service.

—"My research reveals that few, if any, major innovations result from highly structured planning systems."
  —Professor Brian Quinn, Amos Tuck School of Business Administration, Dartmouth College, "Managing Innova-tion: Controlled Chaos"

—"If employees are intimidated rather than helped to do their fundamental jobs by procedures and paper work, they may lose any sense of dedication and involvement they had."
  —Perry Pascarella, executive editor, *Industry Week*

—"We have become the victims of the systems we have crea-ted. Computers, forecasting models, organization charts, and new methods of quantification have been idealized as solutions. Business has become austere and stifling."
  —Mary Cunningham, former vice-president, Bendix Corporation

—"Service systems that are low on the friendliness scale tend, by their very design, to subordinate convenience and ease of access for the customer in favor of the convenience of the people within the system."
  —Karl Albrecht and Ron Zemke, *Service America*

In their passion for systems and technology, technomanagers are oblivious to the Frankenstein monster they are creating: a powerful but thoroughly imbalanced organization that relies on "technology and systems" in conjunction with management to the exclusion of leadership (people) skills. The technomanagers bring in more and better technology systems. Employees become less committed. Management then "techs up" and "tightens down" even further . . . and on goes the dance in tighter and tighter circles.

"You do not lead by hitting people over the head, that's assault, not leadership."

As managers' frustration levels go up, so does their determination to "eliminate the human factor." They complain bitterly that "nobody wants to work anymore." They're partly right: nobody wants to work anymore for *them*. The net result is a further widening of the so-called we/they gap: "we, the managers," pointing the accusing finger at "they" the workers. Nobody benefits from the result.

Yet another problem in technomanagement-driven organizations is the lack of trust that permeates the system. Mistrust is built in to the original assumptions on which the turn-of-the-century efficiency expert Frederick Taylor based his theory of scientific management. Faced with largely rural and uneducated factory workers, the famed theoretician separated the "brains" of management from the "brawn" of production. Taylor saw workers as the source of error and sought to minimize their involvement in systems, procedures, and technology. However, in the rapidly changing world of the eighties and nineties, these assumptions have become very costly.

Eliminating the Human Factor

In *Ten Thousand Working Days*, Robert Schrank comments: "Managers are always complaining about 'those workers—if only they would do as we tell them, we would surpass our quotas.'" Looking at workers as an exotic type of hardware will result in workers looking at their jobs as an exotic type of money machine. In both cases, the incorrect point of view will lead to disastrous results. Machines are meant to serve people and people are most effective when they are participating and not being subservient.

A story is told of a group of scientists from all the major industrialized nations who after years of work finally produced the ultimate computer, a machine which was theoretically able to manifest the ultimate in knowledge and intelligence. After some debate, the first question the group put to their creation was *"Is there a God?"* The machine whirled, twirled, and spewed out its response: *"There is now."*

"Man has such a predilection for systems and abstract deductions that he . . . is ready to deny the evidence of his senses only to justify his logic."

—Fyoder Dostoyevski

The Japanese provide useful examples of alternative assumptions and where such alternatives can lead. Robert Cole's comparative research work in U.S. and Japanese auto plants found, on the domestic side, six to seven layers of management separating the plant manager and the chief executive officer. In Japan there were two layers at the most, and the plant manager was often on the board of directors. Cole also discovered interesting evidence of what the we/they gap can do to erode the system from within. Mistrust can only add to the already heavy procedural load in virtually any business. In Japanese car plants, about 2 percent of salaried staff were found in finance and accounting. In American firms, the equivalent statistic was 8 to 10 percent. Building on leadership and people skills, the Japanese organizations were clearly more concerned with bringing in more beans than in counting the ones they already had.

It follows that managers in technomanagement-dominated organizations who feel the need to control communication and information from the top down need complex monitoring systems. In contrast, researchers like Cole have noted that balanced organizations tend to use their monitoring systems less as tools of distrust than as criteria for distributing rewards and implementing solutions. "Their information systems," Cole writes, "identify problems, perform preventative maintenance, and provide raw materials for problem solving."

Innocent Ignorance?

There is one hypothesis that goes a long way to explain why technomanagers don't practice leadership. *They don't know how.* It makes sense that a manager with weak leadership skills and a resulting lack of confidence would veer toward autocratic, impersonal, systems-influenced management.

Low confidence levels caused by poor leadership skills explain why technomanagers are quick to put systems and technology in charge. Unsure of how to deal with the spontaneous, emotional, or unpredictable behavior of human beings, they take cover behind the skirts of technology and management, issuing memos, formulating policies, establishing procedures, investing in equipment, and fine tuning operations. Instead of communicating clear performance expectations, giving constructive feedback, and correcting problem behavior, low-confidence managers use bells, buzzers, and time clocks to herd employees.

This kind of behavior leads an organization to mediocrity. Somewhere down the road employees and customers will decide they have (to paraphrase from the movie *Network*) "had enough and won't take it anymore!" Not even clever commercials or witty slogans will stop the customer from taking his business elsewhere. Similarly, employees — especially "gold-collar" professionals — will leave the organization. (One employee was overheard to say, "We have an open door policy around here all right. If you don't like the way management runs things, the door is always open.") Customers and employees will not be fooled for long by technomanagers who see excellence as the end rather than the means.

PUTTING IT ALL TOGETHER: A BALANCING ACT

"Scientific and humanist approaches are not competitive but supportive, and both are ultimately necessary."

—Robert C. Wood

The balancing act high-performance organizations engage in is a delicate one. Achieving the correct balance of technology, management, and leadership is a most difficult task. Technology and management present difficult choices, sure, but the choices are among tangibles: systems, hardware, costs. Using leadership skills as a catalyst to multiply the power of technology and management, to make them work for people — as opposed to making people work for them — demands choices among intangibles, variables with no fixed limits. Making these choices can be agonizing. And yet organizations grow to high performance by making such decisions and by balancing contradiction, paradox, and dilemma.

Before you can hope for balance, all three elements of the triangle must be present. Is your organization equipped to handle a "technology showdown" with the others in your industry? If not, you're out of the game. (The recent adoption of the Japanese-style "just-in-time" inventory system is already forcing out smaller suppliers who were unable to gear up to provide quick delivery of short-run orders within explicit time guidelines.) Are your management systems in working order? We're not talking about the extreme of "management madness," but we're not advocating shoe-box accounting either. The baby ought not be thrown out with the bath water; there is much that simplified management systems can bring to an organization.

EITHER/OR, AND/ALSO

Often it appears that technology, management, and leadership contradict each other, forcing the technomanager into an either/or decision. A "balanced" leader understands how to develop a third set of options from two seemingly opposed viewpoints. He also understands the need to put together a diverse team to complement his strengths and reinforce his skills in areas in which he may be lacking.

Mastering paradox is a necessity if one is to survive in today's rapidly changing world. Studies show that highly effective leaders can get into fine detail in one situation and stay at a strategic level in another. They can delegate a lot — and a little. They can be close and supportive, yet remote and demanding. They can rely on spoken communication one day and written the next. They may analyze some problems for months and move with speedy intuition on others. They can talk a great deal — and also be terrific listeners.

"There are three sides to every story. Yours, mine, and all that lie between."

–Jody Kern

THE HORNS OF A DILEMMA

Following are examples of the either/or, and/also choices faced by managers. Choosing one over the other could be disastrous. To keep things in perspective is to practice leadership.

On the one hand: You must meet shipping dates.
On the other: You must meet rigid standards of quality.

On the one hand: You want to maximize proven products, methods, or services.
On the other: You would like to experiment with new products, methods, or services.

On the one hand: You believe in keeping the guidelines for employee assignments loose.
On the other: You must have tight control over customer service, product quality, and respect for co-workers.

On the one hand: You must invest time and money in long-term wealth development.
On the other: You need to strengthen short-term profitability and cash flow.

On the one hand: You feel the need to control your employees' time.
On the other: You would like to build commitment through trust.

On the one hand: You hold employees accountable for performance and results.
On the other: You want to build self-esteem, confidence, and pride.

On the one hand: You set optimistic revenue goals.
On the other: You need conservative financial planning.

Although they are considered undesirable in our North American culture, ambiguity and paradox are accepted in the East. Asian cultures believe that life demands a constant balancing of opposites. The Chinese see everything as composed of two opposite forces, yin and yang. To them, the struggle for balance is ongoing, constant, and dynamic. It is the stuff that life itself is made of, and they know that to choose one or the other is impossible.

In North America we prefer to take one side or the other so as to avoid messy uncertainty and paradoxes. We crave "the truth," the unshakeable facts, the right answer. Ambiguity, uncertainty, and doubt are considered signs of weakness. As Louis Barnes states in "The Paradox of Organizational Trust": "The reconciliation of apparent contradictions underlies some of the most truly creative discoveries of science, not to mention most religions, while the suggested unity of opposites permeates the works of great writers . . . to buy when others are selling, to ask questions when others expect answers, or to give new autonomy when subordinates expect tighter controls, are all actions that make sense under certain conditions."

Barnes credits George F.F. Lombard of the Harvard Business School with what Barnes dubs Lombard's Law: "Hard drives out soft." In other words, the side with the most hard evidence is the strongest. When hard facts and figures contradict feelings and intuition, the hard side usually wins. However, in managing a balanced organization, there must be room for both. Creativity consultant Roger Van Oech says: "A good analogy [is] a potter making a vase. . . . It is a lot easier to shape, mold and throw clay if it has some softness. By the same token, after the vase is shaped, it has no practical value unless it has been put into a kiln and fired. Both the soft and the hard elements are required *but at different times.*"

"The test of first-rate intelligence is the ability to hold two opposed ideas in the mind at the same time, and still be able to function."

—F. Scott Fitzgerald

Building a leadership "base" is a difficult, but doable task. Through the study of outstanding organizations, key steps have emerged. The heart and soul of a balanced organization is a vision of the preferred future framed by a set of core operating values. Unlike quantifiable goals or objectives, this vision appeals to the gut. It is "bait for emotion"; it provides a focal point, like the North Star, to guide strategy and plans. Values, meanwhile, declare boundaries for behavior. They can be a cost-effective substitute for the policy manuals that Tom Peters refers to as the Book of Excuses. Once locked in, values allow employees to make on-line judgments, solve their own problems, and manage the organization's most valuable asset: themselves.

"A company cannot increase its productivity. People can."

—Robert Half

A Foundation for Quality and Productivity Improvement

You can't build anything — not even an outhouse — without a solid foundation. Zenger-Miller Research Manager, Roland Dumas, conducted an extensive study of quality improvement efforts in the United States over a four-year period. He concluded: "Many companies are building 1990s 'high-tech' buildings on 19th Century foundations, because sophisticated systems, like Cost of Quality, Just-In-Time, Employee Involvement or Statistical Process Control are not built on a strong leadership skill base. Most are floundering as a result."

People skills must be the starting point for improvement efforts:

—"In our company, the greatest productivity improvements have come when we have enlisted the hearts and minds of our associates on the factory floor."
—Walter C. Minnick, president, Trus Joist Corporation

—"The failure of scientists and engineers to convince NASA . . . to postpone the ill-fated space shuttle flight is a tragic reminder that technical professionals frequently lack the influence skills necessary to affect managerial decisions."
—George Klemp, senior partner, Charles River Consulting

—"In too many cases, quality initiatives sincerely launched and desperately needed are born without a heartbeat, or lack the vitality to survive. While leadership without management can lead to chaos, management without leadership is sterile."
—Dana M. Cound, vice-president quality, Diversitech General, and president, American Society for Quality Control

---

Balanced organizations recognize the importance of ongoing training and development. They regard leadership-skill building as part of a longer-term overall plan to upgrade the people portion of the organization—on the principle that continually exercising a muscle is healthier than occasionally taking violent exercise. It is not possible to get one shot of development and be set for life. The "soft," intangible, and "fuzzy" skills of leadership require constant building and exercise to remain strong. Use them or lose them.

A study by Harvard's Wickham Skinner and Earl Sasser of successful and unsuccessful managers supports this: "Most of the failures we observed were those of previously successful managers. What had always worked before was precisely what caused the failure. Operating skills can never be considered set—they must always be renewed, reconsidered, developed."

Soft Skills? Anything But!

People power? Pampered employees? Participation? For the first-time analyst of skills, there is usually an assumption that organizations adopting these attributes create a soft or cushy environment for their people, an environment in which people are allowed to do more or less as they please. In fact, the opposite is most often true: employees are more likely to "get away with murder" in a technomanaged organization than they are in one that balances the people components of leadership with other factors. In a technomanaged organization, employees can hide behind rules and policies, names and titles, and turn in good "technical" work while at the same time snubbing their fellow workers and providing mediocre customer service. However, in a balanced organization that has a clear set of values, an overall vision, and people who have mastered the skills of working with each other, there is simply nowhere to hide. In a balanced environment you have what Perry Pascarella refers to as "hard humanism," an environment in which everyone expects the maximum from everyone else and where compromises simply will not be accepted.

Skill development, like organizational performance, is a journey, not a destination.

SKILLS AND BALANCE GO HAND IN HAND

"Intellectuals love the idea of humanity but do not necessarily love the actual individuals who compose it. Insensitivity to the needs and views of other people is a characteristic of those passionately concerned with ideas."

— Paul Johnson

Tolerance for ambiguity and the ability to manage paradox will increase in proportion to skill building. As managers in balanced organizations become confident and competent leaders, their need for certainty, their insistence on "being right," and their

---

Leadership Is the Catalyst

The Carnegie Foundation did a study to determine what contributes the most to a person's success, regardless of career. They found that only 15 percent of a person's career advancement was determined by technical skills, and that 85 percent came from people skills — their ability to manage themselves, their attitudes, and their lives.

Leadership skill is the catalytic agent that determines how well management and technology are used. Where there is a low level of leadership-skill development, money is often poured into other things — like technology and management — in an attempt to compensate for the deficiency.

A large shoe manufacturer embarked on a plant-wide leadership-skills training program. The payoff from improved leadership was a *40 percent* increase in productivity. When senior managers from a competitive plant toured the facility, they were surprised to find it to be old and dingy; its equipment was obsolete, and its management systems were crude. But because this company was obsessed with building a strong leadership base, the less-than-ideal plant had become many times more productive than the visitors' plants.

---

desire for autocratic control decreases. They roll with the punches. Their confidence level is higher, and they can see options and alternatives where previously there were only problems and difficulties. Having sharpened the skills of leadership, they become leaders. They walk the fine line among the complex elements of the organization: its diverse and alien technology, its rational and analytical management, and its people-driven leadership.

Our experience shows that organizations can, with proper attention to skill building, bring themselves into balance.

CHAPTER THREE

Vision: "Skyhooks" for the Soul

"Great men are they who see the spiritual as stronger than any material forces; that thought rules the world."

—Ralph Waldo Emerson

INTRODUCTION TO VISION INTEGRATED PERFORMANCE

A few years ago we were working with the productivity-improvement department of the telecommunications-equipment giant Northern Telecom Ltd. Various parts of the organization were successfully using our approaches. The productivity people wanted us to develop an introductory video to bring the skills and elements of leadership together. Building on our earlier, performance-improvement models, we created the Vision Integrated Performance leadership blueprint. This evolved into the VIP Strategy.

VIP is both complex and simple. Its complexity results from the blending and balancing of four different elements, with four special sets of leadership skills as catalysts.

Its simplicity, paradoxically, results from its complexity. Like a sunny day, which blends the right amounts of light, fresh air, and gentle breezes, the components of the blueprint, once understood, are singularly clear.

When you have read the discussion of vision and values, you will immediately understand that every major accomplishment of yours was possible because, at a fundamental level, you *already* practiced vision and values. And when you have absorbed the section on environment and behavior in the context of the modern organization, how they result directly from (and work in harmony with) vision and values, and how the combination of all four, in turn, affects true bottom-line performance, you will think— AHA!—that nothing could really be more obvious.

What This Book Is All About

Imagine a complex machine composed of many interrelated systems, turbines, engines, levers, pulleys, and widgets. The main sections of that machine are then labeled according to four separate elements: "vision," "values," "environment," and "behavior." To work on or refine the output of the machine, you need not only tools that will correctly fit the delicate moving parts, but also a blueprint or template, so you can be certain that the repairs you are making to one section will not adversely affect any other section at a later stage.

The machine is your present organization. Vision, values, and environmental and behavioral elements you already have in place whether you realize it or not. The tools you will now need to work on these systems are what we call leadership skills. And the template you will need to use to make sure that adjustments done to one system will work in harmony with adjustments made to other systems is the "VIP" leadership model.

The VIP Strategy, once grasped, is itself as clear, obvious, and refreshing as a sunny day. However, like a sunny day, it is difficult to whip together without exactly the right mix of elements — especially if this is the first time you've tried to make one!

The VIP Strategy outlines the direct relationship between what the members of an organization contribute to it (vision/values) and what the organization produces (performance: quality, innovation, and service). The four basic skills of leadership become the mechanisms or catalysts that release the energy contained in vision, values, environment, and behavior.

These basic elements affect all organizations whether or not they recognize it. (Gravity doesn't ask your permission each time it operates!) We have found that high-performing organizations who may not deliberately have adopted the terminology of the VIP Strategy are none the less already following its template each and every day of their organizational lives. And those organizations that have unfortunately wandered far afield from the paths of performance are as likely as not to be ill using the strategies of VIP on a regular basis—although, if pressed, they may be unable to express what they are doing "wrong."

Like the steering wheel on a car, VIP, merely a tool on its own, can be used to control the development of even the largest and most powerful organization—as well as individual departments or divisions, or even much smaller enterprises. To understand the model is good. To develop the skills to use it—*that's* where the payoff lies!

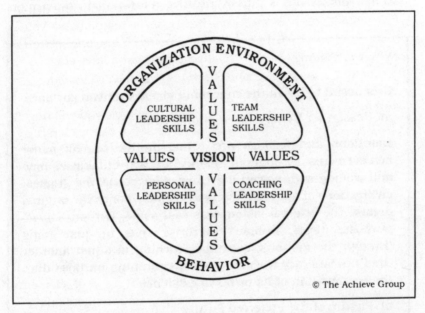

© The Achieve Group

Vision is that igniting spark of purpose that can energize and inspire people to do what has to be done. Vision gives meaning where meaning is lacking, and it enhances meaning where meaning already exists. Vision reaches hungrily out to the future and drags it into the present. Vision is proof positive that the spiritual side of mankind will not be denied. Tom Peters is finding that "developing a vision and, more important, living it vigorously are essential elements of leadership."

"There is no medicine like hope, no incentive so great, and no tonic so powerful as expectation of something better tomorrow."

—Orison Swett Marden

When he was assistant to the president of Standard Oil, O. A. Ohmann coined another term for this creative spark in his classic *Harvard Business Review* article: he called it "skyhooks." Ohmann explains: "[It] came in the heat of a discussion with a group of business executives attending the Institute of Humanistic studies at Aspen, Colorado. As we debated the limits of the rational and scientific approach to life, it occurred to me that science appears rational on the surface, but at its very foundation typically lies a purely intuitive nonrational assumption

---

What Is Vision?

It is useful to break the concept of vision into two parts:

a) Reason for Being (the emotional catalyst)

Emotions and feelings are prime motivators. All major achievements throughout history are attributable to men and women with powerful dreams. Conversely, the greatest civilizations of our collective past crumbled once the original dream, the original vision, was cast aside. Without cause, purpose, ideals, human enterprise ends up just going through the motions, eventually turning into just another tired bureaucracy with no other over-arching purpose than the preservation of its own sad existence.

b) Picture of the Preferred Future

What we get is what we see. A growing amount of evidence is showing that the image, or picture, we have of the next golf shot, business week or coming year, we bring to pass. Today's behaviors are determined by our expectations of tomorrow. Unconsciously or deliberately, we turn our vision of the future into self-fulfilling prophecies.

Pictures of the future already exist at personal, unit and organizational levels. When they are negative, conflicting or uncertain, fear, resistance and weak performance usually follow. Establishing and rallying team or organizational members around a compelling picture of the *preferred* future is the first step to exceptional performance.

---

made by some scientist. He just hooked himself on a 'piece of sky out there' and hung on. It was a complete leap of faith that led him."

Vision — or skyhooks — when properly nurtured, shored up by values, and harnessed by skills, can ultimately lead to a personal, dynamic, and uniquely individualized experience for each member of the organization.

Vision creates energy. The creation of corporate energy involves everyone. Employees at every level have a part to play. The energy springs from something deep inside people that makes them want to work with their hearts and heads as well as their hands. When the vitality of an organization's people is focused and combined, almost anything can be accomplished.

"If we try to renew, it's because we have a vision of something worth saving or doing."

—John Gardner

Vision sets our expectations — what we, at a core level, believe to be possible. Immense visions lead to immense possibilities. Stunted or unformed visions have the opposite effect entirely. Playwright George Bernard Shaw said, "Our conduct is influenced not by our experience but by our expectations." As our late colleague, Dr. Edward Lindaman, former director of program control for manufacture of the Apollo spacecraft, continually stressed: "A fundamental determinate of how we choose to behave today is our conscious or below-conscious expectation of what the future could hold in store." He actually simulated pictures of what the moon landing would look like and had these mounted on the walls at Rockwell Standard so the work teams would get the picture. Every Monday morning via an in-house TV network, Lindaman would interview a different team, demanding that they verbalize what the moon landing would be like for them! There were hundreds of these contractors all together. The flow chart in the project control room covered four walls, ceiling to floor.

Lindaman's preoccupation with visioning inevitably kept things humming. For example, when an engineer lamented about the impossibility of improving the performance of a particular part from one failure per five thousand to one failure per five million, Lindaman replied: "Before you get into telling me your troubles, *what would it look like to you if the problem were resolved?*" His insistence that everyone share and espouse a vision of a "preferred future" kept people focused, energized, and on target. It empowered them to do something that, in fact, had never been done before.

"Some men see things as they are and say 'why'? I dream things that never were, and say 'why not'?"

—George Bernard Shaw

Writers of science fiction understand the raw power of vision. First they figure out where they're going with their stories, and

---

Shooting for the Moon

"I believe that this nation should commit itself to landing a man on the moon and returning him safely to earth before this decade is out . . . . No single space project will be more impressive to mankind or more important to the long range exploration of space . . . but in a very real sense it will not be · one man going to the moon, it will be an entire nation."
—John F. Kennedy, 1961

Charles Garfield spent nineteen years studying more than four hundred "peak performers" in the worlds of art, entertainment, sports, academe, and business. The one common denominator he repeatedly identified was *vision* (or mission). His own personal quest for high performance began when he was a mathematician and computer analyst on the Apollo program: "I experienced as never before or since the magnitude of what can be achieved through the power of people sharing a mission. I saw . . . excitement and pride come alive, affecting everyone around them, kindling imaginations with the possibilities that arose from what we were trying to accomplish. One thing became very clear to me — it's not the goal but the ultimate *mission* that kindles the imagination, motivating us toward ever higher levels of human achievement."

---

then they create an entirely new set of internally consistent laws and actions — sometimes even entire universes and galaxies! — to make sure they get there. They are limited only by their own imaginations. They make the impossible possible.

Visions are pro-active, not reactive. They are positive, not negative. They pertain to the future, not the past. They are alive.

Depending on how vision is used, it can be a blessing or a curse. The choice is ours. We are free to fill the vacuum between our ears with positive images of a preferred future, or to sit back and play host to whatever random chatter and negative images our mind may conjure up. Visions become reality; and the result of negative visioning is far from pretty. The wife of the late Karl Wallenda, the most celebrated aerial artist of all time, observed that, before her husband's final, fatal accident off the high wire, he was more obsessed with falling than at any time in his career. Clearly, each one of us behaves on a day-to-day basis according to our own internal visions. Perhaps, rather than blame the results, we should look to the cause — and make corrections ("paint new pictures") while there is yet time.

"Where there is no vision the people perish."

—Proverbs 29:18

Erich Fromm puts it this way: "Not only does the individual live by hope. Nations and social classes [also] live through hope, faith and fortitude . . . and, if they lose this potential, they disappear either by lack of vitality or by the irrational destructiveness they develop."

Vision makes the unreachable reachable. It permits us to get a finite grasp on the infinite. Harvard professor Rosabeth Moss Kanter, after five years of examining how dozens of successful organizations deal with change, speaks of the need for a "leap of imagination, a leap of faith." She says: "Change efforts have to mobilize people around what is not yet known, not yet experienced."

Think of a tree growing from a seedling. The tree takes root in reality (the nurturing ground) yet it sets its sights for the open sky. A tree not only has a vision of where it is going (up) but also where it will go when it gets there (*farther* up).

We often mistake a goal for a vision. A vision encompasses goals, whereas goals by themselves do not necessarily add up to a vision. *Vision contains spiritual and metaphysical elements that transcend goals.* And so this should be, for organizations themselves contain certain spiritual and metaphysical components that transcend technology—these "components" are its own people! Vision is to people what data is to a computer: a key input so important, so vital, that without it the very purpose of existence becomes questionable.

What about the difference between strategic planning and vision? Vision is compelling but not controlling. It shows you where you want to be, but not exactly how to get there. Vision is the power; planning is the tool. A plan shows you how to get so far, but then, to get further, you need another plan. It's been said, "The minute you lay down a plan it's out of date." *A vision shows you where you're going—and why you are going there.* Visions are flexible, dynamic, organic. They welcome change and diver-

---

Vision: A Context for Goals

Vision provides the broader themes or directions for goals:

GOALS	VISIONS
—are based on a need to accomplish	—are based on a need to accomplish continually
—are measured by results	—are measured by results and feelings
—are rational	—are rational and intuitive
—are conscious	—are conscious and subconscious
—lead to adult maturity	—lead to adult maturity and childlike creativity
—are linear, one-dimensional	—are holistic and multi-dimensional
—create focus	—create purpose and focus
—motivate	—align
—provide direction	—create energy
—are based on past performance	—can establish new possibilities

---

sity. Plans are static and moribund. In our work with clients, we often find excellent strategic plans poorly implemented. Without vision, there is insufficient energy to make the plan work.

Ancient seafarers used to set their course by the North Star. They never expected to reach the star itself—but every move they made was based on its position. And the North Star served them well: whatever happened to throw them off course, it remained true and in a fixed position. When they needed it, it was there. When people get blown off course, a well-entrenched "reason for being" (a vision) can provide a guiding light that will help them reorient themselves. Even if a company has to change its business plan radically, drop product lines, or drastically alter organizational structure, its employees will not feel abandoned if a compelling "reason for being" exists. Vision will keep the team members focused.

"The only way to lead people is show them a future: A leader is a dealer in hope."

—Napoleon Bonaparte

Vision promotes trust, and trust is the foundation of any successful human enterprise. Trust (or faith) binds people to an ideal, sets aside doubts, casts away fear. Trust makes things happen. Those who trust, who believe, will align themselves with the vision and do what has to be done. Those who don't trust, who don't share the common language and common purpose of the vision, will have great difficulty working together. They will instinctively turn away and choose another path. The most powerful team-building activity is the collective development of, and commitment to, a shared vision.

"The heart has reasons that reason does not understand."

—Jacques Bénigne Bossuet

Vision and trust transcend barriers, provide a common language, and make available shared goals. Labour/management relations can be very productive if both parties share exactly the same vision from the start. Without vision, however, individual needs inevitably take precedence over the needs of the organization, and self-centred behavior replaces group-motivated behavior. People then mistrust other people as a matter of course. Instead of one great vision, you will find many smaller, lesser visions, each fighting for its particular place in the sun. And performance suffers.

Vision comes right from the heart. You don't get dreams from a machine. And you don't find excellence in a financial statement. It has been said, "Somewhere in the background of every great business is a man bigger than the business." Robert Haas, president of Levi Strauss, speaks plainly of his personal vision "to make everyone who is associated with the company a spiritual stakeholder." Or consider the company Tom Watson, Sr., joined in 1914, when he was forty years old. Then it made only meat slicers, grocery-store scales, time clocks, and primitive tabulators known as punch-card machines. Ten years later he gave his company a new name to match his vision: International Business Machines. (Years after that, he was asked the question "At what point did you envisage IBM becoming so big?" His answer: "Right at the beginning!" Tom Watson, Jr., verifies it: "Father always talked and acted as though IBM were a billion-dollar corporation.")

"A rockpile ceases to be a rockpile the moment a single man contemplates it, bearing within him the image of a cathedral."

—Antoine de Saint-Exupery

Thomas Bata, Sr., the founder of Bata International, was once quoted as saying: "I was put on the face of the earth to shoe mankind," and that vision has continued to guide his footware-manufacturing company long after his passing. The company now serves more than eighty-five countries worldwide. (Peter Drucker adds: "Typically men of this type have a gift for words . . . . But they are not men of ideas. They are men of vision. And what makes them important is that . . . they act on their vision.")

UCLA professor James O'Toole, a former director of the Work in America Institute, sees dire consequences if North American business is allowed to roam free without vision or context: "Business [has become] merely a game; and there is no purpose to a game—it is an end in itself. Without a purpose, one cannot do long range planning. All one can do is to engage in tactical maneuverings designed to win the current round of the game. Here the planning activities of the Old Guard tend to be reactive, incident-driven, episodic and short-term. That's why [certain organizations] went into tailspins when their charismatic leaders retired."

A vision is never completely defined. This built-in ambiguity makes it more valuable than mere goals. It is not so much a set of precise instructions as a roadmap. When one is lost, the original instructions are not much help. A roadmap, however, allows the traveler to change plans while maintaining the same destination.

Properly exercised, vision draws upon the creative visual side of the human mind. As an example: ask someone to tell you quickly exactly how many windows are in his home. He will probably

---

What Makes Work Work?

William O'Brien, president of Hanover Insurance Company, said: "We each are influenced by our own mental picture of what we are building with our efforts. I call these mental pictures visions and they play an important role in determining what our company becomes." (Hanover was nearly bankrupt in 1969 before the company developed a shared vision that all the employees embraced. Today Hanover is a leader in its field and has grown 50 percent faster than the industry average.)

McBer and Company, a Boston consulting firm, reports: "Fifty-one percent of the 79 percent [surveyed] who thought they could improve the quantity of their output said they could increase it by 20 percent or more, if conditions were better." Added McBer CEO Richard Boyatzis: "The basic message that people are sending out is that companies aren't doing much with the talent they have . . . . People want to work but not necessarily for the person they work for. They are committed to the strategic will to win, and need a sense of belonging to something that they feel proud of. They are looking for a theme or sense of what the organization is — a way of identifying with it, so they can feel proud of belonging to it. *However, they want to belong only to a company that is winning.*"

---

come up blank. Next allow the same individual to try a "visioning" exercise, walking "mentally" from room to room in the house, counting each window one by one as it is encountered. Usually, the person will respond with the exact answer.

"To give life meaning, one must have a purpose larger than oneself."

—Will Durant

A powerful vision seems almost to pick and choose those who will be *permitted* to approach it. We often compare vision to a magnetic force that draws people to it and then heads (or aligns) them in precisely the same direction. To continue the analogy, individuals who do not espouse the vision would be repelled by it, the same way two mismatched poles of a magnet repel each other.

A vision unexpressed or kept secret, on the other hand, is like a television program that never goes on air. If the vision is worth something to you (or your organization), it is worth sharing. Unshared, the vision lacks substance, lacks belief. An unshared vision will fade like the shadowy, incomplete specter it really is.

In the late 1920s the leading manufacturer of soft drinks was a Boston-based company named Moxie. But Moxie saw itself as being in the business of selling "herb-based" soft drinks, whereas an upstart company calling itself "Coca-Cola" had a vision to quench the thirst of a nation.

"Life has value only when it has something valuable as its object."

—Georg Wilhelm Friedrich Hegel

Vision gives people a reason for being; it cuts to their very essence. As Jean Ribaud, president of Schlumberger, speculates: "In the past the Church gave people the values of life . . . . It is now the organization for which they work that gives meaning and purpose."

Proper utilization of vision can lead to a creative, empowering organization rather than a stifling, dehumanizing one. In Charles Garfield's words: "People who were once supposed to be engulfed and depleted by organizations are now using those organizations to extend individual, distinctive, missions toward peak perform-ance."

Garfield also understands the synergy of vision (mission), that it can bring about results greater than the sum of individual con-tributions: "Alignment occurs when individuals perceive that contributing to an organization produces direct contributions to their personal mission. *The more opportunities an organization*

How Leaders Use Vision

Warren Bennis and Burt Nanus studied ninety top leaders in the fields of business, academe, sports, and the arts. They concluded: "[These leaders'] visions or intentions are compel-ling and pull people toward them. Intensity coupled with commitment is magnetic. And these intense personalities do not have to coerce people to pay attention — they are so intent on what they are doing that, like a child completely absorbed with creating a sand castle in a sandbox, they draw others in. . . . VISION GRABS. The visions these various leaders conveyed bring about a confidence on the part of the employees, a con-fidence that instilled in them a belief that they were capable of performing the necessary acts . . . . All organizations de-pend on the existence of shared meanings and interpreta-tions of reality, which facilitate coordinated action. The actions and symbols of leadership frame and mobilize mean-ing. Leaders articulate and define what has previously re-mained implicit or unsaid — then they invent images, meta-phors and models that provide a focus for new attention. . . .

To choose a direction, a leader must first have developed a mental image of the possible and desirable future state of the organization . . . with a vision, the leader provides the all-important bridge from the present to the future of the organization . . . . Under these conditions, the human ener-gies of the organization are aligned toward a common end . . . . All the leaders to whom we spoke seemed to have been masters of selecting, synthesizing, and articulating an appropriate vision of the future. Later, we learned that this was a common quality of leaders down through the ages."

---

gives to its people to align their personal missions with its own, the more likely it is . . . to succeed."

Employers all too often assume that the employee has no vision beyond the desire to collect a salary when, in fact, nothing could be further from the truth. One of many similar studies on the

---

Vision: Key to Innovation

Brian Quinn, a professor of management at the Amos Tuck School of Business Administration, has spent decades studying innovation. His conclusion is that the process of managing innovation is "controlled chaos." At the heart of this process, Quinn found, successful managers make use of the power of vision:

> Innovative managements—whether technical or not—project clear long-term visions for their organizations that go beyond simple economic measures. As Intel's chairman, Gordon Moore, says: "We intend to be the outstandingly successful innovative company in this industry. We intend to continue to be a leader in this revolutionary [semiconductor] technology that is changing the way the world is run." . . .
>
> Such visions, vigorously supported, are not "management fluff." . . . They attract quality people to the company and give focus to their creative and entrepreneurial drives. When combined with sound internal operations, they help channel growth by concentrating attention on the actions that can lead to profitability rather than profitability by itself.

William Bricker, chairman and CEO of Diamond Shamrock, has much the same reaction: "Why has our vision been narrowed? Why has our flexibility been constricted? To my mind there is one central reason: our strategies have become too rigid . . . a detailed strategy is like a road map [telling] us every turn we must take to our goal. . . . The entrepreneur, on the other hand, views strategic planning not as a road map but as a compass . . . and is always looking for a new road."

---

subject was conducted with 57,000 employees of a major gas company. Asked to attribute weights to key factors in job satisfaction, pay came out fifth on a list of ten possibilities. (Management was absolutely convinced it would be first.) More important were job security, enjoyable work, career advancement, and quality of work.

"People who think only of profit in the next twenty years won't make any profit."

—Paul Bougenaux

Nor are "winning" or "profits," by themselves, the substance of a fully formed vision. In isolation, each lacks context. And neither is the stuff that can truly rally the spirit, fire the imagination, and galvanize the faithful. When Johnson & Johnson elected to recall Tylenol [TM], they were not operating out of a pure profit motive, since, had they been unsuccessful in regaining market share (as the experts predicted at the time), the recall would ultimately have cost them millions. In the final analysis, the market applauded J&J's quick response, and Tylenol returned to its dominant position.

Having a vision doesn't automatically mean peace and tranquility, or even unanimity in all areas. Having a vision means absolute unanimity on only one thing: the vision itself. Consider an analogy between the organization and a group of people in a lifeboat. The lifeboat, for those inside it, becomes the context, and rescue becomes the vision. Lesser goals and strategies may be implemented to achieve the vision, but some of these may cause damage to the boat if they don't work. Damage to the boat "above the waterline" (by, say, collision with an overhanging tree), is an acceptable risk. Damage "below the waterline" (from a submerged stump), however, is not. The trick is to keep the vision whole. Similarly, a company that seeks to make profits by illegal bidding or bribery or wrongdoing is doing damage "below the waterline." It is violating its vision (and its values).

Once a shared vision is accepted, disagreements may occasionally develop, as they do within a large family. The conflict, whatever the result, always yields to the larger context of the mission, the love, within the healthy family. It may be a fight, but the opponents are fighting for the same thing.

"Profits are to a corporation what breathing is to human life. We cannot live in a private enterprise system without profit. But breathing is not the sole purpose of life, and profits are not the sole purpose of the adventure we call business management."

—Fletcher Byron

Visioning is the ultimate team-building process, far surpassing the traditional exercises like "lost in the desert." We have watched senior teams collaborate on sensitive strategic plans that, prior to visioning, would have resulted in dogfights and turf warfare.

The waterline analogy works equally well when applied to the "profit or purpose?" conundrum. As John Naisbitt and Patricia Aburdene observe in *Re-inventing the Corporation*: "Vision ultimately gets translated into sales and profit growth and return on investment, *but the numbers come after the vision.*"

Vision is very much a function of perception. Just as fish have trouble "seeing" the water they are in, so people have trouble working with visions that contain elements that are foreign to them. This rule has also been expressed as: "Carpetlayers have trouble seeing the chandeliers."

In Detroit during the complacent sixties, executives had a vision (albeit a limited one) of providing the customer with exactly what they thought the customer wanted, no more and no less. This vision proved to be limited by the fact that the cars of choice common at that time in Michigan (the cars the executives themselves saw as their chauffeurs drove them to work each day) were not what consumers were actually looking for. Those executives would have got a clearer picture by commuting to work in southern California, where buyer tastes of that era were truly being sculpted. Here, the goal was adequate but the perceptual framework, the vision, was lacking. Similarly, an executive who has never been a "worker" would have trouble grasping a vision of an organization as a place where the "workers come first."

To achieve dreams such as these, your organization must first realize that it is no stronger than its weakest link. It is possible to create a context for even mailroom clerks that allows them to join in the organization's overall purpose—provided that the skills needed to contribute toward that purpose are developed. (*STAY TUNED!*)

Just Imagine What It Would Be Like If . . .

SERVICE

—the people who used your products or services got just what they wanted when they wanted it!

—your staff regularly uncovered and incorporated into your business little things that, in the perception of your customers, set your organization apart!

QUALITY

—your customers believed that your products and services provided superb quality and value—and your employees were constantly seeking out new avenues to keep it that way!

—quality was an uncompromised tradition that permeated every level of your organization!

INNOVATION

—your employees embraced change as an opportunity to "meet the future."

—your staff had an ingrained sense of common purpose. They just kept finding better and better ways to get the job done!

PRODUCTIVITY

—there was a powerful feeling of focused energy and vitality evident the moment you walked through the door of your organization!

—your staff members had the necessary skills not only to do their jobs but to be good team players!

CHAPTER FOUR

Values: Vision on the "Flip Side"

"Ideals are like stars; you will not succeed in touching them with your hands. But like the seafaring man on the desert of waters, you choose them as your guides and following them you will reach your destination."

— Carl Schurz

Have you ever wandered into a restaurant, taken a look at the surroundings, and then marched back outside muttering to yourself, "I'm not eating *there*!"? You might have been upset by the lack of cleanliness in the room, a sad-looking assortment of food on display, the unsavory demeanor of the chef, or perhaps even the dowdy customers that the place catered to. Compare this experience to that of entering a "four-star" establishment that boasts gourmet food, a spotless appearance, and international chefs, and that won't allow *you* inside without a suit and tie! The fundamental issue in each case is the same: *values*.

It has been said: "Before you can win the game, it helps to know the rules!" In a business, values are the sign language by which people communicate to outsiders (and themselves) what they are all about. At a more profound level, values are the foundation of the organization's actions, on which it builds and upon which the organization's members climb to new heights day after day.

In 1913 James Cash Penney was one of the first businessmen to prepare a corporate constitution in which his organization's obligations to its customers and staff were clearly enumerated:

1. To serve the public, as nearly as we can, to its complete satisfaction.
2. To expect for the service we render a fair remuneration, and not all the profit the traffic will bear.

3. To do all in our power to pack the customer's dollar full of value, quality, and satisfaction.

4. To continue to train ourselves and our associates so that the services we give will be more and more intelligently performed.

5. To improve constantly the human factor in our business.

6. To reward men and women in our organization through participation in what the business produces.

7. To test our every policy, method, and act in this way: "Does it square with what is right and just?"

"Golden Rule principles are just as necessary for operating a business profitably as are trucks, typewriters, or twine."

—James Cash Penney

Vision and values are interconnected. Vision is shaped by values, and values come alive through vision. The net result, carefully honed by the proper skills, creates an environment of performance, a place where people don't just talk about achieving, they do it!

Michael McCaskey, who manages the Chicago Bears, says values "are the moral compass that give you direction when things get rough."

Ideally, values, once clarified, should have special meaning for those who make them come alive. There is no need to go overboard: the correct value, once identified, will fit like a tailored suit. It will complement the individual or organization that chooses it. Each spring, does the oak tree say, "This year I am going to produce excellent leaves"? No, that is part of its very nature. Each year, being an oak tree, it will naturally do the very best it can.

Properly chosen values in an organization do the following:
—They create an atmosphere of common purpose and trust. Since everyone knows what to do, you can get out of the way and let them do it! More is accomplished; autonomy and entrepreneurial spirit rule the day.
—They provide a clearer focus for feedback and performance reviews.
—They create a qualitative means to reach quantitative objectives.

—They help everyone set priorities and sort out "information overload."

—They direct training and development activities.

—They avoid the "program-of-the-month" syndrome and the resultant shifting priorities that waste energy.

—They discourage the "beat-the-system" confrontational mentality and reduce politics and gamesplaying.

—They provide guidelines for selecting and orienting new employees, who will in turn need to spend less time trying to figure out what the organization is all about.

Anchors in a Sea of Change

Properly used, values are the anchors to which an organization can cling when buffeted by change. Values that draw on the history of the organization can provide refuge from a storm. Many organizations have demonstrated this over the years.

—Jean Coyle, vice-president of management development at Bank of America says: "We articulated our values in four key dimensions—strategy, marketing, people and technology—that we can trace back to the founder . . . . They [the values] got out of kilter as the bank became regulated . . . . We've polished them off and they're back in the forefront again."

—The Ford Motor Company, when fighting the import invasion of the sixties and seventies, gained breathing time by reminding customers of the original Model T, and how simple basic transportation was. That effective transportation continued to be its goal.

—Imperial Oil, going through a nasty down-sizing program in 1982, had to find a way to deal with reducing costs while at the same time being true to the values upon which the firm had been founded. After thorough introspection, the company concluded that laying people off was not in sync with its hundred-year history. Instead, early retirement and leave-of-absence programs were used.

—They simplify rules and policies to a manageable level.
—They build an element of predictability into the organization. People who know what is expected of them are more likely to do it!

"Not everything that counts can be counted, and not everything that can be counted counts."

—Sir George Pickering (often repeated by Albert Einstein)

Buck Rodgers, retired marketing vice-president, was a key player in IBM's phenomenal growth of the last few decades. He speaks of three commitments (values) that are central to everyone, from the CEO to the mailroom clerk, at IBM:

1. The individual must be respected.
2. Each customer must be given the best possible service.
3. Excellence and superior performance must be pursued.

IBM has a history of responding to any service request within twenty-four hours. This policy may not be minutely detailed in the "big three" listed above, but, like any positive value, it is clearly understood, followed, and believed in at virtually every level of the organization. Therein lies the power of a value system. It creates momentum and builds upon itself. In the words of Al Williams, a former IBM president: "It is not bigness we seek, it is greatness. Bigness is imposing. Greatness is enduring."

Johnson & Johnson's CEO, James Burke, appeared on the *Phil Donahue Show* to explain why the organization took a multi-million-dollar financial gamble in recalling bottles of Tylenol that might or might not have been tampered with. He said: "We believe that our first responsibility is to the doctors, nurses and patients, to mothers and all others who use our products and services." Not surprisingly, the statement earned a rousing round of applause from the audience.

There is a lot of discussion today about the need to improve communications in organizations. All too often there is nothing wrong with the communications; the problem is in conveying what the organization's real priorities are. Blaming communications is like saying the telephone is not giving me the information I need. The problem is not with the equipment or the volume of information conveyed; the problem is that employees don't understand what's really important. When values are clear, the organization's leaders can free themselves to achieve by allowing their employees to make their own day-to-day operating decisions within their assigned responsibilities.

In our first book, *The "I" of the Hurricane: Creating Corporate Energy*, we said: "Leaders never create core values, they discover active or dormant beliefs that they and a critical mass of potential followers care about. Then they shape or evolve them into a focus for energy."

"The way to gain a good reputation is to endeavor to be what you desire to appear.

—Socrates

The Good Guys Finish First

The Center for Economic Revitalization, a Vermont-based investment-research group, selected a group of "good" firms based on the following criteria:
— production of nondestructive goods and services, contributing to the overall quality of life;
— responsible employee/labor relations;
— participation in community/public-service work;
— support of philanthropic or public-service programs;
— demonstration of ethical concern for and response to major social problems and issues.
The resultant "good guys," which included such well-known companies as Levi Strauss and Johnson & Johnson, were then tracked (in terms of market performance) back to 1974, the year of the stock market's last great low. Over the period 1974 to 1984, it was found that, while the Dow itself went up only 55 percent, this group increased in share value an average of 240 percent! The conclusion? Those who behave ethically are those who profit the most over time!

—*From Beyond the Bottomline: How Business Leaders Are Turning Principles into Profits*, by Tad Tuleja.

Clarifying Core Values

At AVCO Financial Services, a cross-section of employees put together the following statement of values for management to debate, refine, and commit to.

"Many companies have talked about excellent service but few have defined what they mean by it . . . . At AVCO, providing that service is a challenge. We must:
— respond to the customer in a caring manner at all times. Actively listen to customers. Demonstrate empathy by putting ourselves in their place and thoroughly understand their situation.
— project a professional image. Maintain a professional office appearance and personal manner. Dress so that our customers feel confident in dealing with AVCO.
— build customer relationships. Put customers first and show genuine interest in satisfying their ongoing needs.
— develop expert product knowledge. Be able to deliver the product which best meets the customers' needs.
— conduct all business in an honest and ethical manner. Act within the intent and spirit of the law and company policies at all times."

Values provide the boundaries. Values determine what the organization will punish and reward, what it prizes above all, and what its highest priorities really are. The patterns of collective behavior in organizations are almost always an expression of the organization's values, whereas values themselves are almost always looked at in the context of vision.

"All the bountiful sentiments in the world weigh less than a single lovely action."

— James Russell Lowell

Like vision, values have two critical parts. First are the intended or declared values. These exist in philosophical statements, mission statements, policies, and the like. The second type, the lasting values, are what's lived on a daily basis by members of the organization. Too often there is a significant gap between those values management and employees would prefer and those that are being expressed in day-to-day behavior.

VALUES ARE CONTAGIOUS—ARE YOURS WORTH CATCHING?

Values taken to heart cause others in the organization to follow by example. In his classic *Study of History* Arnold Toynbee speaks of mimesis, the process by which people mimic their leaders. When

---

Foundation for Team Building

The great British statesman and political writer Edmund Burke observed, "No men can act with effect who do not act in concert; no men can act in concert who do not act with confidence; no men can act with confidence who are not bound together with common opinions, common affections, and common interests."

The more powerful and effective a team is, the more likely it is to contain strong, diverse individuals—thoroughbreds, mavericks, champions, entrepreneurs. A process for clarifying shared values is the essential glue that binds such a team together, especially during turbulent times:

—"An inordinate amount of energy gets used up in fighting 'the system'. But when an organization can come up with a strong, consistent set of implicit understandings, it has effectively established for itself a body of common laws to supplement its formal rules."

—Richard Pascale, lecturer at Stanford Business School and coauthor, *The Art of Japanese Management*

—"Reasonable people often disagree . . . . However, it is essential that managers agree on a process for dealing with [such] dilemmas."

　—Bowen H. McCoy, Managing director, Morgan Stanley and
　Co., Inc.

---

leaders send a clear signal, their effectiveness as role models for their organization is enhanced.

"Strong beliefs win strong men, and then make them stronger."

—Walter Bagehot

In this way, leaders can signal values, and the organization will quickly march to the beat. Lee Iacocca did this when he cut his salary to $1 a year as part of his commitment to a renewed Chrysler corporation. At IBM, Tom Watson, Sr., noted early on that repairpersons did not dress as well as other members of the organization, and the treatment they received—both from co-workers and from customers—only reinforced this impression of second-degree status. Watson insisted that all IBM technicians wear a shirt and tie, a practice that has persisted to the present day.

The plant manager for a large auto manufacturer refused a shipment of plastic trim because the color match to the adjacent metal trim was not perfect. Investigation later revealed that the dye had been mixed correctly, but that metal "took" the dye differently than plastic. The manager didn't care: he refused the shipment anyway, demonstrating an obsessive commitment to Quality.

The most effective role model for values is contained in only six words: "Do anything you see me doing." Effective leaders, we've found, are tight on values and loose on operational details, whereas technomanagers are tight on operational details and loose on values.

Values can be imparted by proximity, provided the person doing the imparting has sufficient stature inside the organizational context. When Charlie Sporck, president of National Semiconductor, wanted to turn around the performance of a division in trouble, he moved his desk next to the general manager of that division. Improved results inevitably followed.

Values are like rabbits—they multiply. It therefore behooves the organization to choose *in advance* what sort of values it wants.

Values can be quickly reduced from the vague to the specific. Present the issue in a simple yes-or-no fashion. "Is the customer always right—yes or no?" "Will we go to any lengths to win a contract—yes or no?" "Are we to treat the customer with a small account just as we treat those with large accounts—yes or no?" This kind of simplified exercise shows how values evolve, take shape, and ultimately breathe life into the organization's vision. By directing the daily actions of the organization's members, values bring the organization into alignment with its chosen destiny.

"It is not who is right, but what is right, that is of importance."

—Thomas H. Huxley

BRINGING VALUES TO LIFE

Often the terms *values* and *core values* are used interchangeably, and with good reason. Values cut to the core. They are at the core of every organization's or person's being. Values define who or what we really are.

Perhaps the importance of values can best be understood by looking at what happens when there aren't any. No values mean no vision, and no vision means that each member of the organization is committed only to saving his or her own bacon. In organizations without values, anything goes. It is like a country in which no one speaks anyone else's language—like the Tower of Babel. There is no common bond, no shared intent, no understood goal. Communication and trust break apart. The organization mires itself in mediocrity and collapses under the weight of the very rules and regulations it first promulgated to maintain control.

A hotel chain had seven key executives whose values were both unclear and unexpressed. If two of them visited the same property to check operations, their reports would often contradict each other because *each saw entirely different priorities that needed acting upon.* Ultimately, the sales arm of the corporation came to change their pet name for the executive offices from the Ivory Tower to Puzzle Palace. No one knew what priority or new strategy would be issued next.

Similarly, at Atari Corporation, before a major management change, one manager was heard to remark: "You can't imagine

how much time and energy around here went into politics . . . .
There were no rules . . . there were no clear values. Two of the men
at the top stood for diametrically opposite things. Your bosses
were constantly changing."

Values in Action

At Levi Strauss, an executive who produced excellent results
was fired because he mistreated employees. A top executive
described the firing this way: "We wanted to send a clear unambiguous signal to everyone in the company that abusive
behavior would not be tolerated. If this individual couldn't
get away with it, it would be obvious to everyone in the
company that no one could . . . . [We were] telling all our employees that no matter how much money you may be making
for the company, there are some things you just can't do."

"Men do not stumble over mountains, but over mole hills."

— Confucius

Values are a no-nonsense thing. They demand an immediate
response, a recognizable individual action. Values are like a
flashlight in a dark room. If the light isn't there, you are likely to
spend a lot of time walking into walls.

Expressed skillfully, core values can:
1. specify the goals to be reached;
2. establish the methods by which the progress to those goals
and the organization's vision will be determined;
3. set out the appropriate social contract between members of
the organization to maximize effectiveness and trust;
4. indicate what behavior is acceptable or unacceptable, as well
as what behavioral-control mechanisms within the organization
are acceptable and appropriate;
5. lay out in no uncertain terms how the organization wants to
deal with — and be perceived by — those outside the organization.

Examples of powerful value statements follow:
Leo Burnett: "Make great ads."
Caterpillar: "24-hour parts service anywhere in the world."

Du Pont: "Better things for better living through chemistry."
Sears: "Quality at a good price."
Dana: "Productivity through people."
Chubb: "Underwriting excellence."

"It is truly enough said that a corporation has no conscience; but a corporation of conscientious men is a corporation with a conscience."

—Henry David Thoreau

What is the difference between values and rules? Values are the tree; rules are the leaves. The rules may blow away and change each year but the tree stands. When an individual is discharged from an organization, he or she is more likely to be let go for violating a value than a rule. Organizations occasionally lose sight of this distinction — with horrific results. A rule for its own sake can only add to bureaucratic double talk, pull the organization down, and detract from its energy. Successful leadership-based organizations understand this: they are generally "tight on values, loose on rules." Each subsidiary has discretion to get the job done its own way — within the confines of the organization's values.

Values Challenge Maslow?

Abraham Maslow's doctrine of the hierarchy of human needs suggests that people act predictably according to what is important to them at the moment. They satisfy their own needs before helping others. Yet contrast this behavior to actions like those observed during the Second World War when starving prisoners gave up their food to help the weak and dying. Maslow's hypothesis would suggest the opposite: that the stronger would take the food for themselves, leaving the weaker to fend as they might. But Maslow misses the spiritual dimension of man, the dimension of values. Humans look for meaning in their actions and that meaning supersedes animalistic drive. Even starving people are not immune to the lure of higher values.

Values should also be distinguished from rituals, which got stuck on the evolutionary trail. Rituals, like the handshake between masons or a surgeon's "seven-minute scrub," do help to express values; but they lack dynamism, and they cannot change or adapt to new situations. Rituals can in fact derail the originally stated values and lead to an evolutionary dead end. Interestingly, bureaucracies all around the globe have inundated themselves with these lifeless rituals—"That'll be three copies in triplicate, please." Bureaucrats have traded their souls and their creativity for meaningless charades that might have meant something to somebody long ago, but mean nothing today.

The Value of Values

Industry Week executive editor Perry Pascarella, after interviewing dozens of top executives and surveying thousands of workers, concluded that productivity was essentially a human matter. He continually found that values played a central role in high performance:

—"If people are to work together effectively, they must have a set of shared beliefs."

—"There must be values on which they agree so they can establish trust and common purpose."

—"*Values [are not] a one-way street*. The organization behaves like a marketplace allowing values to be exchanged as people strike a deal for relationships that permit certain jobs to be done."

—"The more people-oriented a corporation is, the more relevant it becomes to society's needs and the more likely it is to capitalize on what people are willing to commit to."

—"Workers in don't care companies don't mind calling in sick; [those] participating in a humanistic setting, on the other hand, realize the burden they put on fellow workers and the possible economic harm their absence will cause."

—"With values, ethics not rule books set the standards for behavior."

Values must be held and practiced consistently. Executives who say one thing on Monday morning and (often unknowingly) do the opposite on Monday afternoon do inestimable damage to their organizations. Values should also be balanced, so that results in the short run are not in conflict with desired results in the long term. A classic example of unbalanced values was provided by a newly hired president who told his executive team that he wanted their participation in turning the company around. He held a retreat and asked for their insights and concerns. The following week, several of the executives were fired. James O'Toole speaks of "creative balance," a viewpoint that looks after "shareholder interests in the short term" while at the same time "investing in the future."

And, finally, values need to be supported by people with the skills to make them work — a process that is often not quite so obvious as it seems.

One simple way to discover your organization's values is to ask a member of the organization what some of the likely grounds are for which he or she could be fired. If the person seems to flounder after the obvious things like "theft," "incompetence," or "negligence," this could indicate that your organization doesn't really have a set of values at all. An experienced manager says: "To find ingrained values, values you may not even know you have, look for things that get people mad — and then ask them why they got that way!"

Another interesting simple test: Imagine yourself ten or twenty years in the future. What would you *look back on* with the greatest satisfaction?

More tests:

— Go back to your roots. Look at those who founded the organization, and try to identify their values.

— Look hard at what exactly separates you from your competitors.

— Ask a new person in the organization for his or her views on the above questions.

— Bring managers from one level together in a working environment with managers from other levels, and see what results.

And finally, here is a quick test to see if your vision/values package is in good working order: *look for pride*. Pride, for vision and for values, is where the rubber hits the road. If the vision/values set is working for the individual, then he or she will have pride in what is being achieved and will believe in the organization's processes. A lack of pride is a serious danger sign: it means the vision/values set is not in tune with the day-to-day realities of the organization's activities.

Surely the most difficult thing about values, once you have clarified yours, is putting them into practice and making them stick. It's not as easy as it looks. For one thing, the values must be understandable to everyone. An incomprehensible value is clearly a value that can never be shared. Next, the values must be reachable — or at least "mainly reachable." Bob Haas at Levi Strauss says that some of Levi's values may *not* be reachable, but at least the organization constantly aspires to them. One of Levi's most astounding bits of cultural folklore is that, during the Second World War, the company refused a federal order to skimp on the weight of the denim used in its jeans.

"Always do right. This will gratify some people and astonish the rest."

— Mark Twain

Values and Ethics

With stock-market scandals and stories of corporate con games in the news, many top executives have issued the decree: "Teach our people some ethics." But can you really teach ethics? Isn't ethical behavior an outgrowth of the organization's implicit value system? And if managers are recruiting ethically questionable people is that not a reflection of the organization's lack of commitment to values? How often are values and ethics explored and used as hiring criteria in today's technomanaged organizations?

Irving Kristol, writing in the *Wall Street Journal*, may have struck at the heart of the problem: "One of the reasons the major corporations find it so difficult to persuade the public of anything is that the public always suspects them of engaging in clever public relations, instead of simply telling the truth. And the reason the public is so suspicious is because our large corporations so habitually do engage in clever public relations instead of simply telling the truth."

In determining how values fit into the modern organization, theorists have had to pose some very thoughtful questions. Are profits (or products, or size) an end in themselves? Do people work only for their paychecks? Does the organizational end justify the organizational means? Peters and Waterman, in a piece of research done prior to *In Search of Excellence*, found that companies whose articulated goals were financial did not perform nearly as well in terms of dollars and cents as companies with broader sets of values. And a 1983 study at Boston College scrutinized the performance over eight years of thirty companies that were judged to be "socially conscious"—that is, having strong explicit core values. According to survey leader Ritchie Lowry, the companies examined performed 106 percent better, based on standarized financial criteria, than their less-principled counterparts.

In 1983, in *The Corporate Conscience: Money, Power and Responsible Business*, David Freudberg reports that James Burke of Johnson & Johnson asked his own staff to find out whether there was any statistical proof that serving the public led to long-term profitability. His staff looked at twenty-six companies (such as McDonald's and IBM). After the screening criteria were modified, the number dropped to fifteen. The selected organizations had outstanding records. Their average growth in profits over the thirty-six year period ending in 1982 was 11 percent. In a nearly comparable period, the Fortune 500 experienced a growth in profits of only 6.1 percent.

In fact, virtually every organization that is successfully marching the hard road to higher performance—every organization that, over a protracted period of time, has built a reputation for quality products, outstanding service, and sustained growth—has since its inception espoused a strong identifiable set of positive values and ideals, values, by the way, that reveal themselves not only in the products, services, and business practices through which the organization deals with the public, but that are clearly reflected in the way it deals with each individual member of its own enterprise, from the CEO down. Shared values produce shared results. And people work harder if they feel they are working for something that aspires to a higher purpose, a greater good.

The jury is in. Values are at the core of exceptional performance.

CHAPTER FIVE

Environment and Behavior: Where the Rubber Hits the Road

"We are or become those things which we repeatedly do. Therefore excellence can become not just an event but a habit."

—Albert Einstein

Two men were walking along Wall Street at lunch time. "Listen to that cricket," said one. But his companion could not hear it. The first man was a zoologist who had, over many years, trained himself to distinguish such sounds in even the noisiest surroundings. He pulled a silver dollar from his pocket and dropped it onto the pavement. A dozen or so people immediately turned their attention to the dropped coin. "We hear," said the man, "only what we are conditioned to listen for."

So it is with an organization. Unless you pay attention, unless you give heed, you may not be aware of the environment you and your staff are so industriously creating every day. This environment—or "culture"—may even be at odds with your organization's goals and purpose without your knowing it.

CORPORATE CULTURE: WHAT IS IT?

These days, everyone is talking about "corporate culture." Countless books, magazines, and management consultants claim it is the key to organizational effectiveness.

Webster's New Collegiate Dictionary defines culture as "the integrated pattern of human behavior that includes thought, speech, action, and artifacts, and depends on man's capacity for learning and transmitting knowledge to succeeding generations."

"The secret of all victory lies in the organization of the non-obvious."

—Oswald Spengler

Marvin Bower, former managing director of McKinsey and Company, puts it more simply: He says culture is *"the way we do things around here."*

In Search of Excellence offers this observation about culture: "The excellent companies are marked by cultures, *so strong you either buy into their norms, or get out."*

In their study conducted for the American Business Center, Donald K. Clifford, Jr. and Richard E. Cavanaugh set out to identify common traits in high-achieving organizations. Each of the top-drawer mid-size companies they looked at had annual revenues of between $25 million and $1 billion, and, as a group, all had more than doubled in size and profits in the five years previous to the study (1983), significantly outperforming the Fortune 500 list. The authors identified four recurring aspects of corporate environment/culture in this group:

1. a sense of being "special," a sense that the organization stood out from the crowd and deserved to be noticed for what it had accomplished;

2. a pervasive "evangelical zeal" or enthusiasm that ran through every level of the organization. Even the mail clerks felt they were making an identifiable contribution;

3. entrenched communication systems that kept people informed about what the organization was doing, provided feedback, and allowed individual ideas to find expression;

4. a view of profit as the "inevitable byproduct" of excellence. Money or profits by themselves were never the goal, merely the rewards for reaching the goal.

Culture or environment is really no more than a "superset" of ingrained habits, an outgrowth of the set of assumptions that people carry around in their heads all day—assumptions about co-workers, about customers, and about clients. Bob Waterman describes organizational environment as: "The collection of shared values an organization has that tends to drive people's day-to-day behavior way down the line."

"A company is known by the people it keeps."

Such "invisible" grids of values, assumptions, and attitudes are the essence of corporate culture. Corporate culture and behavior patterns are much like weather patterns: *it doesn't matter if you notice them or not, you get some every day!*

Each division, department or section has its own unique environmental or cultural pattern. Like a stained-glass window, each miniculture contributes its own color and shape to the overall picture. In turn, the larger culture, like the larger pattern, heavily influences each miniculture. Where top managers are effective cultural leaders, the mosaic is rich and strong. Where organizational leadership is weak (as in technomanagement), the result is confusion and inconsistency.

"That which has become habitual becomes, as it were, a part of our nature."

—Aristotle

Culture, once established, perpetuates itself. Habits or patterns of behavior crystallize to form the ambient culture of the organization. That culture in turn screens out new behavior that is inconsistent with the established norm.

There is an endless loop between behavior, on the one hand, and organizational culture or environment, on the other. (That's why our VIP model shows these two elements as forming a circle.) Which came first, the chicken or the egg? Is behavior the input and culture the output? *In the long run it makes no difference.* Understanding the relationship between culture and behavior is the first step to being able to affect both!

CHANGING THE WEATHER?

It has been said that culture, like weather, just is. It cannot be changed. We have found, however, that not only can you alter your existing organizational culture, but also — if higher performance and achievement are your ultimate goals — you *must* do so.

To begin the process, it is important to examine the very roots of culture. To argue that "managers get the culture they deserve" is perhaps a bit harsh, but it is consistent with our experience. A lackadaisical organization or a division that doesn't pay attention to its direction or its output will create an environment based on

Environmental Factors

There are a multitude of factors influencing and defining an organization's patterns of behavior, or "the way we do things around here." In the past few years, "corporate culture" has become a popular topic. This has lead to a confusing array of models and definitions of culture.

The clearest and most useful analysis of the elements affecting an organization's environment or culture comes from Tom Janz of the University of Calgary's Faculty of Management. Using a process called "factor analysis," Tom isolated the four most common clusters or methods that answer the question: "How do we influence our employees to do what needs to be done?"

Using these factors, Tom worked with Achieve to design an assessment instrument. Called the "Vision Integrated Performance Audit," this analytical tool shows that all organizations have the four factors present to a greater or lesser degree. The most effective organizations have fewer of the "push/manage our staff" factors represented in the first two and more of the "pull/lead our staff" found in the latter two.

Tom has also discovered links between the first two factors and unionization.

Factor 1: Through written rules and regulations.
Examples of this factor are:

›We follow rules and procedures manuals. ›People go by the rules, seeking permission from the proper authorities for exceptions. ›The rules spell out who has the right to tell someone else what to do, and we stick to them. ›The rules guide our decisions when we come across unusual situations. ›My immediate supervisor makes sure the rules are followed.

Factor 2: Through power and manipulation.
Examples of this factor are:

›People try to make other departments or people look bad to get ahead. ›Flattering my immediate supervisor can help me get what I need. ›My immediate supervisor notices only mistakes, oversights or problems. ›It's *who* you know and not *what* you know that gets you ahead in our group. ›People try to keep an advantage for themselves by concealing information. ›My immediate supervisor talks down to me when I don't meet his or her expectations.

Factor 3: Through working towards a shared vision.
Examples of this factor are:

›We understand and work hard towards accomplishing what this organization stands for. ›People manage themselves by common vision. ›My supervisor will try to change a new policy if it interferes with what we stand for. ›People who disagree with our organization's vision and values often end up leaving. ›We reward people who contribute to our organization. ›Achieving our common vision is as important as personal ambition around here.

Factor 4: Through support via listening.
Examples of this factor are:

›My immediate supervisor takes the time to understand my new ideas. ›My supervisor walks around the workplace, listening to people on the job. ›My supervisor helps us out, taking corrective steps when we get overloaded. ›My supervisor compliments people for good tries that do not work out as planned. ›People here listen eagerly to anyone with ideas that will help them get the job done better.

its very lack of direction just as assuredly as a department that is committed to a goal will forge its own way of doing business through will and intent. The difference between the two will be the *type* of culture that is created: the intentionally shaped organization will likely generate a pro-active, visionary, leadership-inspired culture; in the case of non-shaped organizations, a pot-luck culture will be spawned, a culture of unkempt weeds, so to speak.

Employees Learn What They Live

If an employee lives with fear,
He learns to avoid risk taking.

If an employee lives with deceit,
She learns to stretch the truth.

If an employee lives with small expectations,
He learns to have a limited scope.

If an employee lives with a heavy hand,
She learns to beat the system.

If an employee lives with ridicule,
He learns to keep his ideas to himself.

If an employee lives with formality,
She learns how to be a bureaucrat.

If an employee lives with mistrust,
He learns to be suspicious.

If an employee lives with hostility,
She learns how to fight.

If an employee lives with indifference,
He learns not to care.

"Only the man of worth can recognize worth in men."

—Thomas Carlyle

THE STARTING POINT

Unfortunately, many companies are totally ignorant about the roots of their own culture. All too frequently organizations shape culture by stumbling into it.

Richard Pascale suggests that, for culture to be correctly used, the whole picture must be considered, not merely ad-hoc policies

---

If an employee lives with appreciation,
She learns to make an extra effort.

If an employee lives with leadership,
He learns how to take initiative.

If an employee lives with openness,
She learns how to be honest.

If an employee lives with experimentation,
He learns how to be innovative.

If an employee lives with clear values,
She learns how to set priorities.

If an employee lives with customer respect,
He learns how to provide outstanding service.

If an employee lives with encouragement,
She learns to be confident.

If an employee lives with positive visions,
He learns how to perform miracles.

If an employee lives with challenge,
She learns how to master change.

—Jim Clemmer (Inspired by Dorothy Law Nolte's poem "Children Learn What They Live")

---

and piecemeal decisions: "[Certain organizations] may not even be conscious of precisely what they are doing. Moreover, when one examines any particular aspect of their policy toward people—how they recruit or train or compensate—little stands out as unusual. *But when the pieces are assembled, what emerges is an awesome internal consistency that powerfully shapes behavior.*"

It is this "awesome internal consistency" that is of vital concern. Pascale's research identified a number of the footprints of a strong and deliberate shaping of culture. Among them are:

1. A vigorous screening and selection process to make sure not only that the organization chooses the candidate but that the candidate chooses the company. (Some organizations even involve the spouses of candidates directly in the interview process.)

2. The deliberate creation of stress situations during selection to force candidates to come to terms with their own true values.

3. Consistency in the promotion and reward systems.

4. An 'open door' policy for suggestions and gripes.

5. A steady focus on the higher aims and values of the organization to encourage individual sacrifice to a greater good.

6. A highly identifiable folklore (for example, Bell Telephone's keeping systems functional through disasters; IBM's meeting its twenty-four-hour service pledge even if the service technician has to get her sleep on the airplane).

7. Identifiable "human" characters (role models) at each level of the organization to act as signposts for what behavior is expected and what is rewarded.

Productivity is Holistic

Noland Archibald, president and CEO of Black and Decker, declared: "Until U.S. business learns to think of productivity on a system basis—engineering, manufacturing, marketing, sales, customer service, distribution, product service—it will continue to lag. The Japanese superbly manage productivity on a system basis . . . . American industries need to link all parts of their systems. High productivity in manufacturing coupled with low productivity in engineering, marketing, sales, or distribution *still spells failure.*"

CONSIDER THE ROLE OF MANAGEMENT

What is the relationship between management and culture, supervision and environment? Effective managers, managers who manifest leadership skills, understand that their job entails managing people, not just systems and machines. They see and understand the larger picture and relate to the organization not merely in terms of goals and planning and rules, but also in terms of vision, values, and individual behavior. They consciously develop their own skill sets to augment and reinforce the skill sets of those they work with every day. *Successful managers shape their environment by reinforcing the desirable traits of those they work with; unsuccessful managers allow performance patterns ("habits") to form with no strategic purpose. The successful manager steers the course; the unsuccessful manager tags along for the ride.*

"It is something to be able to paint a particular picture, or to carve a statue . . . but it is far more glorious to carve and paint the very atmosphere and medium through which we look . . . "

—Henry David Thoreau

By shaping culture with intent, high-performance organizations have demonstrated that environment *properly used* is an asset, not a handicap. Environment ultimately makes the difference between an individual contributor who decides to get out and do something versus one who, after looking around, concludes that nothing can be done.

All environments have their roots in the attitudes, values, and belief systems of the individuals who collectively create that culture. And, once you know what clues to look for, culture becomes obvious, it "gives itself away" to the sharp observer. One top telemarketing specialist says: "When I call the president of a large organization and get rude and indifferent treatment from his secretary, I immediately have a handle on the way the man himself conducts his affairs. Clearly, he must be as rude and indifferent to people as his secretary—or they would not be able to work together!"

The founder of an organization initially creates an environment that others choose or reject. Later on, however, succeeding layers of individuals, as they come to the organization, pick that environment up and guide themselves accordingly. Like attracts like, and opposites repel.

Cultural or behavior patterns determine how everyone in the organization looks at everyone else. Would an outsider be treated with more or less courtesy than the mail clerk? Would the switchboard operator be any more or less polite if she were talking on her own home phone? Organizational culture is the collection of all the interactions between people.

A manager who believes that customers are a necessary evil, just a means of converting products into cash, will never successfully engender an environment that serves customers — and will not know how customer handling could be improved. On the other hand, a culture that promotes treating customers like kings

---

Style Training: Fun, Insightful and . . . Ineffective

In the field of management development, "style training" has become very popular. While approaches and labels vary, the basic aim is to teach managers what their personal managerial style is and its impact on others. Trainees are shown various models for responding to different situations and conflicting styles. The primary goal is to increase the versatility of managers.

In our early years, we offered style-awareness training but dropped it when it became clear that style awareness did not usually change behavior. Although participants gained insight and enjoyed the exercises, little changed back on the job.

Behavior didn't change because the managers had not developed necessary *skills*. A revealing study by the U.S. Department of Agriculture came to similar conclusions: "Training employees in leadership styles or in special techniques associated with specific technical managerial skills without changing the organizational environment is, by itself, unlikely to increase employee productivity."

---

will readily spot any conduct that fails to meet its lofty ideals. High-aspiring cultures give their organizations power by increasing their perception of what can be done to make things better.

THE "FISH-TANK FACTOR"

Before behavior and culture can be redirected in a more positive way, yet another important factor has to be looked at: the vision or expectations that management has of its employees. Culture and environment are not abstract concepts: they are very real to the assembly-line worker who, for example, has to ask her supervisor's permission to use the washroom; or to the telephone operator who can't spend extra time with a distraught customer because the computer that monitors his use of time would record the event as inefficient.

How people respond to an attempt to improve service or products will depend on how they themselves are viewed within the organization. It is a peculiarity of human nature that *people's accomplishments expand to fill the available expectations*. Increase the expectation and you increase the results. Keep the expectations confined and you get predictable, mundane, and reliable mediocrity.

"What we expect, that we find."
—Aristotle

Treating other people as you yourself would like to be treated changes things. Treating others as though they were already the people you hope they will someday become will cause a transformation. Psychological studies have verified the "Pygmalion effect," a label derived from George Bernard Shaw's famous play (best remembered as the musical treatment *My Fair Lady*). When the heroine Eliza Doolittle describes the metamorphosis she has undergone, she says: "The difference between a lady and a flower girl is not how she behaves, but how she is treated."

Organizations, often unintentionally, use that same principle every day in their dealings with people! Matthew Goodfellow is executive director of the Chicago-based University Research Center Inc., an employee-relations, union-avoidance research group sponsored by some six thousand businesses. He says: "Plant managers are often not aware that they are setting a poor example for their foremen. They do it because of pressure on them." He goes on to cite "a classic study whose title says it all: 'Don't Shoot the Foreman: Aim at the Plant Manager'." Setting a poor example for staff creates a daisy-chain effect that continues down the line. People will treat others much *as they themselves are being treated.*

"He's fair alright. He treats us all the same — like dogs."

Our expectation of ourselves and others—as nurtured and reinforced by others in our environment—determines how *we* act, which in turn determines how *those around us* act, which in turn establishes the *culture* of the organization!

We call this reality the "fish-tank factor." Goldfish will grow to the size permitted by the size of their tank—and no more! The size of an employee's fish-tank is determined by the expectations communicated to him by the organization.

Tom Peters makes the point that even a small thing like the label placed on a particular position might constitute a limitation on the ability of the person to service the customer and, accordingly, the organization. Peters notes that in the hotel industry many workers are routinely called by negative-sounding names like "hourlys," "temps," "non-exempts," and "parttimers." Yet, in the service industry especially, these same people have, on average, more meaningful contact with the paying customer than the company president or CEO. What kind of significant performance can you expect from someone who gets up in the morning and sees the word "temp" on his forehead? (In a lighter vein, Peters relates that an executive at a fast-food organization, after taking one of Tom's seminars, wrote to brag that the word "employees" had been forever stricken from the organization's environment. "I pay anyone in the company $10 if I forget and use the "E" word.")

FLOWERGIRL OR LADY?

Goethe said, "If we take a man as he is we make him worse, but if we take him as he ought to be, we help him become what he can be."

Results consistently bear this out. With experience ranging from professor to university president, Warren Bennis reports: "In a study of school teachers, it turned out that when they held high expectations of their students, that alone was enough to cause an increase of 25 points in the students' IQ scores."

Robert Townsend, the man credited with turning Avis around, comments: "Do you realize that your people can't make long-

---

What Else Could You Expect?

J. Sterling Livingston has been chief executive of Peat, Marwick, Livingston and Company and Harbridge House Inc., among other firms. As a business professor at Harvard he wrote the classic article "Pygmalion in Management," identifying such examples of the "Pygmalion effect" (or fish-tank factor) as the following:

—An experiment at the Headstart program for sixty preschoolers compared the performance of pupils under (a) teachers who had been led to expect slow learning and (b) teachers who had been led to believe they had top students. The second group, although not quantifiably different from the first, still performed better.

—An interesting experiment was conducted at Metropolitan Life's Rockaway district office. Three teams of salespeople were deliberately assembled, with "high," "average," and "low" expectations based on the past performance of the individuals involved. The top or super group showed outstanding performance, and the bottom group performed below even its own normal worst-case scenario. Significantly, the middle group, led by angry managers who refused to accept the "average" label thrust upon them, showed marked and unexpected overall improvements.

—In a study of the early managerial success of forty-nine college graduates who were employees of an operating company of AT&T, David Berlew and Doug Hall examined the career progress of these managers over a period of five years. They discovered that their relative success, as measured by salary increases and the company's estimate of each person's performance and potential, had a correlation of 0.72 to the company's initial expectations. The researchers described their findings as "too compelling to be ignored."

---

distance calls without filling out a report? Do you know what they have to go through to hire somebody? — or buy something? Stop running down your people! It's your fault they're rusty from underwork."

"There is no rule more invariable than that we are paid for suspicions by finding what we suspected."

— Henry David Thoreau

A simple thing like a time clock sends a message that probably ought not to be sent. Do you not trust your co-workers to come in on time? Is it not possible for supervisors to handle latecomers individually rather than hiding behind a system? One of our clients, after participating in a program dealing with cultural leadership, paused to reconsider her use of time clocks in terms of the stated values (and degree of trust) that her organization was aspiring to. In one plant, she ripped out the clocks — and now relies on old-fashioned trust. The message got through — people responded to the increased expectations of the organization by increasing their performance and, in this case, minimizing tardiness. Now the only time these employees get to see a time clock is when one wins the best-attendance award: the award itself is an old time clock encased in plastic and mounted for the occasion.

"Some people, without knowing it, carry with them a magnifying glass, with which they see, when they wish, other people's imperfections."

— John Wanamaker

Utah-based management consultant, Stephan Covey goes further and compares trust to an "emotional bank account": "When trust is high, communication is easy. It is almost effortless and instantaneous. Some people say it takes time — what takes time is to build the emotional bank account and trust level . . . . Think of people with whom you have a high trust level you can communicate with them almost without words."

"Confidence placed in another often compels confidence in return."

—Livy

James O'Toole contrasted high performance assumptions in a Motorola policy handbook with those that seemed to underlie more "traditional" management practices.

"OLD GUARD" (fishbowls)

1. Workers are paid to do, not to think.
2. Workers have few productive ideas.
3. People work solely for money.
4. Workers are all alike.
5. There is one best way to manage others.
6. Managers manage; workers work.
7. Employees shun responsibility for their work.
8. Capital and management are the keys to productivity.
9. Worker participation programs are softheaded at best, socialistic at worst.
10. At the first chance, workers will goof off.

MOTOROLA (fish tanks)

1. Workers are intelligent, curious, and responsible.
2. Workers who care will do whatever is required to get the job done.
3. People will work for money and for a higher purpose.
4. Workers are individuals.
5. There is no best way to manage.
6. Workers and managers are really trying to accomplish the same thing: produce.
7. Employees want to take pride in their work.
8. Leadership and people skills are an untapped source of productivity.
9. An involved employee makes things happen.
10. Workers rise to the levels of responsibility and expectations set them.

"You must expect to be treated by others as you yourself have treated them."

—Seneca

CHOOSE YOUR CULTURE?

For organizations struggling to come to grips with a culture that simply isn't doing the job for them, we offer this provocative corollary to the "fish-tank factor": people who work for other people tend to adopt the values of the people they work for. *Management seldom recognizes its own values and behavior when they are being mirrored back.*

The degree of consistency between the stated values and the actions of corporate decision makers determines the environment. The environment combined with the skills of the organization's members to function within its confines determines behavior: how the people within the organization treat each other is how they relate to the outside world.

This formula works *both* ways. Not only does the environment affect how people behave, but people's behavior in turn creates the environment. As Thornton Bradshaw, former president of Arco, said: "It must be all of a single fabric. From the organization's so-

---

What We Get Is What We See

An immigrant approached the gates of a great city. When asked by the gatekeeper what the people from his old city were like, he replied, "They were selfish, mean, spiteful people. They hated everyone and fought constantly." The gatekeeper shook his head sadly, "I am sorry to say," he said, "but that's exactly the kind of people you'll find here. You'll never be happy in this city." The man departed.

A second hopeful immigrant approached the city and was asked the same question. "They were kind, considerate, and caring," he responded. "They constantly helped each other and worked together." Whereupon the gatekeeper threw open the gates and proclaimed, "Come in, my friend. That's exactly the kind of people you'll find here."

---

cial posture, through the way it treats its employees, to the care it takes in the artistic decor and style of its buildings, everything must manifest a commitment to quality, to excellence, to service."

In her analysis of segmented versus integrated organizations, Rosabeth Kanter looks at organizations striving to be more innovative and argues: "As long as segmented structures and segmentalist attitudes make the very idea of innovation *run against the culture grain*, there is a tension between the desire for innovation and the continual blocking of it . . . . Where there is a history of teamwork and cooperation, where multiple centers of resources exist and are eager to invest them, and where integrative sentiments prevail over segmentalism, then the efforts of innovators, in the stage where they seek the support to move from idea to action, are more likely to succeed."

Money as Motivator: Management's "Big-Buck" Theory

Many managers believe that all their employees really care about is money. The end result is a culture with a hedonistic predisposition to individual gain.

In "Why You Should Train Now to Prevent Strikes Later," Matthew Goodfellow, an employee-relations expert, states that strikes and labor problems are not motivated primarily by money. Money is important, he notes, but the desire for higher wages and benefits is a "rational" one and "amenable to negotiation." What is not rational, however, is something that can be prevented: worker willingness to punish a firm, to hurt it, in order to push back against power, rules, and regulations.

A.H. Whyte, the Cornell University authority on industrial relations, looks at "people power" versus "money power" and concludes: "The argument that strike action is based on some form of rationality is false. I have observed workers taking strike action not because of financial considerations but because they believed they had to demonstrate their opposition to management actions, managerial dominance, and managerial refusal to pay attention to the sentiments of the work force."

"The man who is worthy of being 'a leader of men' will never complain about the stupidity of his helpers, the ingratitude of mankind, nor the inappreciation of the public. To meet and overcome them, and not go down before them in disgust, discouragement or defeat — that is the final proof of power."

—William Boetcker

"What goes around comes around" is an appropriate axiom in the world of organizational environment. Like begets like. Trust creates more trust. And suspicion closes doors as surely as loyalty and communication open them. Treat an employee irresponsibly and he or she becomes irresponsible. Engage in favoritism and you end up with politicians, not producers. As Tom Peters says: "I conclude that there are only two kinds of managers in the world—and not many shades of gray in between—the one who thinks 73 percent of his people are turkeys who would rip the organization off if they could get away with it; and then there's a manager only 25 feet away, drawing from the same population with the same demographics, who thinks that 98 percent of his/her people are superstars if only they trained the daylights out of them. . . . The second manager is the one that *ends up with superstars!*"

Organizations perturbed about their inability to inspire performance might do well to take a critical look at the corporate culture they expect to grow the "performance" in. You can't grow strong trees in poor soil, and you can't create an effective organization (one with attention to quality, service, productivity, and innovation) in an environment that will not sustain those traits. Much as "holistic" medicine is beginning to challenge traditional medicine, the organization that looks at its culture as a whole is challenging the more traditional, segmented type of company.

In the final analysis, altering or changing cultures can be as easy as changing lifelong habits—or as difficult! What the leaders of change-seeking organizations have to decide is *which habits they are going to reinforce and which habits they want to weed out.* Vision, values, and skill-building techniques are, we have found, the keys to success.

In outstanding companies, deliberate choices have been made to have the culture and behavior work for, rather than against, organizational goals. By deliberately setting out to alter behavior (via a skill development program, for example), culture will ultimately change. Vision and values are the catalysts that stimulate such change. Once the transformation process begins, the cycle starts to work in favor of the organization instead of against it.

"Excellence is an art won by training and habitation. We are what we repeatedly do. Excellence, then, is not an act, but a habit."

—Aristotle

CHAPTER SIX

Leadership Skills: The Bridge to Improvement

"If you build castles in the air, your work need not be lost: That is where they should be built. Now put foundations under them."

— Henry David Thoreau

The need for a sound leadership base is critical. Understanding the use of vision and values is vital. Appreciating cultural habits is essential. Assessing the current status of your organization in these areas is a giant step toward high performance.

But . . . unless your organization develops the ability to integrate skillfully the use of vision, values, environment, and behavior, you'll still be a victim rather than a master of change. Analysis, surveys, discussions, and models are useful. They build awareness and may even point to the need for change. But they do not activate the process of change. They will not bridge the gap between plans and actions, between clarifying values and living them, between painting a vision and moving towards it, or between identifying a culture and making productive use of it. *Only the skills of the organization's members can produce change.* Leadership skills are the bridge between knowing and doing.

LEADERSHIP: WHAT IT IS, WHAT IT ISN'T

What does the word leadership *mean in the context of our VIP model?* A country's president or prime minister "leads" the country, but if people at lower levels lack leadership skills, then the leader's energy might never reach the common citizen. The president's or prime minister's leadership, without skilled supporters, amounts to nothing.

The modern organization is no different. The leader at the top can only set the tone, the pace, for leaders all through the organization to join in and move toward the organization's vision. We steadfastly refuse to endorse the traditional elitist model of leadership. *Leadership is a series of actions, not a position. Leadership is a pro-active state of generating energy to catalyze change and encourage performance.*

Beware of Leaders Who Don't Lead!

Laurence Peter, developer of the Peter Principle ("people rise to their own level of incompetence"), says: "Many are called leaders by virtue of their being ahead of the pack or at the top of the pyramid, and that is one definition of the word leader. But being out front or on top denotes only position and not the qualities of leadership. There is a significant difference between being in charge and being a leader."

Too often senior people fail to exhibit leadership skill. They are most often adequate or even exceptional managers, bosses, executives, supervisors, technocrats, or even technomanagers—but poor leaders. On the other hand, unofficial leaders among the non-management staff may be effective leaders in action, if not in name. Unfortunately, what they have to offer is usually passed over or ignored. Their energy, skill, and resourcefulness go unharnessed and sometimes are even used against the organization.

In Chapter 2 we looked at how organizations that don't understand the interrelatedness of technology, management, and leadership invariably throw money at the first two while paying lip service to the last. This is ironic and unfortunate. Emphasizing technology and management over leadership in an organization that is already imbalanced (as many are) usually only accentuates problems. It is a lot less costly and more productive to beef up leadership skills than it is to modify technology or make changes to management systems.

"So much of what we call management consists of making it difficult for people to work."

—Peter Drucker

Technology, Management, or Leadership?

The need for balancing technology, management, and leadership was clearly illustrated by a GM joint venture with Toyota. After launching programs worth billions of dollars to increase the use of robots (technology) at its plants, GM was shocked to discover that the quality of work emanating from its Fremont, California, plant—a plant devoted exclusively to the Japan-U.S. co-venture—*exceeded that of all the other plants in GM's operation!* The reason wasn't hard to fathom: the Japanese used leadership skills, coaching ability, and "people power." *This was a case in which a technologically inferior plant with "recycled" American workers outperformed everyone in the General Motors organization.* Leadership skills made the difference!

"Let's get rid of management," read the provocative headline of an advertisement in the *Wall Street Journal.* "People don't want to be managed," it explained; "they want to be led." Bennis and Nanus agree: "Our top executives [spend] roughly 90 percent of their time with others. . . . The problem with many organizations, and especially the ones that are failing, is that they tend to be *overmanaged* and *underled.*"

"He who does something at the head of one regiment will eclipse he who does nothing at the head of a hundred."

—Abraham Lincoln

So what *is* leadership? We can tell you what it's *not.* Leadership is not just charisma or charm. Reading through the daily paper or watching the TV news, it is easy to confuse leadership and personality. Don't be fooled: expecting charisma to be a hallmark of leadership is like expecting every tail to have a dog attached. *Vision, values, and skilled behavior* are the hallmarks of leaders; charisma is often a byproduct.

An equally erroneous viewpoint posits that leaders must, by definition, exist only at the *top.* Bennis and Nanus, looking at this particular issue, argue: "We may have played into this myth unintentionally by focusing exclusively on 'top' leadership. In fact, the larger the organization, the more leadership roles it is likely to offer. General Motors [for example] has thousands of leadership roles available to its employees."

We refer to this delicate balance as "persuasion power" versus "position power." To achieve long-term results, persuasion power must rule the day. If the leadership energy is correctly employed, everyone coming into contact with it will adopt it and pass it along, irrespective of his or her rank on the organization's totem pole.

One of the signs of an organization manifesting persuasion power is a team attitude. Where leadership is shared "sets of energy," everyone has room to grow and perform *regardless of job title*. Individual contributors are given maximum room to exercise their capacity for decision making and judgment within their assigned areas of responsibility. Supervisors become true coaches instead of mere taskmasters, and they coordinate individual inputs for maximum results.

Now that we know what leadership *isn't*, let's consider what it *is*.

Leadership is powerful. Leaders are restless with the status quo; they are always trying to improve, to create visions, and to push back the limits of possibility. In the words of George Bernard Shaw, "[Leaders] are great believers in circumstances. . . . If they don't find the circumstances they want, they change them."

Leaders are driven by definite values, principles, and ethics. To lead means to gather people around a problem, to coach their efforts and to inspire action. To lead is to empower teams and team members to get things done. At any level, a leader is one who initiates rather than reacts. Leaders in management roles see their positions as a means, not an end. They are thermostats, not thermometers. Leaders work to gain participation and commitment, to harness diversity, and to build consensus. *Leaders don't just use people, they improve them. Leaders are developers. They develop the organization and each other.*

Leadership is the missing link in management theory. It bridges the gap between knowing and doing and makes things happen. Peter Drucker says: "Leadership is lifting a personal vision to higher sights, raising a person's performance to a higher

113

"Leadership is the ability to get a man to do what you want him to do, when you want it done, in a way you want it done, because he wants to do it."

—Dwight D. Eisenhower

Persuasion Power Replacing Position Power

In the new organizaton, a power based on the ability to "pull" others rather than "push" them is in demand. As Tom Janz discovered, vision and support are more effective than power and manipulation or rules and regulations. Among those who agree . . .

—Marilyn Kennedy, managing partner of Career Strategies, says: "Position Power goes with a person's place in the organization. *Influence Power goes with people skills.*"

—Olle Stiwenius, director of Scandinavian Airlines' management consultants, states: "I think it's time we turned the 'pyramid' upside down. We need to put management on the bottom, in a supporting role. If you [do that], you start to think about words like 'support,' 'facilitate,' and 'balance.' This gets managers to think about their responsibilities in a completely new way."

—Futurists John Naisbitt and Patricia Aburdene remark: "During the last few years, the shift is from managers who traditionally were supposed to have all the answers and tell everyone what to do, to managers whose role is to create a nourishing environment for personal growth. Increasingly we will think of managers as teachers, mentors, developers of human potential. . . . The challenge will be to retrain managers, not workers, for the re-invented, information age corporation."

—Rosabeth Moss Kanter says: "Managers are increasingly less able to exercise the authority of command, and it is increasingly less appropriate to what their organizations need. They need instead to have 'political' skills such as identifying issues, persuading, building coalitions, campaigning for points of view, and servicing constituencies, including subordinates. . . . *The need [is] for managers to persuade rather than order."*

Symptoms of Leadership Skill Deficiencies

Like doctors, we are often called in when a client is experiencing aches and pains. And as with bodily pain, where an organization hurts is not always the real source of the problem. Doctors call this phenomenon "referred pain"; as, for example, when a back pain is really a kidney problem.

We find that most organizational problems and performance shortfalls can be ultimately traced back to *weak leadership skills*. Like an antibiotic, many consultants prescribe quick fixes to relieve symptoms, but such remedies often fail to cure the underlying cause.

Symptom: Poor communications.
Common Initial Response: Beefed-up newsletters, writing-and-presentation workshops, surveys, internal "marketing" campaigns.
Potential Root Causes: Inconsistent signals from management teams, "open doors" but closed minds, fuzzy vision and values, poor supervisor-employee relationships, weak feedback and confrontation skills, poor examples of communicating by senior managers.

Symptom: Low morale.
Common Initial Response: "Go get 'em" messages to supervisors, motivational speakers, tapes, books, videos. Incentive/recognition programs.
Potential Root Causes: Weak coaching skills, celebration and "hoopla" not ingrained in culture, low support and reinforcement, constantly shifting priorities and directions, poor team skills.

Symptom: Labor-Management conflicts.
Common Initial Response: Tougher negotiations; threats to move, lock-out, bring in labor lawyers; tougher rules and regulations.
Potential Root Causes: Autocractic management using position power. "We/they" gaps, "participatory management" that is actually manipulative; weak listening skills and scanty bottom-up flow of information; poor conflict resolution.

standard, building a personality beyond its normal limitations." Henry Kissinger said: "The task of the leader is to get his people from where they are to where they have not been."

According to Harvard professor John Kotter: "Millions of technical, professional, and managerial jobs today require much more than technical competence and professional expertise. They also require leadership."

"The most important single ingredient in the formula for success is knowing how to get along with people."

                                                 –Theodore Roosevelt

THE PLEXIGLASS PREDICAMENT

Managers, in their zeal to inject leadership into the organization, sometimes bite off more than the organization can chew. They often adopt systems and call their people to action even before the ink is dry on their business plan. The danger here is that *without proper skills* such organizations become top-heavy with raw enthusiasm.

We use the term "plexiglass managers" to describe those who, caught up in the excitement and rhetoric of an organization renaissance (with, for example, the keynote "Quality" or "Excellence"), find that their own skills are inadequate to meet the needs and demands of the "new" achievement-seeking organization. Like fish who bang against the sides of their aquarium without understanding their reality, these fired-up, inspired organizational members will, without leadership skill, bang repeatedly into invisible walls that they can neither see nor appreciate.

The plexiglass in this analogy is forged by the culture (behavior and environmental habits) in which many managers must operate. Managers at all levels will *say* one thing and unintentionally *do* another. They talk about coaching for higher performance, teamwork, and cultural change—but they are not able to deliver. *The result is an invisible barrier that prevents results from ever meeting expectations.* And predictably, after a few false starts, after bashing into the plexiglass a few times, employees are unlikely to want to rekindle their enthusiasm for new ventures into improving performance, service, or quality.

The Expanding Roles of Management

Today's managers and supervisors are finding demands placed upon them that are without precedent. Lower-level management, especially front-line supervisors, are expected to fill much larger roles today than they did a few years ago. Let's look at some of the differences between the traditional demands and the expanded ones.

TRADITIONAL: Managers get results primarily by directing people.
EXPANDED: They involve people and build personal commitment.

TRADITIONAL: Good managers encourage good followers.
EXPANDED: They need to encourage good initiators.

TRADITIONAL: Managers get people to understand good ideas.
EXPANDED: They get people to generate good ideas.

TRADITIONAL: Managers manage people one on one.
EXPANDED: They also build collaborative, interdependent, and supportive teams.

TRADITIONAL: Managers concentrate on developing strength within their own work units.
EXPANDED: They also develop strength between units and among peers.

TRADITIONAL: Managers also implement directions from above.
EXPANDED: They encourage the initiation of new ideas and directions from anywhere.

TRADITIONAL: Managers help people change when directed and help them make the best of it.
EXPANDED: They generate positive innovations with people without those changes being imposed from above.

TRADITIONAL: Managers should communicate well.
EXPANDED: They must be masters of interpersonal relationships.

Employees in these well-intentioned but unskilled organizations may *seem* to reside in an environment that is airy, full of sunshine, with ample room to move about and grow. *In fact, however, they reside in an environment that is highly defined and confined.* The employees' territory is clearly marked by heavy-duty (albeit invisible) walls that keep them in their places, walls held in place by weak leadership skills.

Before buying in to any ideas that are sent her way, the worker in a plexiglass environment will recall what happened the last time she tried to "join the team." She will become a silent cynic—one of many within the organization.

Performance-seeking organizations must constantly monitor culture, the environment that is being created and recreated. Organizational output is shaped by both behavior and environment. Trying to change output by changing only the environment is like setting the fish free by smashing a hole in the side of their tank. Although the barriers are gone, the fish are limited by their inability to breathe. Similarly, the organization's members, if "let loose" in an unrestricted environment, will suffocate if they lack leadership skills. These skills will allow them to survive in the new environment.

"No matter how much work a man can do . . . he will not advance far if he cannot work through others."

—John Craig

DRIVERS, RESISTORS, AND JACKASSES

The motivational theorist Frederick Herzberg was a strong advocate of improving organizational performance the direct way—by eliciting greater commitment from individual contributors. He was one of the first to draw attention to the fact that every member of an organization has a client somewhere, an identifiable person whom he should take pride in serving. But even Herzberg insisted that, without the proper skills to supplement this approach, carefully nurtured feelings of camaraderie and other motivational hoopla will do nothing to increase either job output or satisfaction.

In "Asinine Attitudes toward Motivation," Harry Levinson asserts: "People inevitably respond to the carrot-and-stick by trying to get more of the carrot while protecting themselves against the stick. This . . . has led to the formation of unions, frequent sabotage of management's motivational efforts and employee suspicion of [manipulative] techniques." This, according to Levinson, leads to a "jackass response": "When employees sense they are being viewed as jackasses, they will see management's messages as manipulative . . . and they will resist."

Removing the Restraints to Motivation

Most organizations are torn between the following:
A. *drivers*
—compensation and benefits
—pep talks
—internal hoopla and PR
—setting of objectives and goals
—pride in accomplishment
—discipline
—competition
—ambition

B. *resistors*
—low management expectations
—ineffective coaching
—poor team leadership
—unsupportive or inconsistent culture
—undefined vision or values
—poor communication skills

Most managers stress drivers and pay only lip service to removing the resistors. Removing resistors, which are often entrenched in the organization, is not an overnight process. The key to getting rid of resistors is upgrading leadership skills. This requires time and resources but, *on balance, it is less costly to remove resistors (by leadership-skill building) than it is to add drivers to an already crowded list.*

Unfortunately, many organizational performance programs are based on increasing what behavioral scientist Kurt Lewin's behavioral diagnostic model, "force-field analysis," calls "drivers" to performance: merit awards, salary increases, position and prestige perquisites. What this approach misses is that performance can often be more effectively improved by reducing the number of "resistors"—things that hold people back. Removing negative behavior patterns, negative expectations, communication barriers, and other impediments can have the same net affect as adding complex motivators. And cost a lot less!

VISION AND VALUES ALONE AREN'T ENOUGH

We have looked at the power of vision and values in the organizational setting. Vision and values give purpose, substance, and meaning to even the smallest day-to-day business activity. Vision and values in high-performing companies show up consistently as high priorities. They are readily understandable and relatively easy to communicate.

Developing strategies, plans, structures, visions and values are useless if the requisite leadership skills are not in place. Conversely, leadership skills are of no use unless plans and visions are there. "It takes two to tango."

"Great ideas need landing gear as well as wings."

—C.D. Jackson

Management consultant, William Fonvielle, makes this observation: "People don't possess a collection of individual values, but rather an interrelated system in which each value is tied to and reinforced by other values. *Changing any one cannot be done in isolation.* Just telling someone that 'satisfying customer needs' should be a primary value may conflict with other values, or may generate conflicting priorities when trying to convert those values into actions . . . . More than anything else, an organization's character and culture . . . influence how groups and individuals behave . . . . People may want to do things in a different way . . . but are frequently constrained by the organization's very design."

Fonvielle sees behavioral change, skill building, and "explicit standards and expectations for performance," as the key. Not that attitudes and values are not important, he quickly adds, but simply "in real life . . . the links between people's actions and their attitudes are *circular,* so that while attitudes influence behavior, behavior influences attitudes . . . . *As a result, organizations that successfully change the way people behave eventually benefit from a change in attitudes and values that reinforces the new behavior."*

Successful change, Fonvielle suggests, reflects a "reinforcing cycle." Real and permanent change results from having "a clear view of the desired behavior change followed by encouragement of new behavior through the creation of a consistent and rewarding organizational environment."

LEADERSHIP SKILLS UP CLOSE

The *Modern American Dictionary* defines skill as an "ability that comes from knowledge, [and] practice." We help organizations control their own destinies by working on specific trainable abilities that we call "leadership-skill" sets and by establishing a self-perpetuating process of cultural reinforcement that strengthens the organization's vision and values.

As we noted at the beginning of this chapter, leadership has a dual meaning. In the first, more traditional usage, the leadership role is generally played by someone who consciously assumes the status of leader — for example, the CEO, division manager, or department head. The other meaning, no less important but not as commonly employed, is at the heart of our skill-building system: it focuses on the *action* of leadership — the power assumed by those who take the responsibility for getting things done. While it may not be possible for everyone in the organization to assume leadership roles, everyone can take leadership *action.*

We divide leadership skills into four key groups: personal leadership, coaching leadership, team leadership, and cultural leadership. The next four chapters are devoted to exploring each area of leadership skill in depth. What follows here is a quick overview.

Personal Leadership
No one is an island. Society honors us for our individual achievements, but it also grows and prospers by our collective ef-

forts. People working together can collectively create something bigger than the individual is capable of. Just as a chain is no stronger than its weakest link, so an organization lacking the skills of personal leadership can quickly drag itself down to the mud and mire of technomanagement. "One burnt-out bulb on a Christmas tree can make the whole tree go dark."

"Some people grow under responsibility, others merely swell."

–Carl Hubbell

What's Motivating You to Manage?

People with accomplished leadership ability are not necessarily motivated by power. Effective leaders often discover that, by the time they reach the levels to which they have aspired, it is not the thrill of responsibility but the zest of creation and the excitement of trying to meet challenging goals that provided the impetus. Power, like money, is most important when you don't have enough.

   Some thoughts on motive:

–As president of Sterling Institute and former president of Management Systems Corporation, J. Sterling Livingston has actively managed hundreds of MBA graduates: "Many . . . who aspire to high level management positions are not motivated to manage. They are motivated to earn high salaries and to attain high status, but they are not motivated to get effective results through others. They expect to gain great satisfaction from the income and prestige associated with executive positions in important enterprises, but they do not expect to gain much satisfaction from the achievements of their subordinates. Although their aspirations are high, their motivation to supervise other people is low."

–J. Willard Marriot, Jr., says: "Let's admit it: in a lot of companies there is a hostile attitude. There are people who like to fire people. Some managers may not know it, but they have created a fear-oriented climate."

Coaching Leadership

There is a lot more to management than giving orders. The skilled manager or supervisor creates a context, an environment, in which all those she works with come to share a common goal, a common vision, a common purpose. She is able to communicate with her staff in an effective and encouraging manner. She establishes performance expectations and provides constant feedback. When performance slips or disruptive behavior appears, she is able to hold her staff accountable while maintaining their self-esteem. A common mistake organizations make these days is underestimating the average employee's sense of fair play. Treat someone badly and, somehow, someday, he'll find a way to get even. The old reliable "do for" or "do to" approaches traditionally taken by management simply won't work anymore; such notions put workers and supervisors at opposite ends of the playing field.

Communication Is Central to Leadership

The best ideas or plans, if poorly expressed, usually fall short. It's not enough to know what's to be done. A leader at any level of the organization must be able to mobilize others to action. With the erosion of position power, communication skills become more important. They produce persuasion power.

Communication skills are essential for senior managers in this electronic age, more so than in any age preceding it. As today's market is global, so today's leaders must be able to communicate globally. This does not mean mastering hundreds of languages, but rather mastering the ability to communicate ideas. John Kennedy had these skills. Jimmy Carter, on the other hand, is thought to have lacked them. Kennedy modeled his communication skills on those of Winston Churchill, a man he revered. Kennedy once said of the English statesman: "Churchill had the unique ability to send the English language into battle. He had the ability by words, phrases, stories, sentences and paragraphs to give hope to the weary, to give tenacity to those that seemingly had lost all hope. Words are powerful."

The optimal approach is "do with," and that means creating supervisors, managers, and executives with the skills to align the employees in the direction the organization needs to go.

"Half the world is composed of people who have something to say and can't and the other half who have nothing to say and keep on saying it."

—Robert Frost

Team Leadership

People who participate in the creation of ideas, concepts, and systems ultimately becomes "stakeholders." They *care*. They will work harder and smarter to make sure things happen. The best solutions to organizational problems lie not with consultants and gurus but with the people who do the job. Provided they are empowered to do so, these people are the best equipped to find solutions. To use their own problem solvers, organizations must first create a context, an environment, that makes workers feel that their input matters. Are your teams working for you or against you? Are your meetings constructive and positive or a waste of time? Are your quality circles "going around in circles"? Do you have the skills needed to work collectively with other people, to make each project a *team* effort?

Cultural Leadership

Does the organization's vision start with the executive, the CEO — or does she gather around herself those who *already* have a common goal or purpose and catalyze it? Who is more important in the organization: the CEO who meets and contacts forty people a day, or the frontline employees like switchboard operators who deal with ten times that number? Who has the more powerful impact on the organization's image? Remembering that you can't grow large oak trees in flower pots, ask yourself the following questions: Where does corporate culture come from? Can an organization *really* accommodate and nourish vision of performance excellence? Cultural leadership molds itself around common aims and goals that the individuals who form the organization believe in. Just as a chain is no stronger than its weakest link, so an organization wanting to improve performance has to foster and create an environment of leadership that carries its messages to every member and customer through *every miniculture within or outside of its corporate environment.*

"The obscure we eventually see. The completely obvious, it seems, takes longer."

—Edward R. Murrow

ALL LEADERSHIP SKILL LEVELS ARE JUST DIFFERENT SIDES OF THE SAME COIN!

At first glance, our leadership-skill sets seem to match up neatly with the chain of command. Personal skills, for example, directly affect the individual worker at the base level; coaching skills help the supervisors or line managers communicate with those who look to them for direction on a day-to-day basis; team skills are within the domain of middle managers, whose positions often require them to facilitate and communicate with others at their own level; and cultural skills seem aptly suited to the needs of senior executives, the people at the helm.

We have no quarrel with that explanation of leadership-skill levels. Indeed, for many companies, it offers a menu from which they can pick and choose which level within their own organizations has the greatest need to improve. There is a problem, however, with the "worker/supervisor/middle manager/executive" explanation of the levels of leadership skills. It's too narrow.

Limiting particular leadership skills to a specific level of organizational responsibility puts you in the same trap organizations themselves get into when they assume, for example, that customers are solely external to the organization. *Restrictive definitions lead to restricted results.* As the best organizations consistently demonstrate, everybody at every level of the enterprise has a customer—somewhere. And the same can be said of leadership. *Everybody in the modern organization has someone who needs leading—including themselves!* When a switchboard operator functions hundreds of times each day as the first positive contact the outside world has with the organization—who is to say she is not acting in the role of a leader? When a line supervisor, frustrated by an intermittent mechanical malfunction, asks the machine operator for suggestions as to what the problem could be, are not both taking on responsibility for production? When a manager tries to improve her department's pride, isn't she really exercising cultural leadership?

The point is worth restating: Although we have neatly parcelled leadership-skill building into identifiable categories, it does not follow that one skill set works to the exclusion of others. Mastering one level of leadership skills expands possibilities available to the individual.

LEADERSHIP-SKILL BUILDING: WHEN THEORY IS NOT ENOUGH

For the majority of organizations on the road to improved performance, the ultimate paradox is that the key elements in such a transformational process — *vision*, *values*, and *environment and behavior* — *already* exist in their enterprise. The foundation is *already* laid down. The irony, we have found, is that once organizations become aware of this foundation, they often wish that they hadn't! All too commonly they realize that the organization's current visions, values, and environment do not mesh with the goals they have set.

Leadership Makes the Difference

Management at all levels would do well to keep the following in mind: "He was hired for his grasp of technology. He was promoted for his ability to manage. And he was fired for his failure to *lead*."

  —Jack Zenger

So what to do?

Change what you don't like. If the organizational vision is wrong, change it. If the values aren't compatible with the desired outcome, shift them. And if your culture is more supportive of unproductive weeds than performance roses, then alter that as well.

But how?

Improve the four sets of leadership skills throughout your organization.

"Here lies a man who knew how to bring into his service men better than he was himself."

—Andrew Carnegie's epitaph

Skills are what distinguish a craftsman from a tinker, a virtuoso from a shower soprano, and a computer whiz from an after-hours hacker. Skills impart the ability to take raw material and produce something better.

Skills can transform your organization.

And what is the mechanism of this transformation to be? One obvious method—once you accept that dealing with the organization's workers is what it's really all about—is to fire everyone

---

What Is Your C.O.S.? ("cost of skills")

Today it is common to talk about the "cost of quality"—the real cost to the organization of "not doing it right the first time." This cost is generally acknowledged to be 15 to 30 percent of sales.

But there is another hidden cost, the cost of not having the right skills in place to do the job.

Such C.O.S. components include:

—*high turnover*, especially among the "gold-collar" professional and managerial staff compounded by the *high costs of retraining* with accompanying losses in productivity and time;

—excessive *paper shuffling* caused by people's weak ability to communicate with each other directly;

—*high overhead* resulting from too many management layers and excessive systems;

—*lost customers* who quietly take their business down the street;

—*wasted time* resulting from ineffective meetings, politics, needless conflict, disgruntled employees, union-management scraps, and a general lack of motivation;

—*wasted ideas* that, having nowhere to spring from, never appear. The lost opportunities from *that* source alone are unimaginable.

---

and replace them with a better lot! But is there a better lot to be had? Or, more to the point, is there a way to improve the people you *already* have?

"To lead an untrained people to war is to throw them away."

               —Confucius.

The answer is leadership-skill building. Effective skill building is powerful: it strengthens the people you already have.

In dealing with the ever-present question, "How do we get *there* from *here*?" skill building not only gives you a method, but assumes that you've already completed part of the journey. You've got the people. You've *already* invested in them.

Don't just throw words at them. Theories are impressive (except maybe to the poor bumblebee who resents the flight theorist's insistence that he must perform his daily chores on foot because, from a designer's viewpoint, he's not built to fly) but actions speak more loudly than words.

The power of leadership-skill development is that it changes perceptions and gets the organization's people thinking in new constructive ways. The law "like attracts like" suddenly starts to work *for* the organization instead of against it. Those not in tune with the new thinking, those not wishing to go "to the max" for quality and service, find they have nowhere to hide. They either shape up—or ship out.

"If you're waiting for your ship to come in, start working days, nights, and weekends building the dock."

             —Paul Micali

Knowledge—even with raw, natural ability thrown in—simply won't suffice! Skills must be learned, practiced, mastered, reinforced, and perfected. Robert L. Katz, consultant and former CEO, put it this way: "*Human skill cannot be a sometime thing. . . . To be effective . . . [a] skill must be naturally developed . . .* and demonstrated in the individual's every action. It must become an integral part of his whole being." Wayne Gretzky, the best hockey player in the world, still practices the basics of skating, shooting, and passing. And he still listens to a coach who, from a performance standpoint, couldn't carry his skate laces.

In a nutshell: To get there from here, you need leadership skills. Because theory is not enough.

CHAPTER SEVEN

Personal Leadership Skills: Building the Basics

"The greatest ability in business is to get along with others and influence their actions."

—John Hancock

WORKING "TOGETHER"

Society honors us for our individual achievements, but it also grows and prospers by our collective achievements. There is an exercise from group-dynamics classes that never fails to make the point. The participants are divided into two sections and asked to locate a hidden prize. Each section is given a certain number of clues to start with. Within minutes, an atmosphere of frenzied competition and rivalry ensues. Usually both groups fail to locate the treasure and tempers are cut to the bone. At this point the group leader makes two observations:

1. Nothing in the rules precluded the two groups from working together (although, inevitably, both groups *assumed* they had to work separately).

2. No indication was ever given that the treasure, when found, would be less than sufficient to satisfy the needs of both groups.

Ultimately, the two groups pool resources and discover the treasure within minutes.

The reason the word *organization* is used in business is because the structure purports to organize (and maximize) the skills and resources of all the different bodies contained within it. There is power to be found when people work with other people, share, contribute, and produce with other people.

The corollary, however, is too often overlooked: if the net result is the total sum of all individual efforts, then individuals *not* in step must be "pulling the organization down" to their level. Just as a chain is no stronger than its weakest link, an organization can be frustrated in its plans by just one person, (or a handful of individuals) unwilling — or more likely unable — to move toward the vision and values.

"One uncooperative employee can sabotage an entire organization because bad spirit is more contagious than good spirit."

–Robert Half

A $50,000 race car comes with tires that are "v" rated, meaning that the tires will cruise safely for hours at speeds in excess of 120 mph. If the car develops even one flat tire, that same car will be lucky to average 5 mph until it gets to the pits.

Even the best, highest-scoring organization is no more than a conglomeration of people. And the organization's performance is really only a magnification of those people who collectively make it up. Take any outstanding organization, replace its people with a

---

The Balance of Power?

Employees hold the balance of power in today's organizations. Since the "front line" far outnumbers management, employees hold sway. They decide whether the hundreds of tiny "moments of truth" with customers will be positive or negative, pluses or minuses for the company. Employees decide whether to let a defective product slip through. Employees choose whether or not to take the initiative to deal with small problems — or do nothing and let them become bigger problems. Employees usually make the difference. Management provides the tools and material, but employees are the ones who use them. The people who get development opportunities beyond technical areas are usually "rising stars" in the management staff. Seldom is the secretary, the shipper, the machine operator, or the assistant given leadership development. That approach could be tragic. As Tom Peters asserts: "Highly trained and thus more flexible workers . . . are a must for constant adaptation to customer needs and constant innnovations."

---

bunch of disjointed, awkward, mumbling employees who can't see beyond their own noses, and even the mightiest corporation will topple like a felled oak.

"Of all the decisions an executive makes, none are as important as the decisions about people because they determine the performance capacity of the organization."

—Peter Drucker

A paradox in modern organizations is that we bring in newer and better technology and management systems to supplant human input, yet our reliance on human input to achieve excellence has never been greater. The story is told of an old rancher who discovered oil on his property. The first thing he bought with his windfall was a Cadillac. Every day he would ride through town in his new car—with two horses pulling it! The old fellow had never learned to drive! Although motivational buzzwords and sloganeering abound in the eighties, a vast amount of human horsepower lies dormant under many corporate hoods.

Along with management specialists we believe that much of the blame can be dumped at the doorstep of organizations that persist in taking a "do for/do to" approach with their employees.

One More Time . . . Soft Is Hard!

Establishing a "do with" relationship means doing away with traditional boss-subordinate or parent-child relationships. It means treating everyone in the organization as a responsible adult. It does not mean, however, "giving away the store," or abdicating management authority. The correct approach, a balancing approach, has been called by Pascarella Hard Humanism: "If you work for me, you're going to have to learn. You're going to have to meet the standards we've agreed upon. We're going to have to sit down and solve problems together. I'm going to tell you when you do well, and I'm going to tell you when you screw up. You and I are going to share some problems and work on them together. We're going to win a few, we're going to lose a few."

"Do for" thinking was prevalent in the industrial period. ("Do for us and we'll give you a gold watch" was the message — an interesting proposition if you feel that twenty-five years of your life is a fair trade for a timepiece.) "Do to" was the approach taken when companies brought in quality-control circles, and other magic fix-its, to add variety to the humdrum tedium of the job. Organizations that successfully nurture their employees' commitment to improving service, quality, innovation, and productivity are doing so using a "do with" approach. The cornerstone of such an approach is to ensure that members have strong personal leadership skills. Everyone has the responsibility (and, through skill building, the potential) to solve performance problems and initiate improvement. Employees and managers will treat each other as peers once they all start behaving like leaders.

PERSONAL LEADERSHIP PROVIDES THE BASE

For each individual, personal-leadership skills are circular in nature. The circle starts with the individual's innate values, goals, and ability to translate desires and energy into reality. And it continues through to the people that this individual interacts with in the day-to-day environment.

Uncommunicated ideas are like eggs — good perhaps for a quick snack. But if you permit the eggs to grow into chickens, you could have food for years. Similarly, if you communicate your ideas, they too will grow. To make ideas work, to make *anything* in life work, you have to go to the next step: sharing with and involving other people.

Communicating with others is not like delivering the mail — you don't just toss an envelope into a slot and return days later to see if there's a reply. Communication is a *dynamic interactive process*. You don't simply express an idea, you create an environment in which the idea can be expressed. There is a flow of energy here, there is give and take on both sides. Even our language reflects this to a limited extent: we say we "work on" cars, toasters, or typewriters. But we "work with" Joe, Betty, and Fred. (Sometimes we slip and say we "work for" the boss, but that is more of a cultural anachronism than a meaningful statement about work — although some backward-thinking bosses would disagree!)

"Ninety percent of the friction of daily life is caused by the wrong tone of voice."

Knowing what we want to say is not enough. Just as a traveler in a foreign country must be able to identify his wants in the language of the foreign land, so must an individual communicating with others be able to do so in a context that is *meaningful to the other person.*

By communication, we mean the ability not just to listen to but to understand what another individual is saying to you. Too often in life we allow our own value sets and information banks to filter what others are saying—just as a "pickpocket looks at a saint and sees only pockets." To communicate, individuals must hear and understand what others are trying to convey, not just listen to the particular words or expressions.

And, of course, the flip side of hearing someone else's thoughts is conveying your own correctly. The ability to say what we mean, to communicate our thoughts, is what separates a good speaker from a bad one, a well-received toastmaster from one who goes through the motions. Surely it can't be simply grammar or diction: George Jessel, one of the most famous and popular toastmasters of the century, had an accent so thick and a delivery so obscure that his style was mimicked by comics. But Jessel knew the secret of story-telling; he knew how to *communicate* with his audience.

QUALITY, SERVICE, INNOVATION, AND PRODUCTIVITY

Meeting the increasing pressure for better productivity, innovation, quality, and service depends on the ability of the organization's people, collectively, to deliver the goods. Strong teams require strong team skills, tough skills. Humanistic, to be sure, but powerful at the same time.

"It is not sufficient to know what one ought to say, but one must know how to say it."

—Aristotle

Personal Leadership: The Foundation for Performance Improvement

You can't light a fire with a wet match, and you can't improve performance without the spark that comes from a skilled team.

— "One of the most prevalent skill deficiencies today has to do with interpersonal relations — the ability to show care, concern, and courtesy. What looks like poor work attitudes often stems from the lack of social skills. For example, the store clerk who shakes her head and walks away in response to a customer's question is not necessarily hostile. She may be afraid of dealing with strangers and lack the simple social skills of looking someone in the eye and speaking clearly. These shortcomings dampen that person's self-esteem and make the work an unpleasant experience. . . . In the past, training in [these] interpersonal skills was confined primarily to managers and sales personnel, but now the rewards of exposing all employees to it are becoming apparent."
   — Perry Pascarella

— "Businesses in general spend too little time training and motivating their front-line employees, whom they treat as the lowest workers on the ladder. The tendency has been to economize on the training process by designing service jobs to have the fewest possible skills. That keeps employee mistakes to a minimum but . . . [makes] it difficult for workers to use their heads."
— "Pul-eeze! Will Somebody Help Me," *Time*, February 2, 1987

— The billion-dollar Service Master Company has a twelve-year Return On Equity averaging more than 30 percent after taxes, one of the highest in the United States. Their successful service focus revolves around a philosophy stated by their chief executive officer: "Before asking someone to do something, you have to help them be something."

The foundation for improvement is laid when the organization's average, non-super-star employees become leaders. When invoicing clerks, computer operators, truck drivers, machinists, expediters, engineers, and other individual contributors improve their leadership skills, improved performance results.

Employees become leaders when:

1. they understand that outstanding external customer service depends on strong internal customer service;

2. they can communicate effectively, listen to and hear what others are saying, express their own thoughts with assurance, and deal constructively with confrontational situations;

3. they participate in meetings and group situations, work effectively with others, and give and receive help to build more effective work or management teams. As one professional said after developing these skills: "We don't hide behind memos anymore. We talk to each other";

4. they deal with change and learn from it, resolve crisis situations as they arise, and find something positive in each experience, no matter how serious things may look at first glance;

5. they are able to take initiative to improve their unit's effectiveness and influence the direction of the larger organization.

We believe some 90 percent of all serious problems in organizations are people problems. If there is a "computer error" then somebody somewhere likely programmed the machine incorrectly. If a customer receives a bad product and complains about it, then somebody overlooked the opportunity to phone the customer up and tell him how valuable his business was, why the problem happened, and how it will be made right in the next shipment. Quality, service, productivity, innovation—in the final analysis, these are people issues, and only skilled caring people can make them happen. Systems and or technology are only tools.

SKILL-BUILDING AND LEADERSHIP-DEVELOPMENT PROGRAMS

When organizations introduce a personal-leadership-skills program to their employees, they send a powerful message. They are saying: "We believe in you. You have much to contribute to improving the organization. We want to employ your hands, your heart, and your head. We want to put you in a large fish tank."

"All life therefore comes back to the question of our speech, the medium through which we communicate with one another, for all life comes back to the question of our relations with one another."

—William James

Since 1980, we have worked closely with Zenger-Miller, a highly successful training and development firm in Cupertino, California. Our clients use this company's leadership-development programs to improve skills and effectiveness. The lasting and substantial behavior changes that these programs produce have been documented by Stanford University (and numerous other studies). A key to these changes is found in the five basic principles that are hammered home repeatedly during each training session. These principles are the foundation for all four leadership-skill areas. They apply to employees, supervisors, managers, and executives alike. Many clients have emblazoned them on coffee mugs, coasters, posters, plaques, and wallet cards.

1. *Focus on the situation (or behavior, or issue) not the person.* When others feel that they are being criticized personally, they react defensively and emotionally. To avoid such reactions, focus on the facts of the situation, not the person. More importantly, in virtually all situations in which interpersonal skills are being brought to bear, the focus should veer away from the individuals or personalities involved and be directed instead to the subject matter at hand. Experience has shown that, correctly used, this basic principle can defuse conflicts and bring about rapid solutions and problem solving.

"Examine what is said, not who is speaking."

—Arabian Proverb

2. *Maintain the self-confidence and self-esteem of others.*
People need to feel valued and respected as individuals. When people are treated as if they don't matter, have little to contribute or are in the way, they lose interest in doing their job. They stop trying, and performance suffers. One turned-off person can drag

137

down the performance of many others. On the other hand, when people are treated as if the whole organization depended on them, they will surprise you (and possibly themselves) by acting as if that were really the case. Actions that praise, reward, and enhance the self-confidence of individuals create empowered employees.

"There are two ways to get the tallest building in town; tear everybody else's down or build up your own."

3. *Maintain constructive relationships.*

Every contact you have with every individual, no matter how small, contributes a few more "pennies" to the "bank account" of that interpersonal association. People by nature miss little that takes place around them: just as the behavior of a rude sales clerk

---

Customer Service Begins at Home

Efforts to improve customer service are too often short lived and ineffective because they attempt to fix the people who have contact with customers. These attempts include teaching them soft-sell techniques (cross selling), positive thinking ("customers pay our salaries"), telephone courtesy (smile and dial), problem handling and listening (handling complaints and "problem customers").

While this training may be useful, the real payoff comes from making the entire organization customer oriented. To do this, one must begin by showing those large groups of people who don't directly contact external customers (sadly, too many are managers) how to provide internal customer service. By defining the organization as a chain of customer-supplier relationships, all employees and managers are able to trace their contribution to the customer's ultimate satisfaction. They also learn how to exist for the customer, how to understand the value of a common performance standard, and how to separate useful work from bureaucratic activity. Employees serving external customers get the support systems, products/services, and assistance they need to provide outstanding service.

---

may have once clouded *your* day, so your inappropriate conduct with others (even if unintentional) may have surprising—and unwanted—long-term results. This principle simply restates the obvious: treat your relationships like the investments they really are. Strive to create trust, for trust can make any relationship work better and more smoothly. Keep communication pathways open. Take conflicts as opportunities in disguise: use them to build bridges, not to disrupt supply lines. Assume that, with most people, you won't get more than one chance (an excellent assumption!) and do your best to make the most of that chance.

4. *Take initiative to make things better.*
Any car mechanic knows that no problem, left on its own, improves. In fact, it will almost certainly get worse. Taking initiative mirrors perfectly that old maxim: "If you're not part of the solu-

---

Some examples of "hidden" or internal customers are:

—In a hospital, the patients are the obvious customers; the surgeons who rely on the nurses and anesthetists are the "hidden" customers.

—In a manufacturing company, the receivers of goods are the obvious customers, while the shippers who depend on the production workers for high-quality products are the "hidden" customers.

—In a retail store, the shoppers are the obvious customers. The sales staff and the inventory and financial clerks are the "hidden" customers.

Albrecht and Zemke found that in the best service-producing organizations, "management itself is a service . . . . Managers see their roles in the context of helping service people do their jobs better. The role of management in a service driven organization is to enhance the culture, set expectations of quality, provide a motivating climate, furnish the necessary resources, help solve problems, remove obstacles, and make sure high-quality job performance pays off."

---

tion, then you must be part of the problem." This principle holds that, by taking responsibility for her own output and the output of her organization, each individual contributor should strive to be pro-active rather than reactive. Fix things before they break, not after. Deal with problems early, don't let them fester. Take responsibility not just for making decisions but for the results of those decisions.

5. *Lead by example.*
Just as every member of an organization has a customer, so every leader has a follower — or, potentially, yet another leader. People will instinctively tailor their own behavior, their own values, their own attitudes to those of the people around them. Almost every action will ultimately produce a reaction — somebody somewhere will try to copy it. Actions are contagious; make sure yours are worth catching! Just as a father who extols the virtues of being a teetotaler with a martini in his hand will discover that his words lose impact, so those trying to uplift their organization will find that their words fall on deaf ears unless their actions are seen to match their words.

"Example is a lesson that all men can read."

— Gilbert West

CORE SKILLS OF PERSONAL LEADERSHIP

Let's get to the heart of the matter and be specific. The following skills describe the "how to" of personal leadership. Drawn from Zenger-Miller's "Working" program, these skills form the base for transforming a good employee into a contributing leader. They are also the first steps in building stronger supervisors, managers, and executives.

1. *Listening to Understand Clearly*
Too many of us spend our time talking instead of listening. Communication is a two-way street. Good listeners receive more information, earn the respect of their co-workers, and save time in the process.

Listening is a skill you can practice. Show interest in what the other person is saying. Ask questions to clarify what you've heard.

140

Then, if you think you follow, let the other person *know* that you understand by repeating as accurately as possible the meaning of what was said, using your own words wherever possible.

"A good listener is not only popular everywhere, but after a while he knows something."

—Wilson Mizner

2. Giving Feedback to Others

It is difficult to succeed without knowing what we do well and what needs to be improved. No one gets useful feedback unless someone else takes the time (and has the skill) to give it. Giving effective feedback is not easy. Most people avoid offering praise or criticism because they are afraid they will deliver it badly or they will be misunderstood and the recipient will take offense.

Good feedback starts when you state clearly the purpose of the discussion. Describe specifically what you have observed and your honest reaction to what has taken place. Don't get sidetracked with personal issues or characteristics. Where appropriate, offer suggestions. Summarize your discussion and demonstrate your willingness to help the other person take the proper action based on the feedback.

3. Taking on a New Assignment

It's not uncommon to have mixed feelings about taking on a new assignment. With practice, however, the new responsibilities can be incorporated into your work environment almost seamlessly, increasing not only your own efficiency and output, but also your pride and self-respect.

Find out exactly what results are expected. Determine in advance the steps and skills required to achieve those results. Also determine exactly what resources will be needed — and then make sure they will be available. Don't guess about the limits of your decision-making abilities in your new role. Find out what decisions you are expected to make on your own. Finally, spend time with your supervisor or manager laying out a step-by-step action plan and, once that's done, agree in advance on an appropriate time to sit down and review the results of that plan.

4. Requesting Help

Many of us don't ask for help even when it's needed most. Too often we feel that our request might be viewed as a sign of incompetence, or even weakness. We put off asking for help until it's too late, or we never ask at all. When we avoid requesting help, the situation usually gets worse.

Understand that it is okay to ask for help as soon as it is needed. Describe the problem and summarize everything that has been tried to improve the situation. You will find that things work better when everyone knows how to solve problems together and, where possible, can take appropriate action on his or her own.

5. Getting Your Point Across

Presenting an idea that you want someone to listen to deserves an investment of time and thought. As you would when preparing a gourmet meal, you increase the chance of success if you prepare your ingredients carefully and introduce information into the message mix one morsel at a time. Your basic goal is to be understood, and there are specific skills and techniques that can help you to achieve this.

"Blessed is the man who having nothing to say, abstains from giving us wordy evidence of the fact."
—George Eliot

Capture attention as quickly as possible. A sharp opening statement usually does the job. ("I'm going to show you how to save some *real* money!") Get to the basic point quickly and state it. If you are presenting complex information, summarize it and explain why the listener needs to have it available. Finally, present organized data and facts to support your point. Make it clear that your intent is to present serious information. Opinions are fine, but people are more willing to go along with you if you can back them up with facts.

6. Participating in Meetings

Meetings can be a joy or a punishment. Properly used, they present an excellent opportunity for all the people working on a given job or affected by a specific decision to get together and share their ideas, viewpoints, or problems. Every participant deserves to get something out of a meeting, and if the meeting is correctly handled, positive results will surely follow.

The meeting leader ought to state the topic and purpose of the meeting up front and keep attention focused and on point. If someone veers off course, he should gently be guided back to the matters at hand. If you're the participant and not the meeting leader, offer strong facts and ideas while being, at the same time, respectful of the opinions of others. Most importantly, help others to express and contribute their facts and ideas even when they may seem a little contrary. Don't, for example, say, "Jack, I think you're off base with that." Instead, try something like, "Jack, you have had some unique experiences in that area that the rest of us haven't, so, while we appreciate your contribution, it's a little hard for us to share that viewpoint."

7. *Keeping Your Boss Informed*

Passing on critical information to your boss isn't just a form of apple polishing — in fact, such information might even include material that *disagrees* with what your boss is doing! A smart boss appreciates the contribution of those directly involved in activities. When you pass along information, you yourself are more likely to receive, in return, the help and support that you need!

Be conscious of the ongoing need to offer any information to your boss that may be useful. Bosses don't like surprises. In general, whenever something starts to drift away from the plan, the boss should be made aware of it. Be clear, however, about why you think the information is important. Understanding your reasons can help the boss decide what action needs to be taken. Finally, ask for a reaction. Why — or why not? Ask what information your boss wants to be apprised of in the future. Of course, listen carefully to what is said, and use the information to guide your actions later on.

8. *Resolving Issues with Others*

There are four ways to handle difficult situations:
— Avoid or ignore the problem altogether.
— Try to smooth things over by doing something to make the situation less tense, but without really addressing the problem directly.

—Have a win-or-lose confrontation using your power at the expense of the other person.
—Take a problem-solving approach and work with the other person to find a mutually agreeable solution.

"Most entanglements are caused by vocal chords."

To take the problem-solving approach, you need to express your concerns promptly. Describe the situation clearly and calmly, and then ask for the other person's views. If these steps are taken, everyone can then review those facts together and generate some alternative solutions. Finally, the parties involved need to agree on what, exactly, each person will do to resolve the problem.

9. Responding Positively to Negative Situations

Even in the best work environments, people are confronted with circumstances that are negative, unavoidable, and beyond their control. These situations test our ability to stay cool and maintain control. Panicky, impulsive reactions often lead to bigger problems that are hard to undo. These, in turn, can become inhibitors to performance.

It takes skill and maturity to cope effectively with the frustrations and disappointments we face in the course of day-to-day organizational life. People need to deal constructively with their emotions and get a meaningful perspective on even the most trying situations. In a nutshell, making the best of a bad situation means understanding why the situation exists and finding something useful that can be gained from the experience.

"If you wish to succeed in managing and controlling others, learn to manage and control yourself."

—William Boetcker

10. Working "Smarter"

It is important to set priorities, to take initiative, and to get things done, rather than simply waiting for someone else to do it (or, more likely, for someone else to notice that nothing has been done about it). Don't do a task a certain way simply because that is how it always has been done. Be alert for better ways, smarter ways, to accomplish what needs doing.

Some ways to work "smarter" include:

— identifying which tasks and results are most important to you and your team and "prioritizing" situations and events;

— looking always for better ways to do things and for possible improvements. Jot down ideas you may have and, if you need help, bring in others to assist you in deciding whether the ideas have merit;

— contributing ideas and suggestions as the work progresses. If you think you know a way to make something go better, say so. Don't hold back;

— taking the initiative when the opportunity presents itself. By taking action, you nip problems in the bud, or perhaps prevent a big potential problem from becoming a reality.

11. Dealing with Change

Changes are part of the process of getting better. Don't fight change; instead acquire the skills to flow with it, improve with it. The following techniques in particular can help.

— Find out exactly *what* changes are planned.

— Make an effort to understand *why* the changes will occur.

— Find out *how* the changes will affect you.

— Pitch in to help solve the problems associated with the changes.

Following these guidelines, you will make change challenging, rewarding, and, possibly, fun!

12. Being a Team Player

The skilled and well-coordinated team is always the one that wins, both in sporting events and organizational life! But being a team player doesn't mean that you don't have to be competitive at the same time. A sense of competition even within your team helps you and the other team members stay sharp and alert. Competition between equally skilled people keeps performance at its peak.

For a more productive team, be alert to the need to pass along good ideas. Don't "hog" clever approaches to problems. Remember that when the team succeeds, so do you. Always be quick to help others in your team, but first make sure your own responsibilities are taken care of. If your output falls, so does the team's. Give

New Trends in Employee Development

In the past few years employee training has received growing attention. The California firm of Zenger-Miller is a trailblazer in this field of skill development. One of their employee-development programs, "Working," was created as the result of a long and hard process. Taking statistical data from agencies such as the Public Agenda Foundation, the firm began a critical analysis of morale boosting and other employee programs that somehow failed to live up to expectations. Data was gathered through interviews with participants from these programs. A research team conducted additional interviews with first- and second-line managers and trainers and with front-line employees from twenty-five companies in four key industrial sectors: service, high-tech, manufacturing, and health care. The interviewing method used was the "Critical Incident Method," which is designed to obtain information drawing upon key situational examples from the interviewees' own experiences. They were asked to identify job motivators and satisfiers, necessary interpersonal and organizational skills, and personal philosophies and attitudes toward work.

Once all the data was in, the specialists at Zenger-Miller began to draw conclusions about skill needs, employee concerns, and employee-management relations. They also tracked dominant business issues, constantly relating these issues to the study's key findings and thereby keeping a perspective on what type of interactive-leadership program would improve participants' and, ultimately, the organization's effectiveness.

Roland Dumas, the lead investigator on the project reported: "Our approach revealed both the critical skills areas and the clear messages that we feel need to be communicated to individual contributors through the same kind of training their managers are privileged to experience." The result was "Working," a revolutionary interactive-leadership-skills development program for front-line employees delivered by their manager or supervisor.

recognition for things well done. In hockey, the forwards score the goals, but the goalie keeps the other side from scoring against you. Recognize the contributions, in your own group, of both the forwards *and* the goalies! And, finally, don't be shy: let others know what you need from them to get the job done!

RESULTS YOU CAN SEE!

Over the past decade we have worked with both public and private organizations to improve the personal-leadership skills of employees. Like any effort at improvement, the results vary from one group to another. However, we've found that most organizations that really work at it realize the following results:

1. Expectations rise. Employees get a sense that the organization trusts them and is encouraging their growth. Employees learn to expect more of themselves. Self-esteem is seen to increase as skills develop.

Joan Cobourne, an intensive-care head nurse who participated in such a program, comments: "Months ago, when in the middle of a heated situation, I'd become upset, lose my cool, and jump on people. Now that I communicate more effectively, I am better able to convey my concerns."

2. Quality of working life improves. Jobs become more stimulating and rewarding. The whole person is now on the job. A post-training auto worker says: "We don't care how long the problems existed in this plant or who is to blame. We realize now that we have to work together if we want to stay in business."

3. Visions and values come to life. Clear messages regarding the cultural changes sought are interwoven in the skill-building sessions. Concern for innovation and mastering change is shared by all.

"It is easier to fight for one's principles than to live up to them."

—Alfred Adler

4. Leaders create followers, and vice versa. An organization is only as strong as its weakest link; all employees learn skills, so each becomes a better communicator both vertically and horizontally within the organizational structure. (Anyone newly appointed to an executive position at Ogilvy & Mather gets a special gift

from the founder, David Ogilvy — a Russian doll containing five other dolls, each smaller than the other. The attached message reads: "If each of us hires people who are smaller than we are, we shall become a company of dwarfs . . . but if each hires people who are bigger than we are, we shall become a company of giants.")

5. Teams grow stronger. As skills grow, so does the process of collaboration, participation, and involvement. Adversaries become advocates, conflicts are resolved in the context of getting the job done and not stroking individual egos.

6. Managers "build" employees by personally delivering the program to their staff in groups of between nine and twelve people. This has a double effect on managers: they further develop their own personal leadership skills by teaching others, and they reinforce their own management role of coach and developer.

7. Productivity and effectiveness increase. Morale improves. People take responsibility for achieving the maximum, not just filling in time.

8. Relationships improve. People begin to form closer relationships from the training process itself. Also, because management leads the session, communication and cooperation between the two groups are enhanced.

9. Understanding improves. Employees see how what they do is a part of what the organization does. When people are more informed about their work, they feel a greater sense of control.

Nor are the effects of these new skill sets limited to the work or organizational environment. Indeed, these new abilities, new modes of expression, and new precepts of self-worth make the worker feel like "more of a person" — outside the workplace as well as in it. Where formerly only artists and professionals were thought to have fulfilling occupations, and workers' jobs were thought dehumanizing, now, with assistance, support, and skill training, workers are able to find more meaning in their work and contribute to the organization's vision and values.

Skill-building programs aimed at the individual contributor represent the "first step" in taking the modern organization where it wants to go. You start with people, continue with people, end with people. Good people are always ready, willing, and able to do what has to be done. They need to be placed in bigger fish tanks, have the plexiglass removed, and be shown how to swim.

"Working" in Action

The personal-leadership-skills program "Working," was adopted by NCR Comten, a wholly owned subsidiary of the National Cash Register organization. That unit develops, manufactures, and services data-communications systems that manage such critical operations as cash transactions and branch-to-central transactions in the banking industry. NCR Comten identified four hundred employees in "lead" positions — project leaders, specialists, coordinators, administrators, and senior-level employees — who were not supervisors but who needed to develop better management skills to do their jobs more effectively. The results? According to Deb Splett, a management-development specialist with the organization, participants in the program are now acting independently, instead of taking up supervisors' time, giving positive feedback to their peers, taking a more professional attitude to their work, and coming up with ideas that can save the company both time and money.

For example, one employee who had labeled himself an "interrupter" said he discovered that he had begun allowing his co-workers to finish their explanations and instructions. He now listens better, can glean more information from fewer questions, and doesn't make as many assumptions.

Generally, employees who have gone through "Working" have learned how to put aside their personal feelings, deal effectively with change, and be team players. Participant May Duley volunteered that the skills she learned have even spilled over into her personal life: "It's helped me in personal relationships. I was a person with a quick temper. I control [it] now." Adds Duley: "I'm more productive and the people around me are more productive. We've always cared about our work but now that feeling is enhanced. 'Working' has helped us save time and money and improve quality. That's the bottom line."

A colleague of Duley's summarizes: "Everyone is so much easier to work with. There is a new willingness to work together as a team."

Fix Them, But Leave Me Alone

When we talk to organizations about the critical role of personal-leadership skills in improving service, quality, innovation, and productivity, there is a tendency to slot only lower-level employees into such training programs. What a tragic mistake! Management must also improve its skills, for three reasons:

1. Most employees mirror their bosses. If a manager is dissatisfied with an employee's ability to resolve issues with others, to give constructive feedback, or to keep others informed or be a team player, he should look in the mirror for a major source of the problem. Through involvement in a personal-leadership skills program, managers at all levels improve these vital skills and provide more effective role models for their staff.

2. Personal-leadership skills provide the base for the three other types of leadership skills we are about to explore.

3. Managers who huffily sniff that training in personal leadership is "too basic" or "beneath" them are usually the ones who need it most. They don't understand that people skills, like muscles, need constant exercise to remain strong.

"We first make our habits, and then our habits make us."

—Stanford Lee

CHAPTER EIGHT

Coaching Leadership: The Leader as Developer

"You can buy a man's time; you can buy his physical presence at a given place; you can even buy a measured number of his skilled muscular motions per hour. But you cannot buy enthusiasm...you cannot buy loyalty...you cannot buy the devotion of hearts, minds or souls. You must earn these."

—Clarence Francis

MISMANAGED PEOPLE: AN EXPENSIVE PROBLEM

Robert Half, author and head of a New York-based executive-recruitment organization, claims that "time theft"—lack of productivity through employee indifference or mismanagement —costs business more than such recognized crimes as arson, pilferage, fraud, and embezzlement. Half suggests that American industry is losing at least $125 billion a year to the problem. He comments: "Time theft erodes the nation's productivity and feeds inflation by increasing both the costs of producing goods and services and the prices consumers are required to pay for them."

A supervisor in a large manufacturing company insisted that he had experienced *no* disobedience. The man described himself as a mechanic who had been given the position of supervising electricians. Although he knew almost nothing about the trade, he'd taken the job because it was "a promotion." Each morning, he would gather the tradesmen, outline the work that had to be done, and ask their input on how to do it. The rest of the time was spent getting them what they needed to do the job. No one ever disobeyed, he said, because he never gave orders. His crew—significantly—was the highest-producing team in the plant.

151

These two examples depict extremes. The current state of managers' coaching skills lies somewhere between them, but, in our experience, the former situation is more common than the latter. Although most organizations can take comfort from the fact that most of their employees are not deliberately setting out to scuttle the operation from within, neither are people producing to the best of their ability. These organizations are using only a fraction of their employees' potential.

"To every action there is always opposed an equal reaction."

—Sir Isaac Newton

A common mistake made by management is to underestimate the average individual's sense of fair play. Treat people wrongly and they'll find a way to get back at you. In the 1970s, car manufacturers were plagued by workers who deliberately sabotaged their own work by, for example, putting pop bottles inside the doors on cars that were being built. Since it takes a worker *longer* to perform that sort of act, you would logically expect em-

---

A Top Coach on Coaching

"We like our players to play for fun and to be happy rather than afraid. It's like that in any business. If you have employees who work through fear, you're not going to get any ingenuity out of them. You're not going to get any employees who will take a gamble or come up with ideas. All you'll have are robots who are going to do their jobs, have a low-key approach, stay out of trouble. They'll put in their hours and go home. But I'd rather have it the other way . . . . So we talk to people. We don't fine them indiscriminately. A lot of teams have rules that say if you're late or miss a plane, you get fined. We have rules, but we temper them with mercy. We talk to people."

—Arnold "Red" Auerbach, thirty-six years coach and general manager, now president, of the Boston Celtics, "the most successful sports franchise in America"

---

ployees — especially disgruntled ones — to shun such mischief. But you would then be overlooking the human factor. If a worker feels he is getting revenge for a personal slight, real or imagined, he will move mountains to regain his dignity.

Organizations that are overcome with the grandeur of their systems and technology (technomanagement) end up managing everything *but* people. Industy analyst Maryann Keller, referring to the relatively poor showing at General Motors during the mid-1980s, commented that the industry was trying to heal itself with money and technology instead of dealing directly with the skill of managers. *"Those are the harder things to accomplish,"* she said, *"because those are things that require changing people's attitudes and forcing people to change their behavior. It's much easier to order a robot . . ."* Once again . . . soft skills are soooo hard!

Time magazine polled automobile experts and wrote: "[They] agree that Japanese excellence begins on the factory floor. One of [that] country's great tools is that workers are encouraged to devise improvements in goods *as they are produced*, resulting in enormous advances over a short time. Can [North American] firms show similar dedication?"

SO WHAT'S THE REAL ISSUE?

Management consultant and bestselling author Ken Blanchard has observed that many North American organizations are run like SPECTRE in the early James Bond films: "All of a sudden you hear a scream . . . and somebody's down a chute!" He goes on: "Ever wonder why quality circles don't work as well here as they do in Japan?? *Because in Japan, they don't mean their people harm."*

It's bad enough that we treat children like children. Do we have to treat adults like children as well? In many large organizations, managerial and supervisory behavior is based on a parental pattern. The assumption is too often that employees are innately lazy and prefer not to work. Therefore (so the thinking goes) we must show them precisely what we want done and then quickly punish them if they fail to do it. This management style (aka "kick butt and take names") did us only minimal damage in the early part of the century when North America was competing only with its own great expectations, and the typical worker, illiterate and unschooled, was grateful for a steady paycheck.

Today's workers are the most educated in history and, unless they feel appreciated, they just won't produce what they are capable of producing. Today the competition is from countries that not only pay lower wages but sometimes boast of a working population that shares lofty goals and mutual dreams with management. The challenge in the work force of today is that managers can no longer command participation from their people, they must earn it.

"Good leadership consists of motivating people to their highest levels by offering opportunities, not obligations."

— The Tao of Leadership

MOTIVATION . . . OR EXACERBATION?

In one firm, a group of managers brought in a consultant to look for ways to improve their unit's performance. "They're lazy," said management, "and cannot be motivated." "Surely," the consultant replied, "you can think of at least one activity at which they excel?" Management thought for a bit and volunteered, "Bowling. They are very enthusiastic at bowling." "Then," suggested the consultant, "imagine bowling operated like their jobs and let's see what would happen. First, each supervisor will explain which ball to pick up, how to swing the arm, and when to release. Then we'll put a soundproof curtain between the bowler and the alley so that the employee never knows whether or not he has hit any pins. Once a month — if you have time — you will tell the bowler what he's doing wrong. *How motivated would a bowler be under those circumstances?"*

Managers would do well to remember something that all elementary teachers know: unless you're careful, you will spend most of your time managing the people who contribute the least: the few highest and lowest achievers. Those in the middle, the ones whose efforts continually support the organization in its day-to-day efforts, too often go ignored, unappreciated, and unrewarded.

This sad state of affairs is a variation on the Pareto Principle, which suggests that 80 percent of the effort ultimately produces only 20 percent of the result. Managers, being problem solvers by nature, often get caught in this trap: going after the problems, the exceptions. The net result, "management by exception," is deadly to the organization. People don't work best if they perceive that their efforts are being ignored. To achieve maximum results, the organization must have an environment that reinforces and rewards the "quiet heroes" who do 80 percent of the work.

Simply put, the modern organization cannot afford to miss opportunities to get the most out of its workers. One example of a lost "people opportunity" is the selection process itself. Many managers farm out this task to their personnel officers and then moan and groan about the result. Balanced organizations, those that see people as the catalysts of better performance, realize that starting with good people is a critical first step. Such organizations involve senior management in hiring decisions. A progressive series of interviews determines whether the candidates share the organization's vision and values. Extra time spent in the early stages pays for itself later on.

"The secret of success lies not in doing your own work, but in recognizing the right man to do it."

—Andrew Carnegie

PERFORMANCE MANAGEMENT: PEOPLE NOT PAPER

Another "lost opportunity" to coach people is that stormy area called "performance appraisal." Managers and employees are often turned off by the inherent artificiality of the process: a yearly ordeal in which both parties must face each other like distant cousins at a family gathering, brought together to dig up the ghosts of past performance and sift them through the twin filters of ego and money. Too often both employees and managers are frustrated by the procedure.

"A manager develops people. He directs people or misdirects. He brings out what is in them or he stifles them."

—Peter Drucker

155

Appraising Performance Appraisal

—"The annual reviews . . . had become a meaningless routine with managers constrained to be nice to the review subject because they had to work with him or her the next day."

—David Hurst, executive vice-president, Russel Steel Inc.

—"Printed forms for performance appraisals and MBOs are used by incompetent bosses in badly managed companies. Real managers manage by frequent eyeball contact."

—Robert Townsend, *Further Up the Organization: How to Stop Management from Stifling People and Strangling Productivity*

—"Most performance appraisal systems are more noteworthy for the angst they create than the results they achieve"

—Ron Zemke, consultant, author, and senior editor, *Training* magazine

—Honeywell Corporation studied the impact of performance appraisal and found "it was near the bottom of a list of 24 impact items . . . about 4 percent of supervisors, 2 percent of managers and 1 percent of executives said performance appraisal had a positive impact on their careers."

Management trainer Dean Spitzer observed: "Managers are afraid of performance appraisal because they are afraid of their people. They are afraid to confront people and tell them straightaway that they are doing a bad job."

When managers at all levels improve their coaching-leadership skills, performance improves dramatically. Performance appraisals and management-by-objectives processes are only tools. They are no substitute for the day-to-day skills of establishing performance expectations, taking (where appropriate) corrective action, recognizing positive results, establishing (and following up) action plans, and giving frequent, constructive feedback. Performance systems (no matter how good), unless supported by these skills, will deteriorate into a meaningless bureaucratic exercise.

Many managers are afraid to reinforce or even recognize good performance. They argue that employees will use such recognition as grounds for demanding a raise—or will form overblown opinions of themselves. The roots of most performance-management problems lie in the focus of the human-resources staff that determine the approaches adopted within the organization.

Performance management is a people, not a paper, issue. Technomanagers, by their nature, become infatuated with "performance appraisal." They fall in love with paper systems, replete with boxes that need checking, scales that need grading, and observations that need recording. Because technomanagers lack the skill to coach their staff on a day-to-day basis, they often hide behind an impersonal system, while calling their activities rational and objective.

Performance coaching is a people issue. Paper systems and overly formalized processes may be indicators of weak coaching-leadership skills. *Performance-appraisal systems should be the servants not the masters of the performance-appraisal process.*

THE NEED FOR FEEDBACK

The most critical element of coaching-leadership skills is regular and frequent feedback. Feedback that promotes in the organization's workers a common vision and shared values. Performance comments (positive *or* negative) should not be allowed to accumulate like entries on a general ledger with debits and credits waiting to be tallied at year end.

"The wise leader does not try to protect people from themselves. The light of awareness shines equally on what is pleasant and on what is not pleasant."

—The Tao of Leadership

Good or bad, we all want to know how we're doing. We feel as children do: love us, hate us, but don't ever ignore us. An example puts the problem in perspective: a man walked into a drugstore to use the pay phone: "Hello, Acme Widgets, I understand you have an opening for a sales director?" After a slight pause, he continued: "What's that? You say you hired someone six months ago and he's working out just fine?? Okay, 'bye." The druggist, meanwhile, could not help but express his sympathy: "Tough luck, son, I'm sorry they didn't have an opening." The young man, surprised, turned and commented: "Oh, I'm not really looking for a job. That was my own organization I called—and I'm the sales director. *I was just checking to see how I was doing.*"

"Good management consists of showing average people how to do the work of superior people."

—John D. Rockefeller

Feedback is Vital to High Performance

According to Ken Blanchard, many managers with low skill levels rely on a technique he calls "Leave-Alone Zap": "The supervisor notices the unsatisfactory behavior but, not wanting to reprimand [the employee], decides to tolerate [it] just this once. Once then becomes twice and twice becomes three or four times. The employee [is] unaware of his manager's ire. The manager gnashes and fumes, vowing 'next time' he'll straighten the employee out. When he finally does, it's usually with a large outburst in response to a relatively small offense."

Feedback on performance that fails to meet expectations is critical if people are to improve. And feedback is equally important when goals are met. A good coach lets his players know when they've done a good job and helps them establish new, even more challenging goals.

Denis Plumb, chief accountant at Coneco Equipment, used coaching skills he had acquired in a coaching-skills program to deal with one individual whose performance was poor. At the interview he "began by stressing all the things she was doing well before going on to say there were a couple of areas where she could make some improvement, and cited specific examples. It worked well . . . and really built up her confidence and self-esteem. She [now] interacts with other departments, and there has been real improvement."

SIGNS OF WEAK COACHING SKILLS

To be effective, to create an environment that encourages productivity, innovation, service, and quality, managers at all levels must coach their people to go "above and beyond" the call of duty. Classic symptoms of weak coaching-leadership skills include:

—overemphasis on "management by objectives." Details are endlessly adjusted and fine tuned with little regard to leadership-skill development;

—employees expect to be left alone *unless* they mess up. Any intervention from management instills paranoia;

—no reward systems in place *or* those in use are indiscriminate or nonspecific;

—senior management who ignore the fact that their coaching skills are rusty;

—public bullying or ridiculing to *embarrass* marginal performers into bettering their work;

—attention focused on only the very high and low achievers. The rest of the staff are invisible, taken for granted, almost part of the furniture;

—excessive losses from absenteeism, medical leave, and turnover. These are written off as "costs of doing business";

—managers who save gripes until they explode at unsuspecting employees;

—workers who use grievance procedures frequently;

—management by rules not reason;

—senior management that delegates responsibility for employee performance and is not aware of what is going on;

—"snoopervision" in lieu of skill—TV cameras, time clocks, computer work tracking, etc.

SOME SOLUTIONS ... AND MORE PROBLEMS

High-performing senior managers have ceased seeing themselves as paper pushers and instead are starting to view themselves as people movers: "The truth is," says Donald Petersen, chairman of the rejuvenated Ford Motor Company, "I'm finding myself spending much of my time with management issues that were not addressed in my graduate school curricula. I'm coming to grips with teamwork, trust, and respect, how to treat our people and inspire their very best efforts."

Technomanagers not only fail to meet the challenge, they often fail to see it. Management by "brute force" is the substitute used by those who lack the skills, care, or training to take a more effective tack.

"A good manager can step on your toes without messing up the shine."

Let's face it: people today respond better to requests than commands. The trick is to pull people to where you want them to go, not to push them. Coaching has become a mandatory management skill. It requires the careful balance of two seemingly opposite traits: a "hard" results-driven approach, with a "soft"

Focus on: Taking Corrective Action

Specific skill steps for taking corrective action:
1. Point out the difference between present performance and agreed-on expectations.
2. Describe specifically the negative impact of the employee's performance.
3. Get the employee's view of the situation.
4. Ask for ideas on how the employee can correct the situation—and add your own.
5. Explain any steps you plan to take and why.
6. Agree on an "action plan" and a date for a follow-up. [an "action plan"? This is a process that alerts the individual to exactly what performance/behavior is expected and allows the employee to participate, at the time the plan is drawn up, in deciding what reasonable and appropriate gains he or she is expected to make by what stage of the plan. It also lets the individual quantify and determine *on his or her own* if the plan is being met and provides a guaranteed forum (the follow-up meeting) at which both parties can reexamine the plan and the progress made. Where needed, it provides a record of the steps that were taken to correct the behavior [or improve the performance] in the event that stronger measures must be taken.]

---

esteem-building humanistic content. In *Power and Influence: Beyond Formal Authority*, John Kotter quotes one employee's appraisal of Jim Treybert, chief executive at Tandem Computers: "He's loving and caring and all those good Marin County words, but when a tough decision comes along, he's hard and he's tough."

Technomanagers don't even realize that this whole area is a paradox in need of management! In their unrelenting black-and-white world, they either coddle employees—and let them off too easily—or they swing a big stick to produce results. *Effective leaders—performance coaches—do both.* They hold people accountable for high levels of performance while at the same time enhancing and building their self-esteem. Leaders don't protect people from themselves, they look for ways to strengthen them.

7. Express confidence that the employee can correct the situation.

Note that these seven steps follow basic principle Number 1: "Focus on the behavior or situation, not on the person." Corrective action and praise have this in common: people innately want to improve and contribute, but first they must understand the problem. Soliciting the employee's opinion allows the individual to be involved in his or her own corrective process. Finally, the "action plan" provides specific identifiable criteria for judging whether or not the process is providing results.

Rick Baltzer, a foreman at Burlington Transit, used these steps to deal with a co-worker who had an eleven-year history of moodiness and noncommunication. He says: "Our discussion changed [the employee's] work. The meeting was held in the latter part of September. In November, I had to be out of town for a week and for the first time in the eleven years he's been there, he was left in charge. On my return, I got a favorable report from the driver foreman . . . . At one time this guy was the least likely person in the company to be asked to tackle a new assignment."

Athletic coaches in particular understand the payoff in maintaining self-esteem among players. Coach John Robinson of the Los Angles Rams says he "never criticizes players until they're convinced of [his] unconditional confidence in their abilities." At that point, if he spots something that might need improvement, he says: "Look, what you're doing is 99 percent terrific, but there is a 1 percent factor which could make a difference. Let's work on that."

There is a lot of work to be done to make managers at all levels more aware of poor coaching skills — and the potential for bottom-line payoff were they to improve these skills. There is a big

---

Career Coaching: Avoiding the MADMUPS Blues

Flattened organizational structures and slower growth have created a crisis for such "gold-collar" professionals as engineers, systems analysts, and accountants. Terms like MADMUPS (middle-aged, downwardly mobile, underutilized professionals) are now being used to describe these people. Demotivated and discouraged professionals are finding that the likelihood that they will receive a management position as a reward for years of technical work is small. The problem is compounded by management's reluctance to initiate open discussion of this sensitive career issue. The outcome is professional turnover, and an even more costly response, "quitting on the job." Product quality, teamwork, customer service, innovation, and productivity are suffering at a time when professional talent is needed most.

To deal with this problem Achieve joined forces with a Utah-based consulting firm, founded by Brigham Young University's chairman of organizational behavior, Gene Dalton, and the dean of their School of Management, Paul Thompson. Their work, now packaged in a dynamic two-day workshop called "Novations," is based on fifteen years of extensive research while they were at Harvard Business School.

difference between the "carrot-and-stick" approach to behavior manipulation and the use of sound coaching skills.

Carrot (bonuses and rewards) and stick (discipline and punishment) methods can play a role in building commitment to the organization's goals. But in the hands of technomanagers, they become just another system to compensate for weak leadership skills. Effective leaders use reward and punishment where appropriate. These techniques should, however, be used to support the leader's habit of building commitment by frequent face-to-face coaching sessions.

Money is not the magic motivator it is assumed to be. While

It identifies four stages of career growth:

1. Learning the Ropes. During this apprenticeship, the individual is supervised by senior professionals and performs detailed and routine tasks.

2. Making Your Mark. Here, the person is given greater responsibility and the chance to work independently. He or she can develop credibility and a reputation through significant results.

3. Contributing through Others. At this stage the individual continues to make technical contributions, but also becomes an idea leader and a mentor to younger professionals. The person also works with clients or helps develop the business.

4. Leading through Vision. Now the person is able to highlight threats and opportunities to the organization and to develop a technical "niche" or area of competence. He or she becomes a key strategic resource.

The MADMUPS syndrome is being eliminated in many high-performance organizations as managers learn how to career-coach professionals, using the "Novations" four-stage approach. By developing pathways to stages three and four through job assignment, these organizations have revitalized many older, valuable professionals.

profit sharing, employee ownership, and other incentives are often part of a leadership-balanced approach, consultants Stephen Cohen and Cabot Jaffee have found that the following are *more* important to individual contributors than higher pay or more perks:

—opportunities to discuss their performance with (and get feedback from) their manager;

—knowing exactly what is required of them;

—an opportunity to contribute to setting their own job-related objectives;

—assessment of their potential future with the organization;

—recognition for their accomplishments.

"The manner of saying or doing anything goes a great way in the value of the thing itself."

–Seneca

In "Managing Human Performance for Productivity," Cohen and Jaffee make the following point: "We cannot issue orders for a change in personal job behavior. We must create a climate in which performance change is possible and rewarding. The process is highly complex and calls for specific skills . . . . In order for on-job performance appraisal systems to work, they must be designed to develop the skills of managers in ways that will make [people] want to do a better job and be involved in the organization's goals."

COACHING: WHAT IT IS, WHAT IT ISN'T

Napoleon said: "An army's effectiveness depends on its size, training, experience, and morale . . . and morale is worth more than all the other factors combined."

Zenger-Miller's "Frontline Leadership" skills-development program puts it this way: "Opportunities to coach grow out of manager-employee relationships that are built on mutual respect and trust. If your relationship with an employee is strained, is not well established, or is not on solid ground for one reason or another, don't expect a great deal of . . . receptivity to your attempts at coaching." Clearly, where trust, open communications, and an attitude that maintains the self-esteem of both parties exist, the individual contributors will work their best instead of merely logging time.

As executives run about singing the praises of higher quality, improved service, greater productivity, and more innovation, it behooves managers and supervisors to gear up for the task of bringing it all home. Many executives have found to their consternation that they can't just order up these qualities — they have to be grown and cultivated. As Tom Peters said, excellence comes from "volunteerism," an organizational state of mind in which employees are more than an extra pair of hands and feet. Instead they are seen as participants, contributors, partners, and helpers. Managers become effective coaches when they are able to connect the hands, heads, and hearts of people.

As we've discussed, the role of supervision and management in the modern organization is changing dramatically. No longer can the blame for poor service, low quality, and meandering profits be laid exclusively on employees. Management has to look in the mirror and lay blame where it belongs. In the classic words of Pogo: "We have seen the enemy and he is us." Mistreated people will mistreat back.

"The employer generally gets the employees he deserves."
—Walter Gilbey

Management must throw off old attitudes in which they see themselves as responsible for results and not people. Today's more effective supervisors, managers, and executives are those who adopt a strong "performance" bias strive to increase their coaching skills.

The critical elements of effective performance coaching are:
1. sharing your expectations with people;
2. allowing solutions to develop from shared problem-solving sessions;
3. reinforcing positive results. If there is one golden rule, it is "What gets rewarded gets repeated." Through skill development, organizations can create an environment in which people get sold on success, addicted to achievement, and exuberant about excellence.

COACHING AS A SKILL

But knowing isn't doing. Many executives assume they know all there is to learn about coaching leadership. "I must know all that stuff or I wouldn't be where I am." They become what Howard Cosell called "legends in their own mind." Know-it-all executives pollute the environment by sending signals about what matters and what doesn't. These signals, like radio waves, permeate the culture, bounce around the structure of the corporation and, ultimately, are broadcast as poor results.

Harvard professor of business administration Richard Walton, in summarizing his research, makes an important point about the difference between obedience and commitment:

A model that assumes low employee commitment and that is designed to produce reliable if not outstanding performance simply cannot match the standards of excellence set by world-class competitors . . . . Market success depends on a superior level of performance, a level that requires deep commitment, not merely obedience — in this new approach, jobs are designed to be broader than before, to combine planning and implementation, and to include efforts to upgrade operations, not just maintain them . . . . With management hierarchies relatively flat and differences in status minimized, control and lateral coordination depend on shared goals, and expertise rather than formal position determines influence . . . . *The commitment model requires first line supervisors to facilitate rather than direct the work force, to impact rather than practice their technical and administrative expertise, and to help workers develop the ability to manage themselves . . . . The new breed of supervisor must have a level of interpersonal skill and conceptual ability that is, for the most part, lacking in the present supervisory work force.*

"The deepest principle of Human Nature is the craving to be appreciated."

—William James

Expressing appreciation is one example. Robert Townsend, author of *Further Up the Organization*, defines the six-letter word *thanks* as "a neglected form of compensation." Management writer Michael Leboeuf wrote an entire book on the subject of praise, which he believes to be "the greatest management principle in the world." Among the varieties of reward/honor mechanisms he recommends are:

—awards for highest sales and productivity, most improvement, least absenteeism, etc.
—certificates, citations, trophies, and plaques
—public praise for a job well done
—congratulatory letters
—special attention from top management
—publicly announced bonuses or raises
—an empoyee hall of fame

"I have yet to find the man, however exalted his station, who did not do better work and put forth greater effort under a spirit of approval, than under a spirit of criticism."

—Charles Schwab

A St. Louis hardware organization used prizes to solve its problems with absenteeism and tardiness. Workers who were punctual for a month were eligible for a draw awarding one worthwhile prize per twenty-five workers, on average. Workers with six months' perfect attendance were also eligible for another draw offering a larger prize—a TV set! The result was that tardiness and absenteeism dropped substantially—and sick leave costs plummeted by 62 percent.

There is as big a danger in the inappropriate use of rewards as there is in underutilization. A predictable and specific trait of humans is that we will accept any measurable increase in our well-being as though we deserved it. (Offer a family member a package done up in ribbons and bows and he or she will open it up *first*—and ask what it's for *later.*) Organizations that have tried *indiscriminate* use of rewards have achieved results quite different from what was expected.

Ken Blanchard tells of one organization that tried to mete out praise for a successful fiscal year by sending turkeys to all employees. Inevitably there came a backlash from the most unexpected sources: employees who didn't like turkey in the first place,

Focus on: Recognizing Positive Results

Motivated contributors are proud employees. They feel they belong to something worthwhile. They matter. And their performance reflects their self-image. Recognition is a two-way street. Letting employees know how much you appreciate their input makes them more receptive to what you are trying to do. On the other hand, meaningless praise serves only to confuse people about what behavior is desirable and what isn't.

Here are three specific steps that help communicate appreciation.

1. Describe the results you are recognizing as *specifically* and *immediately* as possible. (George, I noticed you giving that customer a refund without any hassle, and you were pleasant through the entire conversation.)

VAGUE	SPECIFIC
"Jane, you are becoming a whiz."	"Jane, this is the second month in a row you've gone ten percent over quota."
"I know I can rely on you, John."	"John, you consistently process over a hundred and eighty claims a week."

2. State why these results deserve your personal appreciation. (I was pleased to see you in action because one of our core values is to exist for the customer.)

3. Reaffirm your recognition and continuing support. (I know I can count on you to go on setting an excellent example of client service for our new employees.)

Jack White, day foreman at Cyanamid (Canada) Inc., after taking a coaching-skills program, said, "It's something I never used to think about. Outstanding work—good or bad—I'd notice, of course, but the consistent worker I wouldn't even think of praising. Yet they are the ones that the entire operation depends upon for success."

employees who felt that the specific turkeys being sent to their co-workers were larger than their own, and, finally, employees who were surprised—and hostile—when they realized that the free turkeys would not be a yearly event! They reasoned that if the handing-out of the turkeys was a form of praise, then withdrawing the gifts must be a form of punishment. Blanchard calls such non-specific trinkets "jelly-bean" motivators, and warns against their use: "Feel free to praise but praise specifically. By flattering people for no good reason they'll come to expect applause, even when they are doing slipshod work."

Robert McNamara summed it up: "Brains, like hearts, go where they are appreciated." Above all, employees must have a sense that they count as people and are not considered cogs in a larger machine. The opposite situation was summed up by one sales director: "The boss and I get along great. I laugh at all his jokes, and he laughs at all my suggestions." Basic principle Number 2 (see Chapter 7) urges that the self-esteem of the individual be maintained at all times. Good behavior must be supported and encouraged. Negative behavior can be dealt with only in the context of a caring relationship. The story is told of a manager who is criticizing one of his salespeople to another worker: "Wally is such a slacker. I asked him to pick up a sandwich for me while he was on his calls and I bet he totally forgets." At that moment, Wally rushes in: "Guess what? I just picked up a $10,000 order!" The manager turned disdainfully to the first employee and said: "See—what did I tell you—he forgot the sandwich!"

"The meanest most contemptible kind of praise is that which first speaks well of a man, and then qualifies it with a 'but'."

—Henry Ward Beecher

The thing to remember about motivators, words of praise, and other forms of feedback is that they must *mean* something. People are shrewd when it comes to evaluating how others really feel—they'll not be fooled for long by insincerity.

Tom Watson, Sr., said, "If we respect our people and help them respect themselves, the organization will profit." Buck Rodgers says: "IBM couldn't afford to spend so much to reward the good performers if we had to subsidize those who do not produce . . . . Honoring those who do superior work is not only motivation for them to continue their high-level performance but also a strong incentive for others. An organization can't be *too* appreciative of its high-achievers. Organizations that take them for granted don't deserve to keep them."

"It is only people who possess firmness who possess true gentleness. Those who appear gentle generally possess nothing but weakness, which is readily converted into harshness."

—François Duc de La Rochefoucauld

RULES . . . OR REASONS?

Our associate John Scherer relates: "Years ago we had a puppy and named him Samson. We wanted to make sure he never got hit by a car so we trained him to stop whenever he came to a curb. He would come screeching up to the curb, slam on his doggy brakes and then sit there panting until we caught up. The system worked perfectly—until we moved to a neighborhood *that didn't have curbs*! Samson would be walking along and then the grass would thin out, and the gravel would increase, and then, the next thing you know, he would be standing right in the middle of the road wondering why we were so upset." The issue, Scherer urges, is this: Do you teach your employees about rules, or reasons? If you respect people's innate intelligence and ability, you will take the extra time and deal with reasons. If not, if you deal with rules only, then you are just another carrot-and-stick technomanager, and one day you many find your best people standing obediently in the middle of a busy intersection, looking to you for their next instruction and wondering why you're so upset.

In Chapter 5, we made the point that people, like goldfish, grow to the size of the tanks they are put in. By allowing self-esteem to increase, by treating employees like thoughtful, intelligent people, by explaining the reasons behind the policy, you increase the size of the fish tank, giving employees more room to grow.

In our "Instructor Certification Seminars," participants are asked to describe the most effective managers they have encountered. From sessions conducted over a number of years, the following characteristics consistently emerge:

— Effective managers give their staff freedom and are concerned about their development. Moreover, they are trusting, inspiring, and honest. They keep their word and protect and fight for the people in their unit.

— They understand that people can learn from failure. They permit staff to challenge them. They are innovative. They make others feel smart and treat them as individuals.

— They are collaborative, good listeners, and display confidence. They are approachable and ask for others' input. They take risks.

Contrast the above responses to those we receive from the same participants when asked for characteristics of *ineffective* managers:

— They ridicule others and seldom ask for other opinions.

— They lump individual employees in with everyone else. They look over employees' shoulders and are abrasive.

— They are evasive, indirect, and avoid eye contact.

— They are free with criticism, stingy with credit.

— They rarely give reasons; instead they quote company policy.

— They seldom support their employees to other managers or departments.

— They offer little feedback. Employees don't know what they really want.

Teaching People to "Fish"

There is an old adage: "You can give a man a fish and feed him for a day, or teach him how to fish and feed him for life." Technomanagers get trapped on a treadmill because they must constantly tell their staff what to do and "snoopervise" to make sure it's done. *Leaders teach people to fish.* The are coaches, not commanders. Developing others initially takes extra time and effort, but it pays off with high individual commitment and less need for costly controls.

Developing employees' skills requires particular coaching skills on the part of the manager. The task must be clearly defined. The steps to be undertaken must be individually ex-

---

plained. Every part of the process must be demonstrated for clarity, and then the employee should be asked to redemonstrate the process to verify learning. Finally, the manager must provide accurate and specific feedback — employees should never have to guess whether or not they are handling the situation correctly.

Lindsey MacKnight, operations supervisor with Midland Transport, was frustrated that his dock workers would not work faster. "My first thought was they were just idiots, or not trying," he recalls. After taking a skills-development program in which coaching skills were emphasized, Lindsey was able to communicate the proper procedures to his people using the steps above. "Before," he says, "it took six guys twelve hours to load four trailers. Now we can do the same job in half the time—with two less people. Efficiency is way up and the guys are really impressed with themselves."

"In judging the thing to do is supply light and not heat."

—Woodrow Wilson

DISCIPLINE: FIRST WE GET YOU, THEN YOU . . . .

A bellwether of an organization's ability to lead (as opposed to push) people is the way discipline is applied. A we/they approach to discipline (like giving out demerit points for offensive conduct, with 350 points in a twelve-month period leading to mandatory termination) creates a self-fulfilling prophecy: employees, eager to protect both their jobs *and* their self-esteem, dig themselves deeper and deeper into a protective shell and become less in tune with the organization's real objectives.

The alternative is known as the "nonpunitive" approach. As David N. Campbell, R. L. Fleming, and Richard C. Grote reported of their experiences with a highly successful nonpunitive management approach at Tampa Electric Company: "It seems impossible that people will become better workers if management treats them progressively worse. The ultimate problem with traditional approaches is that they take problem employees, punish them, and leave them 'punished problem employees.' It leaves the worker freed of responsibility for future good performance. The slate is now 'clean.' [In a nonpunitive approach], the manager reminds the individual that he or she has a personal responsibility to meet reasonable standards of performance and behavior . . . . Together they create an action plan to eliminate the gap between actual and desired performance. The main objective is to gain the employee's agreement to change. A *nonpunitive approach to discipline requires problem employees to make a choice: to become either committed employees or former employees.*"

"Correction does much, but encouragement does more. Encouragement after censure is as the sun after a shower."

—Johann Wolfgang von Goethe

A nonpunitive approach can result in profit increases by reducing high employee turnover and improving morale. The results of a study conducted by Campbell, Fleming, and Grote included: "measurable reductions in absenteeism, dismissals, disciplinary actions, grievances and arbitration." Also cited in the study were "improved morale and respect for management, a reduction in wrongful termination suits, and a sharper focus on the majority of employees who are performing well." Among the organizations studied were: Tampa Electric, Union Carbide, Liberty National Bank, and General Electric.

"Never tell people how to do things. Tell them what to do and they will surprise you with their ingenuity."

—General George S. Patton, Jr.

SKILLS MUST DRIVE THE SYSTEM

Communication is a skill. Making a point, listening to another, giving praise, providing feedback—all these powerful communication modes are used, or misused, depending on the skill level of the communicator.

173

Performance Coaching: A Joint Problem-Solving Approach

Effective managers and supervisors are able to take an employee who is working below his or her potential and *work with the employee* to bring about improvement. A coaching attitude summed up by the words *work with*, rather than *do for* or *do to*, will result in increased employee commitment and self-esteem. Managers who rely on position power or rule books might produce short-term gains but, in the long haul, problems will persist.

To help employees improve, an effective leader/coach will describe in detail the performance that is expected and explain its importance to the organization's objectives. The employees' feedback will be sought, and they will be encouraged to suggest specific ways in which they can upgrade their performance. The effective leader/coach will then give constructive feedback on the employees' ideas and supplement them with his or her own suggestions. An action plan and a date for follow-up should be mutually agreed upon. Throughout, an attitude of encouragement, support, and confidence must be maintained.

Pauline Hinchcliffe, administrative assistant with Sarnia Transit, discovered firsthand how awkward it can be to confront an employee about a behavioral problem: "I had a problem with one employee who was taking a lot of sick time. It was a touchy situation because there was an excuse for a certain amount of it as she was pregnant . . . . In the end I asked her what *she* thought she could do to reduce her sick time, and then asked what *she* thought *I* could do to help her. We agreed that she would lie down for five or ten minutes each afternoon to relieve her tiredness. She was absent a lot less after that. More importantly, we settled the matter without having to take recourse in the regulations."

Professor Joseph Leonard, in an article entitled "Why MBO Fails so Often," says: "Although the MBO process has been used by near-ly half the Fortune 500 firms, some investigations show only a 20-25 percent rate of success. *Poor communication is perhaps the primary reason.*" In determining how the success rate might be improved, Leonard focuses on the feedback process: "Face to face communication provides the most effective feedback." However, the writer concludes, the skills are often not in place to make such communication possible: "[MBO] requires friendly, helpful managers; honest and mature employees; a climate of high mutual trust . . . *but often the manager cannot communicate well with individuals and groups whose perceptions of work may differ.*"

CHAPTER NINE

Team Leadership: Two Plus Two Can Equal Six

"Coming together is a beginning; keeping together is progress; working together is success."

— Henry Ford

Franklin Murphy, chairman of the Times-Mirror Publishing Company, asserts: "People have a stake in an idea if they participated in its creation . . . . They'll work harder to bring it to success." William Dyer, professor of organizational behavior at Brigham Young University, says, "The modern manager is solving problems collectively, involving everyone that has a contribution to make. [He] is a coach, a facilitator, a developer, a team builder."

Peters and Waterman put the matter this way: "If you have a major problem, bring the right people together and expect them to solve it."

Humans are noteworthy not only because of our individual accomplishments but because of our ability to get results by working with others. *Individual* achievers get the attention, but it is the *team* that keeps things hopping. Would Wayne Gretzky, zipping down the ice all alone, be as impressive as he is without his teammates? Could Johnny Carson capture his audience without the NBC technicians and crew chipping in to send his electronic message along its appointed path? Even John Wayne would have run into difficulty without his screenwriter, cameraman, and—never to be forgotten—his horse!

"Two men working as a team will produce more than three men working as individuals."

— Charles P. McCormick

Team Problem Solving Pays Off!

Today's manager can't be expected to come up with the best solutions on his own. The optimal approach to problem solving is a team affair. Paul Matthews, a foreman with FAG Bearings Ltd., felt that his participation in a team-leadership skill-development program paid off handsomely: "To increase employee involvement, three team leaders were chosen and volunteers called for. Considerable latitude was allowed on the projects; the only guidelines were that the problem should be something that directly affected the quality of products that the team provided, and that it be within their ability and scope to resolve the matter." Paul was impressed with the results. "They motivated themselves. All I did was let them know their ideas were welcome . . . . the whole experience was very satisfying. Ten heads are better than one, and I've noticed that the workers' involvement has been more productive, not just in the project but in all their work."

Peter Conacher, a senior technician with Turbo Resources, concurs. His involvement in a program that focused on team skills produced dividends: "All the people in the department thought the brainstorming was great. We developed three ideas [that] saved us between $10,000 to $50,000 a year. We meet every three months for brainstorming sessions now. Whenever there is a problem, I ask the people involved to find a 'doable' solution."

The late Dr. Ron Lippitt, professor at the University of Michigan, a mentor to Achieve in our early days, pointed out that in the first fifty years of this century an average of three people cooperated to develop new inventions. However, the last decade has seen, on average, twelve specialists collaborate in the fostering of every new concept. The benefit of combining with others in groups is *more commitment to the adopted solution, since the people choosing the strategy are the very ones who have to implement it.*

Rosabeth Moss Kanter's reasearch into innovation and change brought teams and team-oriented leadership skills into focus. "Interdependence as a stimulus to innovation is a common research finding," she notes. Teamwork is critical to the improvement of service, quality, and productivity. While technomanagers are pushed to their limits to get compliance and meet minimum standards, leaders are able to inspire commitment, focus lofty visions, and pull their teams to new heights of performance.

The new employee is helping to shift the organization toward broader levels of team effort. Most are no longer content to act as "the hands" for someone else's bright ideas. They feel they have valid contributions of their own to make.

William Ouchi, professor at the UCLA School of Management and author of *Theory Z*, says: "We're dealing with an economic setting that demands teamwork and cooperation. Companies that don't come up with those are going to go out of business. It's as simple as that."

"The point that most needs to be borne in mind is that the welfare of every business is dependent upon cooperation and teamwork on the part of its personnel."

—Charles Gow

TEAMS, TEAMS, AND MORE TEAMS

Business has seen a virtual explosion of team activities. Teams come in all shapes and sizes. Most fall into three classes:

1. Management and Employee Teams

Senior and middle-management committees, executive boards, and management councils are getting more involved in directing the organization. These groups focus on solving organizational problems and setting strategies. They also set tactical plans and review operational performance. Many leading companies like General Electric and the Royal Bank of Canada are experimenting with "self-directed work teams" that operate without an appointed supervisor.

2. Quality and Service Teams

The roots of these teams go back to the quality-circle movement popularized by North America's fascination with Japanese management methods. The concept brings together workers to identify the causes of quality problems and propose solutions. Many "small fish-bowl" organizations were not ready for the "large fish" that quality circles created. Consequently, a number of these early efforts failed, and quality circles often fell into disrepute. But the common sense behind the concept, fortunately, has survived. With wider management acceptance and support, and a multitude of new names, team improvement efforts are with us today under such names as Corrective Action Teams, Service Improvement Groups, Employee Involvement, Quality Teams, and so on.

3. Project Teams

Project teams are temporary, unlike the others discussed here. Such teams draw together specialists and experts from different but increasingly interconnected departments or divisions. With their assortment of professionals, managers, executives, and workers, these ad-hoc committees usually focus on specific problems, or work to develop a particular new product or service.

All three types of teams have the same objectives—bringing together people to set new directions, solve problems, establish action plans, rekindle energy and commitment, and follow through with implementation.

"I make progress by having other people around me who are smarter than I am and listening to them. And I assume that everyone is smarter about something than I am."

−Henry J. Kaiser

EFFECTIVE TEAMWORK . . . WORKS!

A skilled team, carefully assembled and well led, can produce extraordinary results. *Effective* team effort inevitably brings about noticeable improvements in service, quality, innovation, and productivity. The principle of synergy, "the whole is greater than the sum of its parts," is the reason that effective groups out-produce individuals. While performance goes up, the time taken to produce results goes down. (Meetings, for example, accomplish more, yet typically don't last as long as sessions held by unskilled members.)

An exciting and instructive turnaround at the Ford Motor Company centered on teamwork. Traditionally, the line worker's sole responsibility was to put the vehicle together: design and engineering figured out what had to be done, and the worker followed instructions. By 1980, Ford had reexamined this approach. The company reasoned that involving workers at an earlier stage would result in production innovations that could save dollars down the road. So, in the development of the Ford Ranger, hourly workers were asked to contribute their opinions. More than 740 suggestions were received in the early stages of Ranger development, and the company chose to adopt 542 of them. The net result was a more efficient production line and more involved employees, not to mention increased profits.

"It ain't the gun or armament, or the money they can pay, it's the close cooperation that makes them win the day, it ain't the individual, nor the army as a whole, but the everlasting teamwork of every bloomin' soul."
        — J. Mason Knox

Team leaders quickly learn that power is best utilized when it is shared, not hoarded. Paul Reeves, a manager with Harman International Industries, says about authority: "Since I started giving it away, I never had so much."

The beauty of tackling problems with a team approach is that the information and opinions you receive come from people who have a direct relationship with the problem, as compared to consultants whose grasp of your business is theoretical. Dave Ober of Western Textile maintains: "I'd rather listen to three hundred workers who understand the company than a few 'expert' consultants who don't really know what's going on."

Team leadership is to an organization what a nourishing diet is to a youngster. It brings about controlled, healthy growth. It creates an environment where ideas, energy, and enthusiasm can circulate freely. Rosabeth Moss Kanter says: "Innovating companies seem to deliberately create a 'marketplace of ideas' recogniz-

Results of Effective Teamwork

—Quality-based teams operating at the Pittsburgh-based Mellon Bank found a way to reduce the response time for letters from three months to less than a week. Similar team efforts at Mellon's data center analyzed performance data and concluded that savings of up to $3 million a year were possible if the team's recommendations were accepted.

—Fifteen years of team-based operations at the Topeka branch of Gaines Foods showed that team productivity results are not a passing fad. The plant can produce a product identical in all respects to that of its sister plant in Karkakee, Illinois—at a 7 percent lower labor cost.

—At a Honeywell manufacturing facility in Arizona, the use of work teams resulted in a rise in output per week of 1,800 pieces in December 1980 to 4,500 in November 1981, while as a result of the efforts of the problem-solving teams, the number of people involved in production dropped from 120 to 85.

—In 1981, J.C. Penney reported a profit of 44 percent based on a 4.5 percent increase in sales. Success was publicly attributed to a "new management style involving teamwork."

—General Electric's plant in Ravenna, Ohio, invoked a "participation" (team) approach in the mid-1970's. Productivity improved 25 percent.

—An electrical manufacturing plant in Alberta made the move to semiautonomous work teams and measured their progress in relation to the amount of time it normally took to build a particular motor-control device. Full production of that unit dropped from eight weeks to five days.

—At the Kubota tractor factory in Osaka, Japan, a handwritten sign over the grinding machines reminds workers of the productivity increase from the use of "quality" teams. Shift changeover time dropped from two hours to five minutes.

ing that a multiplicity of points of view need to be brought to bear on a problem. It is not the 'caution of committees' that is sought—reducing risk by spreading responsiblity—but the better idea that comes from a clash and an integration of perspectives." Top executives, according to Kanter, feel that "broad-based managers rather than technical experts [are] the wave of the future."

Grocery whiz Stew Leonard knows how to make teams work. When it came time to design a food kitchen for his showcase operation, it was the cooks, servers, and food handlers that he turned to. The result was one of the most utilitarian and cost-effective designs in the industry.

Rockwell International's Gene Little took over a troublesome plant in El Paso and found nothing but wastage, inefficiency, and poor morale. He decided to take the problem right to the employees, telling them individually how important their jobs were and asking their help in putting the plant back on track. Within eighteen months, output increased 55 percent and factory yields went up 80 percent. Absenteeism and employee turnover, traditionally serious concerns in the plant, "all but disappeared."

In a special report entitled "Management Discovers the Human Side of Automation", *Business Week* magazine concludes that "the teamwork movement has been a quiet revolution. Many of the leading companies have not trumpeted their findings, partly because they believed their innovations provided a competitive edge. Now some of the pioneers are opening up a bit, and their evidence of superior performance in teamwork is impressive."

The other special quality of a team with *effective* group skills, as opposed to a collection of talented individuals, is that it is virtually self-policing. Once the greater good is seen to take precedence over individual need, the team begins to drive itself. There is nowhere for slackers to hide. Individual contributions and individual participation are there for everyone to see. A few years back, a manufacturing company decided to try semiautonomous work teams. Employees were permitted to make day-to-day operating decisions. After a very successful year, one supervisor, a company veteran of twenty-two years, quit. It had become apparent to everyone, including him, that he lacked the skills of team leadership and wasn't making a contribution. In other words, the team environment revealed the presence of an ineffective leader.

TEAMS VERSUS TEAMWORK

That same *Business Week* cover story went on to ask, "If teamwork produces such good results, why haven't more companies tried it? We feel [teams] are not used as often as they could [be] because the shift requires a drastic change in management style and method." Many "teams" are really just collections of individuals.

Knowing isn't doing. Changing an entrenched habit or establishing a more participative environment requires new skills, skills whose power is underestimated by most managers. Many can "talk" the language of teams, but few actually "walk their talk."

Technomanagers are inclined to adopt an "appliance" approach to teamwork—they plug in an "employee-involvement program," a "quality-improvement team," or a task force and expect them to work. They look for quick results and, at times, get them. What they don't get are lasting results. *Effective teamwork come from skills, not systems.* Giving people organizational tools (procedures, committees, policies, programs) doesn't create teamwork anymore than blueprints and building supplies alone can create a house. Skilled builders are needed.

Quality circles are a classic example. Since the Japanese culture already encourages teamwork, the Japanese have a strong background to work from; *they already have the skills and the context in which to make the system work.* In North America, implementing quality circles without the team-leadership skills to support them proved foolhardy and counterproductive. It was like taking a novice driver and putting him behind the wheel of a Ferrari. When quality circles started to fail, many organizations compensated by providing facilitators to run the sessions. This let the group leader off the hook and left responsibility for team results with someone outside the group. The results, as might be expected, were less than desirable—increased cost, poorer performance.

A team doesn't only employ hotdogs or superstars. *In sports the most valuable players are not necessarily the highest scorers.* They're often players who help create a situation in which their team scores.

Teams are based on teamwork. Many organizations lose sight of this obvious fact. They engage head hunters who, in turn, go out and hire high-powered technical specialists and topnotch upwardly mobile managers. They put these loners into a room and expect things to happen. When you get too many thoroughbreds on the same track, all you can expect is a race. Races have one winner and many losers.

"It's easy to get the players. Gettin' em to play together, that's the hardest part."

—Casey Stengel

INEFFECTIVE TEAMS: BUILDING ON A SHAKY FOUNDATION

Your organization is no better than the way its teams work together. Teams are a microcosm of the organization. Interdepartmental conflicts, heavy-handed management, uncoordinated efforts, and lack of participation can be traced right back to a management group that is operating without teamwork.

Unfortunately, the majority of supervisors, managers, and executives have weak team-leadership skills. Many have never experienced the power of effective teamwork. To compensate they bring in expensive technology or complex systems.

Signs of weak team skills are often subtle and insidiously linked to other problems within the organization. The three most common symptoms of team failure are: ineffective meetings, technomanagement, and loss of vision.

"Many poorly run group sessions are a meeting of the bored."

1. Ineffective Meetings
Where the team is a microcosm of the organization, the meeting is a microcosm of the team. Meetings reflect how effectively the team is operating. Improve a manager's meeting skills and his team-leadership ability will improve as well.

Studies have found that as much as 70 percent of middle and senior management's time is spent in group actions (in other words: "meetings"). And meetings cost. In 1979, 3M Canada did an internal study and concluded that 2,500 person-hours a week were spent in meetings—at an estimated tab of $1.5 million a year! Andrew Grove, president of Intel Corporation, figures the cost of *any* meeting at $100 per person-hour. A two-hour meeting with ten people, Grove argues, costs the organization more than $2,000! Such a significant expenditure, in the ordinary course of business, would normally have to be approved by senior people, yet, paradoxically, a meeting can be called by almost anyone on a whim.

"Too many committees keep minutes, but waste hours."

Meetings are the ultimate catalyst to people power, an opportunity to bring different viewpoints together, exploit diversity for the good of the group, establish strategies, and obtain commitment to action. Grove puts it this way: "The output of a manager is the output of the various organizations under his control and influence. For every activity a manager performs, the output of an organization should increase. The extent to which that output is increased by any given activity defines the *leverage* . . . . A manager's output is thus the sum of individual activities having varying degrees of leverage. *Meetings, properly led, are a high-leverage activity."*

"The very essence in all power to influence lies in getting the other person to participate. The mind that can do that has a powerful leverage on his human world."
— Harry A. Overstreet

A study conducted by Robert Half International found that executives consider more than 30 percent of the meetings they attend a waste of time. This waste is inexcusable. If capital equipment were to lie idle for 30 percent of its operational time, or if people within the organization twiddled their thumbs for 30 percent of their working days, heads would roll! Yet because people in meetings look busy, massive losses of productivity are ignored — a classic example of confusing "activity" with "accomplishment"! And, as team-oriented approaches grow in popularity, the problem is sure to get worse.

Too many senior managers have twenty-twenty vision for everything except what is in their own backyard. They agree that meetings "out there" may be poorly run, but regard their own meetings as jewels of effectiveness. In matters of team leadership, practice does not necessarily make perfect! As Vince Lombardi said, "Only perfect practice makes perfect." Too often senior managers mistake "comfort" (because of the number of years they have been conducting meetings) and "cooperation" (because of their organizational power) as synonymous with "results." The outcome of poorly led team meetings is low commitment, hidden agendas, confusion, demotivation, poor team spirit, and a host of other "invisible" problems. Worse, the rest of the organization will imitate ineffective meetings! If senior managers feel that their people are not running effective meetings, they need go no further than the mirror to find the reason.

Indicators of ineffective meeting skills include:
—Meetings continually run overtime or wander off topic.
—Attendees contribute little or find the topic doesn't concern them.
—Key people are absent; decisions are postponed or information is incomplete.
—Meeting leaders take too much "air time." If they already have the answers, why call the meeting?
—The purpose and expected outcome of the meeting is not made clear (most common with informal gatherings of two or three people in someone's office).
—*Robert's Rules of Order*, or a similar bureaucratic approach, is used to compensate for poor leadership skills.
—Meetings stall or wander to a close (every meeting *should* end by recapping what was decided and setting up a plan for following-up).
—Basic principle Number 1 ("Focus on the situation, not the person") is violated. Personal attacks, public ridicule, and put-downs weigh heavily on team spirit and enthusiasm.
—Healthy diversity deteriorates into personal conflict.
—Meeting roles and responsibilities are not clear.
—The type of meeting (information gathering, decision making, etc.) is not clear.
—The type of meeting *is* made clear, but another type of meeting in fact takes place.
—The meeting has no agenda.
—Meetings are called for reasons more suited to getting together one-on-one or with a subgroup.

2. Technomanagement (and Its Related Ailments)
Technomanagement interferes with team performance. One giveaway is "manipulation versus participation." For many techno-

managers, teamwork means asking for involvement in a decision that's *already been made*. Accompanying this attitude is usually a thinly disguised contempt for the ideas of others, especially from so-called "unqualified" sources (which is how techno-managers tend to classify most front-line employees).

Another symptom is the "Do as I say, not as I do" approach. Technomanagers too often see team approaches as techniques to be exploited rather than skills to be developed. Rosabeth Moss Kanter calls this approach "where the top orders the middle to be participative to the bottom."

"Shooting the messenger" is also cause for concern. This occurs when visible or vocal team members are routinely shot down (or quietly kneecapped) for contributing divergent views or un-popular information.

When "grunt" work is all an organization delegates, team effec-tiveness suffers. It is difficult to empower a team by handing them only other people's dirty work.

3. Loss of Vision and Abdication

Poor team leadership skills are often compounded by the absence of vision within the organization. Groups that meet by rote with no purpose are moribund. When an organization loses sight of its reason for being, it becomes deathlike or bureaucratic. Real teamwork is sparked by shared purpose.

Another cause of team failure is "abdication." Sometimes, in a futile attempt to encourage participation, unskilled managers throw things wide open, leaving minority views and weaker team members unprotected. Their lack of skill invokes "jungle law," which allows group members to attack each other and play politics. The result—bruised and battered individuals and occa-sionally a clique. Inevitably, unhealthy competition displaces cooperation and politics replace performance.

"Men are never so likely to settle a question rightly as when they discuss it freely."
—Lord Thomas Macaulay

BUILDING A BASE FOR TEAMWORK

The key to effective teamwork is leadership skill. The output of the team is most often a reflection of the leader's skill. The late

Death of the Heroic Manager

Management authors and consultants David Bradford and Allan Cohen believe that the traditional notion of "manager as hero" is rapidly becoming obsolete. In its stead is a new role model, "manager as developer."

The "heroic" manager is a modern-day business version of the Lone Ranger, a problem solver complete with executive assistant who appears at the last possible moment, solves the problems of the poor townsfolk (remember the "body count" in each of his TV adventures?), then skedaddles out of town without a forwarding address, leaving behind only a silver bullet, and the townsfolk's question: "Who was that masked man?"

Among the reputed qualities of the "heroic" manager are omniscience about his particular work unit, superior technical expertise in relation to co-workers, coolness under fire, extreme rationality, and an aversion to a team approach.

The Lone Ranger was an entertaining character but in real life he makes a less than optimal manager. His problem is that he insists on taking *personal responsibility* for making things go right. Team concepts go out the window, along with team commitment and energy. If the Lone Ranger can't solve the problem, then by-gosh-and-by-gum the problem just doesn't get solved.

According to Bradford and Cohen, the days of the Lone Ranger are all but over. Today's effective manager must be a developer of teams, of people, not a solo artist. Today's high-performing managers are more concerned with bringing out the best in the people who work with them than with solving problems and disappearing into the sagebrush. They don't create a situation where the poor townsfolk have to wait for thundering hoofbeats every time problems come up.

James Houghton, Chairman and CEO of Corning Glass Works, describes what he regards as the "indispensable" manager: "He has flexibility, a willingness to learn, and the ability to listen. Lots of managers don't listen. You don't get the job done by yourself. The only way to get the job done is by working on a team."

Norman Maier examined the relationship between leadership skills and effective results in group settings:

AMOUNT OF TRAINING	% CREATIVE SOLUTIONS	% SATISFIED WITH SOLUTION
LITTLE OR NONE	3.4	62.1
MODERATE	63.6	72.7
A GREAT DEAL	85.3	100.0

Among Maier's fascinating insights was that change-related decisions reached by group leaders who had some skill training were better accepted by the groups (95.5 percent) than decisions offered to groups with untrained leaders (50 percent). Also, ideas that sprang up from the untrained leader herself usually were slower to be (a) understood and (b) accepted by the group. Decisions made by the group itself were accepted and understood by the group almost instantaneously. This latter finding is especially significant for those who believe that team dynamics are more costly to the organization than individual decisions. Maier discovered not only that solutions arrived at by a team were higher quality but also that they were accepted and implemented more efficiently.

"The Tao of Team Leadership"

The ancient Chinese sage Lao Tse set down laws of effective leadership. He called them *Tao-te-ching*, or "How Things Work." Psychologist John Heder has adapted these time-honored strategies for today's organizational performers.

—"A good group is better than a spectacular group. When leaders become superstars, the teacher outshines the teaching."

—"The leader who tries to control the group through force does not understand group process. Force will cost you the support of the group . . . . Every law creates an outlaw."

—"The wise leader settles for good work and then lets others have the floor. The leader does not take all the credit for what happens and has no need for fame."

—"Learn to lead in a nourishing manner.

Learn to lead without being possessive.

Learn to be helpful without taking the credit.

Learn to lead without coercion."

THE CORE SKILLS OF TEAM LEADERSHIP

You can't expect to lead a team if your own house is not in order. Team leadership, like other leadership skill sets, demands that you have it all together: vision, values, integrity, personal and coaching leadership skills. Presentation skills are also important to the team leader because he or she depends more on "persuasion" than "position" power. *Before you can rally support for any idea, you have first to express it.* And you have to create an atmosphere of trust and empowerment. If you treat people like turkeys, they'll let you down every day of the year except Thanksgiving.

Ironically, many managers who profess to be able to do their jobs proficiently cannot bear to have *their* ideas challenged. There is a contradiction here. To be a leader, to manage teams, managers must learn how to tie their own egos into the success of the people they manage. Although, intellectually, many managers understand that innovations are the results of free expression and joint action, they lack the skill to create such an engendering environment.

"Few are open to conviction, but the majority of men are open to persuasion."

– Johann Wolfgang von Goethe

Central to team leadership is the ability to help others buy into sharing the group's preferred future. Motorola vice-chairman William Weisz says: "We recognize three basic ideas. One, every worker knows his or her job better than anybody else. Two, people can and will accept responsibility for managing their own work if that responsibility is given to them in the proper way. And, three, intelligence, perspective, and creativity exist at all levels of the organization. And I mean all!" As one senior mill worker with a large textile organization found: "The workers out there know how to do their jobs better than they are, but you gotta get it out of them."

Peters and Waterman say that *what* the team leader decides to do in relation to bringing his or her people together is not as important as *how he or she goes about doing it.* Whereas ineffective

Toward More Effective Meetings

Tom Langshaw, a manager for Paul Revere Insurance, took a skill-development program to improve his team-leadership skills. Whereas formerly meetings within Tom's unit wandered off topic, he now prepares in advance. Of one important meeting he observed: "Speakers were contacted every three weeks to monitor progress on their presentation . . . . Each seminar was planned to last half an hour and I researched the topics thoroughly . . . . By the time the day arrived, we covered all the subjects, stayed on schedule and got good quality participation . . . . All the participants have [since] written to say how successful it was." Michael Wilbur, manager for Great Northern Apparel, participated in a similar program. He explains his meeting technique: "I made a point of informing everyone in advance of the purpose of the meeting and, when possible, sent out an agenda . . . . At the end of each agenda item we spell out an action plan . . . . The result is that people arrive better prepared and leave with a clearer understanding of what action they are to take. A meeting that normally took an hour now takes half that time."

team leaders dive deeply into the task at hand and overlook how the team works together, effective leaders pay as much attention to process as to content.

We've broken the core skills of team leadership into four categories: group problem solving, conducting effective meetings, persuading and influencing, and pulling the team together.

"Problems are only opportunities in work clothes."

—Henry J. Kaiser

1. Group Problem Solving
The key to arriving at decisions that work is to bring together people who are closest to the problem, people who have specialized information to contribute, and people whose support is critical to make it all work. A dual focus, on solutions *and* im-

plementation, demands that group leaders balance disciplined problem-solving processes with the dynamics of group interaction.

Particular skills to achieve this include the discovery of problem areas and the selection and definition of specific problems to work on. Criteria for problem selection should be established by the group before it begins the task. The desired outcome of the problem-solving process must also be clear. Before beginning to analyze the selected problem(s), the possible causes for the difficulty should be scrutinized. This step will involve gathering and sorting specific information. Group members must accept responsibility for this work. After the information is collected and analyzed, some time ought to be spent interpreting the data.

To complete this process of problem solving, the group ought next to agree on criteria for seeking a solution or solutions. Multiple possible solutions are often best; they can then be combined and mixed as the group pleases.

Finally, one solution from all possible solutions should be accepted. There must be group commitment at this point or the process will not work. Once the decision is made, the group should plan actions, delegate accountability, and establish a progress-measurement system.

2. Conducting Effective Meetings
Formal meetings are easy to recognize: they are scheduled in advance, there is a set agenda, and often a set time limit as well. But there are many more informal meetings. We believe that *any time two or more people get together for any reason, a meeting is taking place, and meeting management skills should come to the fore*. The key actions of team leadership, the skill sets, apply to *any* kind of meeting.

High-achieving organizations recognize that the following "non-traditional" type of meeting, skillfully handled, can be more potent than the traditional sit-down-with-agenda variety:
- informal get-togethers
- unplanned discussions
- impromptu problem solving
- hallway and "water cooler" discussions
- "coffee conferences"

"Many ideas grow better when transplanted into another mind than the one where they sprang up."

— Oliver Wendell Holmes

Meetings are critical for performance improvement. After a multiyear study of the manufacturing of air conditioners in the U.S. and Japan, David Garvin, associate professor of business administration at the Harvard Business School, concludes: "The greater the frequency of meetings to review quality performance, the fewer the undetected errors. The U.S. plants with the lowest assembly-line defect rate averaged ten such meetings per month; at the other U.S. plants, the average was four."

Conducting effective meetings is a skill. At the start of the meeting, the skilled leader will make clear the purpose of the meeting and the outcomes expected. Each participant should clearly understand what his or her involvement and contribution to the meeting is expected to be. An agenda should be set and respected: each item, in its order, should be dealt with before the next item is addressed. A skilled leader will quickly catch any digression from the main focus and steer the meeting back on course. Sincere participation that is within the stated bounds of the meeting must be acknowledged. Ending the meeting should be as carefully handled as beginning it: the conclusions reached should be discussed and a quick summary presented. The summary is what people will remember.

3. Persuading and Influencing

A good idea presented poorly comes across as a poor idea. Ideas ought to be presented in a way that helps people remember them. Dale Carnegie summed it up: "Tell them what you're going to tell them, tell them, and then tell them what you've told them."

"The credit goes to the man who convinces the world, not the man to whom the idea first occurs."

— Sir William Osler

Presenting ideas is a skill. Effective communicators capture the group's attention by whatever means is most appropriate

193

(sometimes a polite request will work, at other times something more dramatic might be called for). Then the point is stated. Support or substantiation for the idea should be presented next, in an organized, well-thought-out manner. Finally, the whole topic should be summarized.

Throughout all the steps listed above, an effort should be made to communicate with the other people responsible for bringing about the expected results. Other members of the team must be made to feel involved at all times. When presenting new ideas, take a moment to elaborate the positive benefits to individuals within the team or organization. Get feedback and deal with it attentively. If there are concerns, address them. If support is needed, explain who you expect to provide it. An action plan and date for reevaluation should bring the communication session to a close.

4. Pulling the Team Together

It won't always be smooth sailing. Whenever different people with different points of view get together, problems can and do arise. But skilled team leaders are able to keep people focused and on track.

First, there must be no misunderstanding about why the team members have been assembled in the first place. The team's overall purpose and expected impact on the organization must be crystal clear. Similarly, the roles and responsibilities of individual team members must be understood. If particular resources or procedures are required to accomplish the team's purpose, they should be identified and made available. Team members must be reminded that they are part of a team — helping each other means helping themselves. The foundation for dynamic results is laid by first getting each member to dedicate himself or herself to a common purpose, not a series of individual achievements.

When trouble comes up, deal with it. Promptly. Let the individuals involved know how their behavior is affecting performance. If the disruptive behavior persists, bring the individuals into a private problem-solving meeting and encourage them to present their own points of view. Agree on what problems need to be addressed and allow each individual to suggest possible solutions. Finally, get commitment from each on what he or she will do to solve the difficulty.

"When two men in business always agree, one of them is unnecessary."

—William Wrigley, Jr.

Throughout these processes, the skilled team leader walks a tightrope. On the one hand, he or she *wants* diversity from his or her people because diversity fosters creativity. Diversity is therefore a "group rule," something to be encouraged whenever possible. Similarly, all new ideas ought to be carefully considered *independently* of the person who first proposed them. Often, we judge ideas on the basis of the person's past performance. Ideas should stand or fall on their individual merit.

But diversity can go too far. Whenever a conflict appears, focus on the common areas first. Ironically, you may find that everyone *agrees* on what they are most upset about! That's fine; finding consensus, even on things that are causing conflict, reminds a team what its function really is. Each point of disagreement should then be analyzed and clarified. Steps should be agreed upon to deal with the problems. Finally, once these steps are followed, the attention of the group ought to be focused back on the original business of the team.

In pulling the team together, a skilled team leader doesn't shun diversity or resistance. He or she welcomes it because he or she knows that energy, if managed, can be used to produce a better result. The skilled team leader is like a black belt "judoka" who turns resistance to his or her advantage by redirecting the energy of the adversary.

"When all think alike, no one thinks very much."

—Walter Lippman

The skilled team leader understands that it is more difficult to deal with apathy than resistance. Resistance is really only another viewpoint (which can be considered, weighed, and used if need be), whereas apathy is nothing but dead space. The skilled leader will draw out team members gently — by asking a reluctant participant to comment on another's point, for example. The skilled team leader understands that unless all members are committed to the team's progress — both problem solving and implementation — then the energy of the team itself is diminished.

EVERY TEAM NEEDS A LEADER!

Study a cat with kittens. Its behavior is an interesting model for the potential organizational facilitator or team leader. It keeps an eye on them but allows them to play together and learn from the experience. It feeds them if they ask for food but doesn't insist. If the roughhousing gets too serious, the mother intervenes. The runt of the litter gets special care, and the pick of the litter gets its nose gently smacked if it gets out of hand. If a mouse zips by, the mother cat will resist the temptation to take after it merely for her

---

The Power of Diversity

Calvin Coolidge said, "Progress depends very largely on the encouragement of variety, tends to standardize the community, to establish fixed and rigid modes of thought, fossilizes society . . . . It is the ferment of ideas, the clash of disagreeing judgments, the privilege of the individual to develop his own thoughts and shape his own character that makes progress possible."

Diversity should be encouraged, not stifled. The key to effective team leadership is getting commitment, not acquiescence. General Motors CEO, Alfred Sloan, reportedly once refused to accept support for one of his own ideas at a meeting, saying: "I'm going to table the proposal until next month. I don't like what's happening to our thinking. We're getting locked into looking at this idea in just one way, and this is a dangerous way to make decisions. I want each of you to spend the next month studying the proposal from a different perspective." (A month later, that plan, as the story goes, was voted down.)

General Douglas MacArthur had his own method of encouraging diversity. His practice was to allow the most junior staff officer to deliver the first opinion, followed by the opinions of the more senior officers. While each spoke his piece, the others were forbidden to interrupt. MacArthur always spoke last—and *then* discussion began.

---

own gain—but she may soften it up and offer it to her young so that they can learn.

"It is a great misfortune neither to have enough wit to talk well nor enough judgment to be silent."

—Jean de La Brupère

A skilled team leader is a problem identifier, a rule bender, and, most of all, a facilitator. He or she marshals ideas, encourages the frailest in the group to speak out, and keeps the chatterboxes from going off in the wrong direction. He or she focuses purpose, infuses ideals and values, and leads by example. Members of a group led by a skilled group leader not only solve problems *but, by adopting the behavior of the leader, they develop their potential to lead other teams.*

CHAPTER TEN

Cultural Leadership: Vital Skills for Managing Change

"It takes a long time to bring excellence to maturity."

—Publilius Syrus

Circles have no beginning or end. Yet, paradoxically, anyone seeking to draw one has to start somewhere. A similar dilemma confronts organizations seeking to improve performance via cultural leadership, the final skill set in our VIP model.

Cultural-leadership skills deserve special attention because they form a base for the other skill sets. The best way to improve performance is to clarify the organization's vision and values, the roots from which its environment, behavior, and patterns of performance spring. Logically, this process ought to begin with the senior management team and then cascade down through the organization.

As theories go, that one is pretty good. Our experience with hundreds of organizations suggests that there is no one right way to proceed. A multitude of approaches have yielded results. Some organizations have found it effective to start with middle management. Others have "dug in" at the supervisory level, and others started at the bottom of the organization (or top if you invert the traditional hierarchy and place customers at the head) and worked their way up (or down).

One point *is* crystal clear: without strong cultural-leadership skills throughout the organization, attempts at leadership development are doomed to failure. At best, they will be Band-Aids. At worst, they will remind employees how frivolously management looks at the whole subject of change. People aren't stupid: they can see the differences between faddish classroom

198

sessions and their daily adventures in the organizational world.

Our VIP model (Chapter 3) demonstrates the interplay between cultural and other skill sets. In the outer circle are "Organization Environment" (culture) and "Behavior." Each creates, reinforces, and, ultimately, determines the other. The collective behavior of all the organization's members in turn forms the tens of thousand of "moments of truth" that are played out each and every day with customers, suppliers, peers, employees, and managers. These little dramas are played and replayed every time anyone makes a decision, ranging from invoicing to the correct way to answer the phone. Viewed in isolation, these seemingly random events appear to be a "hair's breadth" short of insignificant. So what if a shipment is a little late? Who cares if the phone rang six times before it was answered? Surely one typo is not going to put the company out of business? But, added together, these moments of truth represent the difference between long-term failure and success. Over time, they collect like so many grains of sand and eventually tip the scales in favor of either high performance or mediocrity.

"Events of great consequence often spring from trifling circumstances."

—Livy

JUST WHO ARE THE CULTURAL LEADERS?

Obviously, the CEO is a key player. Ultimately, responsibility for technology, management systems, and corporate direction rests here. The CEO's personal focus and priorities ultimately translate into structure, strategies, systems, and other components that, collectively, form the organization's environment. As that old business proverb put it, "The footprint of the owner is the best fertilizer." Too often, a boss's words are assumed to be fertilizer.

To stop at the CEO is to fall for that old trap, the elitist model of leadership. True, these people play a major role in setting the tone for those who work under them. However, because an organization is a cultural mosaic, it follows that there must be many cultural leaders, people who quietly influence the creation of "minicultures," like the coloring of tiny pieces of glass within the larger stained-glass window. *The most successful cultural changes we've participated in are those where department heads, team leaders, division managers, and unofficial heads of "minicultures" were given the skills and change processes to shape their environment.*

"The only things that evolve by themselves in an organization are disorder, friction, and malperformance."
—Peter Drucker

Culture is like the prizes boisterously hawked by old-time carnival barkers: "Everybody's a winn-nnn-errr."

Stifling Innovation and Change

Rosabeth Moss Kanter found that segmentalist, low-innovating companies have ten qualities in common:
1. They regard ideas from below with suspicion.
2. They insist that people who need authorization go through several levels for approval.
3. They ask departments and divisions to criticize each other's work—and the "survivor" wins.
4. They criticize freely, and they let employees know they can be replaced.
5. They see problem identification as synonymous with failure (so eventually no one wants to admit there *is* a problem).
6. They control everything carefully and frequently count everything that can be counted.
7. They make decisions, such as reorganizations or policy changes, in secret and then spring them on people. ("Keep em on their toes.")
8. They require requests for information to be justified. ("We don't want information falling into the wrong hands!")
9. They delegate lower-level managers to implement any threatening decisions (layoffs, job changes) made at higher levels.
10. Finally, they believe that senior managers already know everything there is to know. Otherwise, they wouldn't be senior!

All organizations, departments, or divisions have a culture *whether or not it's the one they want.* Some enterprises get "lucky" and foster a high-performance culture seemingly without effort. Why? *Because they already had strong vision, skills and values in place.* The questions are obvious: What culture do you want? Who is going to take responsibility for bringing it into being? And how is this going to happen?

Rosabeth Moss Kanter's extensive research on companies that are mastering change is again enlightening: "Corporate change —rebuilding, if you will—has parallels to the most ambitious and most noble of the plastic arts, architecture. *The skill of corporate leaders lies in their ability to envision a new reality and aid in its translation into concrete terms.* Creative visions combine with the building up of events, floor by floor, from foundation to completed construction."

For a manager to be an architect of culture, a long-term view is needed. Cultures are not moved about like silverware on a dining table. They take time to evolve. A key ingredient is how managers view their role: as running a business . . . or building an organization. There is a critical difference!

To build an organization requires a long-term commitment to growth, not simply an avoidance of trouble by constantly putting out fires. Growth-oriented managers see the glass as half full, not half empty. They look for behavior to reward and reinforce. They recognize that people are a unit's strength or its weakness, and that results come from those people.

If these principles are correctly utilized, the net result is a "culture of pride." According to Kanter: "Success breeds success. Where there is a culture of pride, based on high performance in the past, people's feelings of confidence in themselves and others goes up. They are more likely to take risks and get positive responses when they request cooperation from others. Mutual respect makes teamwork easier."

"Tell me to what you pay attention and I will tell you who you are."

—Ortega Gasset

CUES TO WEAK CULTURAL-LEADERSHIP SKILLS

Too often technomanaged organizations confuse good management with an abdication of responsibility for providing cultural direction. Here are some cues that reveal this deficiency. In a weak organization:

—"implementation details" for pending major changes are delegated, decreed, impersonalized, or systematized;

—"we/they" gaps are reinforced by reserved parking spaces, executive dining rooms, or time clocks;

—strategic planning is mistaken for cultural leadership (the first is a tool, the second a skill.);

—there is an overreliance on "structural" change to create new environments;

—leaders tire of restating vision and values. Their attention lags, and they turn to other things;

—middle and lower-level managers stop trying to influence their minicultures because the organization's culture is moribund;

—territorialism and politics run rampant;

—new people take a long time to find out what the unwritten rules really are;

—managers intimidate and overpower anyone who challenges them;

—few suggestions come from the lower levels;

—employees are confused by conflicting messages from management;

—mistrust and suspicion run rampant;

—managers and executives send supervisors and employees to be "fixed" while their own development activity is minimal;

—vision and values appear in catchy slogans but aren't central to decision making;

—managers see cultural change as "changing them" rather than "starting with us";

—hiring decisions are based on technical and management expertise. Hiring is delegated to people who will not be working with the new recruits;

—anything that can be measured is. Things that can't be measured are deemed not to exist;

—information is hoarded and doled out in small portions;

> Consultants Can't Build Your Culture
>
> In a "culture of pride," nothing has as much potential for dampening enthusiasm as consultants — outsiders brought in by senior management to problem solve and troubleshoot. The message *this* sends is clear: we trust strangers more than we trust our own people.

—waves of new senior managers routinely "clean house," establishing new directions and priorities among people who aren't clear what the old directions and priorities were.

KEY ISSUES FOR CULTURAL CHANGE

In Search of Excellence has become famous for its eight "attributes of excellence" that differentiated "excellent companies" from mediocre ones. In 1983, Tom Peters, its coauthor, collaborated with Zenger-Miller and The Achieve Group to create an excellence-discovering and action-planning process for management teams. Hundreds of organizations have used this process, called "Toward Excellence", to set culture-change plans into motion around five key issues. Discussions on each issue, along with its component "key practices," have spurred many management teams to clarify their larger vision and values while taking specific action to shape their culture.

What follows is a brief overview of the issues or questions raised during the process. Leaders trying to shape their unit's or organization's culture need to initiate organization-wide discussion and planning around these issues.

1. *Taking Innovative Action*
Innovation comes through experimentation, pilots, and trials. The more *experimentation*, the more innovation is likely. Most innovations need what Drucker called a "monomaniac with a mission," a turned-on *champion* who will fight the bureaucracy, inertia, and resistance to new approaches. Management must create a climate that nurtures and protects these "boat rockers" long

enough to give new ideas a chance for a fair trial. This can sometimes be accomplished through projects or *skunkworks* that operate slightly out of the main business stream. A major challenge is to balance promising experiments and *skunkworks* with proven approaches that keep the organization in business. The future growth and development of the organization depend on the success of it innovations.

"In Endymion, I leaped headlong into the sea, and thereby have become better acquainted with the surroundings, the quick sand, and the rocks, than if I had stayed upon the green shore and piped a silly pipe, and took tea and comfortable advice."

—John Keats

2. *Getting Back in Touch*
Large - and medium-sized organizations can easily become bureaucracies out of touch with their customers or employees. A key to preventing this is to have management teams mingle with customers, suppliers, or employees. Management by reports, systems, and upper-level meetings is tempered with "*management by wandering around.*" Seeing effects of rules and procedures or hearing directly from customers helps senior management find ways to *simplify systems* to make the organization more responsive and adaptable. A structural technique to keep the organization lean and effective is "*chunking.*" This involves breaking the organization into autonomous teams, work groups, and divisions. A key result is small, quick-moving teams of turned-on people who perform at much higher levels.

3. *Existing for the Customer*
Countless studies are showing that many innovations happen with organizations that are close to their customers. *Innovating with customers* means paying attention to "non-expert" customers who seem irrational, unreasonable, or petty. *Providing real and perceived service* or *real and perceived quality* means getting the customer to set your standards for service and quality. Since these are subjective or intangible, perception is all you have

to go on. It also means the organization must become truly focused on and driven by the customer in all aspects. Improved quality comes from a mind set that finds ways to do it right the first time. A significant result is higher quality and productivity.

4. Fostering Individual Commitment

Only turned-on, committed people go the "extra mile" needed to improve innovation, service, or quality. Commitment comes from a sense of ownership and involvement. These come from management's effort to find as many ways as possible to *delegate autonomy*. The *sharing* of *information* sends an important signal about how much management trusts its employees and really wants a business partnership. Another signal and key to high performance is *emphasizing training*. You can't get people to excel at a job for which they aren't well-trained. And you can't hold them accountable for something you haven't shown them how to do. Finally, commitment is reinforced and further encouraged when management *recognizes commitment*. A "culture of pride" and motivation to perform is heightened by appreciation, recognition, and celebration.

5. Instilling Unique Values

Anything more than three values is no values because they are too diffused. *Clarifying the core value* involves bringing management teams together to debate and define the key priorities or focus of their unit. These bedrock values remain true and unchanging and form the foundation of shifting strategies and plans. However, they only come to life through the collective actions of managers. *Mundane tools* such as who is invited to meetings, what questions are asked, where management time is invested, or which employees are considered "heroes" and for what actions are used to send powerful values signals. In the end, what gets signaled or lived by management is what is valued and imitated by everyone in the organization.

"What is shown by example men think they may justly do."

—Marcus Tullius Cicero

PROCESS FOR CULTURAL CHANGE

Changing an organization's culture is like redirecting the flow of a mighty river. (Bone-weary cultural leaders might remark that at times it feels like trying to push the river upstream!) Old traditions, habits, and patterns of behavior trickle together to form a cultural torrent.

As the importance of culture has become better understood, seemingly enlightened managers in the "heroic" style have worked diligently to change cultures on their own. They articulate, in their own words, the desired culture. They rearrange organization charts, reward what they think needs rewarding, and bring in management and technology systems.

The success rate of "one-man bands" is spotty at best. (More like "one-man Band-Aids!") Redirecting cultural flow is a big job; it calls for a lot of help and support. It calls for an army of cultural leaders that are marching in step to a mutual destination. It calls for a process that pulls people together around a shared vision and a shared set of values. Terrence Deal and Allan Kennedy identified this need in *Corporate Cultures*: "Many [cultural leaders] look for relatively structured devices for focusing attention on key values."

Thousands of management teams in hundreds of public- and private-sector organizations have transformed their cultures using an organization-wide cultural planning process. Sleepy, stodgy organizations have become dynamic innovative powerhouses. Sales, market share, and profitability have increased dramatically.

Campbell Soup Company, for example, found itself with eroding sales and profits. In 1983 the company's new Canadian CEO, David Clark, took his management team through the five "excellence" modules described above. Each issue facing the company was examined in terms of how the routines of the "excellent companies" "encouraged experimentation," "delegated autonomy," and "provided real and perceived service." With each such technique, the team noted how well they (and the organization) performed in relation to the "excellent" standard.

Next, the group studied and discussed the ratings they had given themselves, asking questions like, "Who are our customers?" "How do our customers perceive us?" and "How do we know?" All these exercises finally culminated in a visioning and action planning process. The group determined where it "saw" itself eighteen months down the road, then brainstormed possible ways to get there. The group finished by establishing thirty-day action plans detailing specifically how the work would be accomplished.

"Action without a name, a 'who' attached to it, is meaningless."

—Hannah Arendt

The outcome for Campbell Canada was vision of "a dynamic, market-oriented growth company, excelling in the 'well-being' business." Their core values were clarified as:
1. a profound respect for people;
2. an obsessive desire to satisfy our customers and consumers;
3. a passion for creative risk taking.

After the executives met, the real work began! The next challenge was to get commitment from four hundred managers and supervisors. Dave Clark remarked: "When the management team decides 'this is what we've got to change,' the decision alone will have zip impact on the organization. Those thoughts must be debated, modified, spread down the organization, and owned by everyone . . . . Because, in the final analysis, it isn't you that's going to implement excellence, *it's the folks on the line*. It's the folks who are making it and selling it. *These people have got to 'buy in' and work it from the bottom up too*."

To achieve that "buy-in," all management and supervisory staff were invited to duplicate the planning process that Dave and his executive team had begun. They wrestled with the proposed statements of vision and values. They debated. They agonized. Ultimately, they took action to change the culture at Campbell Canada.

The impact of the Campbell Canada cultural transformation was awesome. From 1983 to 1987, sales increased 31 percent while profits rose 50 percent. Book value per share was up 54 percent and Return on Equity increased from 15.8 percent to 18.6 percent. Significant to future earnings, Campbell Canada has become one of the most innovative companies in the food industry with a record number of successful new product introductions. Product quality levels have also risen even higher.

The most successful cultural changes in which we have participated followed the process adopted by Campbell Canada: the senior management teams define their vision and values concerning innovation, service, quality, employee commitment, customer satisfaction, and "trivial mundane actions" over a thirty-day period. The management teams reporting to each executive follow the same procedure. *As each level gets involved, the entire culture begins to undergo a powerful transformation.*

Excuses, Excuses Excuses

The following excuses have been stifling change for years.
1. We've never done it before.
2. Nobody else has ever done it.
3. It has never been tried before.
4. We tried it before.
5. Another company/person tried it before.
6. We've been doing it this way for twenty-five years.
7. It won't work in a small company.
8. It won't work in a large company.
9. It won't work in our company.
10. Why change? It's working okay.
11. The boss will never buy it.
12. It needs further investigation.
13. Our competitors are not doing it.
14. It's too much trouble to change.
15. Our company is different.
16. The ad department says it's impossible.
17. The sales department says it's impossible.
18. The service department won't like it.
19. The janitor agrees with advertising, sales, and service.
20. It can't be done (anyway).
21. We don't have the money.
22. We don't have the personnel.
23. We don't have the equipment.
24. The union will scream.
25. It's too visionary.

VISION AND VALUES: KEYS TO CULTURAL LEADERSHIP

Our VIP message is founded on a bedrock belief in the power of vision. And, as we said before, values are the flip side of vision. Effective cultural leaders establish vibrant exciting visions. They clarify values as "the way we do things around here." There is little doubt about where the group is going or what it believes in.

Visioning requires one to have the courage and skill to shape destiny not just for oneself but for others; and to have the ability

26. You can't teach an old dog new tricks.
27. It's too radical a change.
28. It's beyond my responsibility.
29. It's not my job.
30. We don't have the time.
31. It will make other procedures obsolete.
32. Customers won't buy it.
33. It's contrary to policy.
34. It will increase overhead.
35. The employees will never buy it.
36. It's not our problem.
37. I don't like it.
38. You're right . . . but
39. We're not ready for it.
40. It needs more thought.
41. Management won't accept it.
42. We can't take the chance.
43. We'd lose money on it.
44. The payout is too far away.
45. We're doing alright now.
46. It needs committee study.
47. The competition won't like it.
48. It needs sleeping on.
49. It won't work here.
50. It's still impossible.

to communicate dreams to others to help others "paint" themselves into the picture.

Once one person starts to do these things, others with similar disposition and bent will be drawn like a magnet until one day that one person will be surrounded by individuals of common purpose, looking for the same thing—making a shared vision become reality.

Perry Pascarella suggests that aspiring cultural leaders should begin with a long hard look at themselves and then move to a process much like the one we've just examined: "Take stock of your fundamental beliefs. View your role—and your organization's—in the largest possible context. Tell others where you are coming from and where you would like to go. Work toward building a common purpose. Include employees at all levels in discussion. *Set standards of excellence and make them known.* Promote work as a rewarding and fulfilling activity. Reward managers for performance on quantifiable human-resource factors. *Train managers in problem solving, communication, and leadership skills.*"

MANAGEMENT SUPPORT: WHERE GOOD INTENTIONS AREN'T ENOUGH

Wanting to improve quality and service will not make your organization unique. Developing vision and a set of values, however, will place your organization on the starting line along with a select cadre of other organizations. Unfortunately, however, most organizations only get this far.

The problem? A lack of management support condemns many performance-improvement processes to a nasty death. James Olson, president of AT&T, commented: "We must engage *all* our people to take ownership of, and pride in, the entire chain of events that delivers effective products or services to a customer. This requires management commitment."

"Diogenes struck the father when the son swore."
—Robert Burton

Karl Albrecht and Ron Zemke find that "the organization's climate must be ready and the management community must be present for service management to take root and thrive . . . .

Slogans will not do it . . . . Inspirational memos will not do it . . . . *Isolated change and improvement programs tend to run their course, and then run downhill toward the performance level that existed before the program.*"

As the American Society for Quality Control put it: "A quality system cannot succeed without the active, visible, and continuous support of management."

Thomas Melohn, president of North American Tool & Die, believes that, for his own people, actions speak much louder than words: "Sure we use techniques like SPC or SQC, but quality must be in each employee's heart and head or we're dead . . . . [Senior management] have to practice it every day, every night. You can't deviate or the whole crumbles."

Whenever we have examined unsuccessful attempts at cultural change, the problem can inevitably be traced back to senior management. Like a bad dream played out in real life, we watch organizations invest large amounts of time and money in supervisory management only to fail because they didn't properly leverage their investment. *Leverage comes from a comparatively minor commitment of senior management's time in order to learn how to reinforce, support, and coach their managers and supervisors*—in other words, they need to develop the skills to support the junior managers they want to see develop.

Communicating the Vision at General Foods

CEO Phil Smith set out these steps for his managers:
1. Develop a vision that can be clearly communicated.
2. Follow up with clear direction so the organization knows what it has to do to translate that vision into reality.
3. Gain the commitment of the organization to that vision and direction.
4. Establish an environment that is conducive to helping the organization achieve its vision.
5. Develop a sense of trust that flows from integrity at the top and that gives the organization confidence to do what's required—even when it is not necessarily in the workers' self-interest.

If senior managers are not part of the solution, they are likely as not part of the problem. Supervisors will deduce that the principles of communication and teamwork (see the "basic principles" in Chapter Seven) are, for them, only a futile academic exercise because, day by day, they see their bosses disregarding those precepts in action.

"He that gives good advice builds with one hand; he that gives good counsel and example builds with both; but he that gives good admonition and bad examples builds with one hand and pulls down with the other."

–Francis Bacon

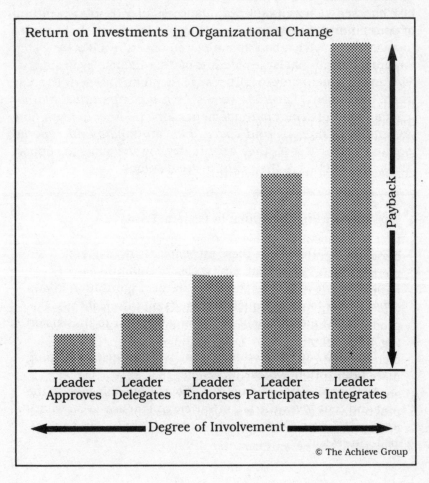

"POCKETS OF LEADERSHIP"

Having emphasized that top management support is vital to cultural change, we are about to reverse ourselves somewhat.

Often, a human-resource person, middle manager or supervisor will see the need for leadership-skill development and cultural change while top management continues with the status quo, massaging its systems and technology. Non-executives in this situation have three options: they can quit; they can float along reluctantly with the cultural stream (wringing hands, gnashing teeth, and complaining); or, they can *take positive action to bring about change in their minicultures.*

"If you can see in any given situation only what everybody else can see, you can be said to be so much a representative of your culture that you are a victim of it."
                                                                    —S.I. Hayakawa

That third route, the one less traveled, is the path of leadership (defined by actions, not position). Leaders don't throw up their hands, point fingers, or make excuses. They are not thermometers, there to reflect the current state of culture; they consider themselves thermostats, actively seeking to adjust culture. Not all succeed, but we've seen many such leaders produce cultural change, at least in their own unit or "cultural pocket".

Instilling Cultural Change the Hard Way

In a large hospital, the education director did not have the budget or management commitment to install the development program she knew was needed. She organized seminars for supervisors and managers to explore leadership topics. She invited other hospitals and charged a fee, thereby producing additional revenues to support her meager training budget! Ultimately, her campaign (seminars, articles, memos, surveys) was noticed by senior management and more budget (and more commitment!) was provided. Today, she is orchestrating a full-fledged leadership-development program. The culture of the hospital has shifted noticeably to greater participation, and employee commitment is evident. The quality of patient care has also improved.

OPEN COMMUNICATION: A VITAL TOOL FOR CULTURAL CHANGE

There is a "communication crisis" fermenting in many organizations. A 1982 report from the Opinion Research Corporation found that "*All employee groups gave their companies poor marks for communications.* Employees said that the company grapevine was their primary source of information . . . . They do not prefer it that way . . . . They would like to get information . . . face to face." The report emphasized: "Management *must* re-establish its ties with employees in order to solve productivity problems and meet consumer needs." Fortune editor Walter Kiechel, III, after considering the ORC study, commented: "If the brass don't wake up soon, they stand to get their sleepy little heads handed to them by the competition. Virtually everyone who has studied the problem — executives, consultants, business school professors — agree that you have to share lots of information with employees if you hope to elicit their commitment". He goes on to conclude: "Surveys confirm this 'numero uno' request among employees: when you talk about strategy, be specific and detailed — the experts say you're kidding yourself if you think that by keeping the strategy from the people who have to carry it out, you can keep it from the competition." Any competitor worth his salt knows anyway.

Kiechel cites a recent survey that looked at twenty-six companies (twenty of which were Fortune 500 firms). They found that executives rate communication *among themselves* as their principal area of difficulty, ahead of such challenges as handling

---

Leading in the Rain

A story is told of a rainy day in 1943 when a battalion was lined up awaiting an inspection by Lord Mountbatten. The officers wore raincoats, but the troops had none. They were soaked. Mountbatten's car pulled up and he quickly emerged, wearing a raincoat. After half a dozen steps, he stopped, went back to the car to shed his coat, and returned to make the inspection. The troops cheered.

---

conflict, holding better meetings, or making decisions. The study concluded: "If you look at the tier immediately below the president, in 80 percent of the cases we find most of the group afraid to share their feelings about problems in the company."

EVOLUTION NOT REVOLUTION

Change can be looked upon as either a threat or an opportunity—the unpleasant giving up of a known and comfortable lifestyle, or the embracing of the unknown, potentially better way of getting things done.

Change by revolution is always costly to any culture that adopts it. In *Vanguard Management; Redesigning the Corporate Future,* UCLA professor James O'Toole observed that "whether it is a planned Maoist-like cultural revolution or the unplanned collapse of a primitive culture . . . revolutionary change is always shocking, painful, disruptive, and undesirable."

Effective leaders are always on the lookout for ways to build on the existing culture. Even drastic cultural shifts can be successful if the prior culture is respected: all organizational members need the confidence and support that comes from a link to the past, the "anchors" of time-tested, historical values. *A good starting point for cultural evolution (not revolution) is the examination of the organization's roots.* What was the vision of the founders? What did leaders of the past do to keep the vision alive? What values were instilled at the organization's founding?

"Historic continuity with the past is not a duty, it is...a necessity."
                                                —Oliver Wendall Holmes, Jr.

For example, when Bill Hewitt took over the John Deere organization, he needed a hook to grab the organization's commitment. The hook was the organization's past. Quoting Deere himself—"I won't put my name on a plow that doesn't have in it the best that is in me"—Hewitt painstakingly convinced a somewhat stodgy senior-management group that they "deserved" the best and the brightest, that it was their due. When the time finally came to build a new headquarters, Bill further demonstrated that the company "owed" it to the principles of its founder to produce an innovative and modern structure of the highest possible quality. Today, the Deere head office takes a back seat to none in terms of quality, innovative design — or efficiency.

TOWARD A LEARNING AND GROWING ORGANIZATION

Cultural change demands innovation, and innovation comes from experimentation. *Try it! Fix it! Do it!* But experimentation is valuable only when it advances the overall body of experience and knowledge. Progressive learning is central to cultural change.

But again the obvious is not so obvious. Few organizations seem to be progressively in a learning or growing state. Consider the example of a teacher with ten years of seniority who was promoted to school principal. Another teacher with twenty years of faithful service demanded to know why *he* wasn't promoted. "Unfortunately," replied the district superintendent to the unhappy aspirant, "you don't have twenty years of experience, You have one year multiplied twenty times!"

Like the school teacher, many managers stopped learning and growing years ago. Their university degrees reflect only dated technology. Their skill levels, once state of the art, now lie in state. They feel that they've paid their dues. They attempt to handle an ever-changing world with policies based on open doors but closed minds. They apply old solutions to new problems. And the results are predictable: low levels of experimentation that stifle innovation. Resistance to change permeates the culture, attempts to "fix the supervisors/workers" stall, nimbler competitors grab market share, and bureaucracy reigns.

The most successful organizations we've been privileged to work with view excellence, quality, and service as a journey, not a destination. They never expect to "arrive." Although they consider yesterday's successes instructive, they never lose sight of the fact that they were *yesterday's* successes. Tomorrow brings new challenges. Successful organizations push managers at all levels to develop the skills needed to solve a never-ending parade of new problems. Experiences, both successful and unsuccessful, are shared so that the organization can learn, assimilate, and advance. As one manager put it: "When you're green, you're growing. When you're ripe, you rot."

RECOGNITION, CELEBRATION, AND MINI-HEROES

Successful cultures, from ancient Greece to the present, have understood the importance of role models and champions. *Exemplary folk don't have to be from the upper crust of the organization* — on the contrary, the most effective organizations, the most effective cultures, foster champions and heroes at *all* levels: the salesperson of the month, the switchboard operator who best handles a crisis, the repairperson who saved the client by working through the night.

"It is easy to flatter; it is harder to praise."
—Jean Paul Richter

It is up to cultural leaders to make sure that heroes and champions not only find space to breathe but also that they receive the nurturing and encouragement they need to grow. Jack Welch, CEO of General Electric, used to interrupt whatever he was doing whenever a purchasing agent phoned to report the latest deal that had been struck. "That's wonderful news," Welch is reported to have said, "You just knocked a nickel per ton off the price of steel" — and then, straightaway, he'd grab pen and paper and scribble off a congratulatory note to the agent who'd phoned. The message these actions sent was clear and unambiguous: We know who you are and what you are doing. We are pleased to have someone like you working with us.

There are a multitude of ways cultural leaders can institutionalize motivating positive reinforcement. Recognition and celebration are limited only by the imagination of managers. The following are a few examples:

—A Holiday Inn regional manager had staff hand out coupons to guests. The guests were asked to write down which employees gave outstanding service. Every employee so noted was personally commended for his or her work.

—"Bragging sessions" are a regular event at Transco Energy in Houston. Individuals and unit representatives stand before the entire department and boast about everything in their bailiwicks from low absenteeism to effective cost cutting.

—McDonald's gives out "Employee of the Month" awards and hangs a picture of the chosen candidate at the front counter for the world to see.

—At Achieve, we developed note pads headed "Recognitiongrams." People receive these notes with a hand-penciled message explaining exactly what it was that deserved the recognition, in response to outstanding performance. (Those who get them feel so strongly about being recognized that they invariably pin them to their wall!) Each quarter, all Achievers vote for the person who provided the best client service as recorded on their Recognitiongram. The winner decides which charity will receive Achieve's charitable donation for that quarter.

—At a popular resort hotel the only "executive" parking spot has a sign on it indicating "Employee of the Month."

—North American Tool & Die has monthly meetings to award its "Super Person of the Month" plaque—along with a check for $50.

—An enterprising home builder rewards exceptional employees by naming streets after them in his developments!

A word of caution: Without strong coaching, team, and personal leadership skills to ensure consistency, these

---

Mixed Messages

Harvard professor Chris Argyris offers "four easy steps to chaos":

1. Design a message that is contradictory or ambiguous, so that it seems to be saying one thing while in fact saying another. This keeps the sender from having to take a position and is guaranteed to keep the receiver guessing. (For example: "*It's okay to take risks and be innovative, but be careful!*")

2. Understand that the receiver of messages will welcome ambiguity because some day he or she may need an "out" to justify poor results. (In our sample message, the receiver doesn't want "careful" spelled out in much detail.)

3. Be totally spontaneous. People who send mixed messages often do so glibly and without much prior thought. Hesitation might interfere with ambiguity and accidentally lead to a meaningful message.

4. Make the message retroactively "undiscussable." The whole point of mixed messages is to avoid situations and not confront them.

---

approaches will lead to cynicism. Employees will feel manipulated instead of motivated!

"A rose on time is far more valuable than a $1,000 gift that's too late."

—Jim Rohn

STICK-TO-IT-IVENESS

At an Achieve client conference, a utility-company manager was asked to address the issue of cultural change. He began by stating: "There are three key steps: 1. Follow through. 2. Follow through. 3. Follow through."

Most employees have lived through the "program-of-the-month" syndrome. As yet another manager enthusiastically returns from a retreat or seminar, the word goes out: "Lie low and play along. This too shall pass." Time has shown that new ideas rapidly become old hat as management and employees slowly but surely lose interest! A great many quality and service activites have unintentionally qualified for this category. They start with a bang but end with a fizzle. One client called these shifting priorities "executive sun spots."

"The strength of a man's virtue should not be measured by his special exertions, but by his habitual acts."

—Blaise Pascal

Cultural change is like rolling a large rock up a steep hill. It takes persistence, dedication, and plain old-fashioned stick-to-it-iveness. Letting up for a moment means the loss of valuable ground. One of our clients has a favorite analogy to explain the need for a long-term executive involvement with implementation. He likens the process of introducing cultural change to what happens with a tree: while senior management may, early in the process, generate sufficient energy to get the branches swaying and the leaves rustling, *very little change will be noticeable at the roots.*

A 15,000-employee telephone company has been aggressively evolving its culture since 1984. Of the many techniques and methods employed, senior management follow-through has been the common denominator. Each quarter, executive meetings review the progress made on cultural-change activities and go over their past personal involvement. New plans are established for the next quarter. This combination of peer pressure and team playing is highly effective. Occasionally, videotapes are made of the review session and sent throughout the organization. They are often used to kick off review and planning sessions at other management levels.

BECOMING A CULTURAL LEADER

As James O'Toole says: "To talk about 'it' is absurd: Culture is 'us'. To talk about top management's role in changing corporate culture is to talk about changing *ourselves* not changing some 'it' or 'them' outside the door of the executive suite."

We've found that culture is often a direct reflection of the person at the head of the organization or miniculture. The more powerful the person, the more distinctive, either positively or negatively, the culture he or she is likely to spawn. Weak, indistinct cultures usually come from weak, indistinct leaders.

The *first step* to cultural change is defining a vision and values that the culture wants to shift toward. The next step is instilling these into the very fiber of your unit. It becomes the pulse, a drumbeat for the group. One client who successfully shifted his culture toward greater innovation, higher quality, and employee involvement notes: "In the final analysis, *vision and values get defined not by words but by actions.* We even have a statement we developed to remind us about that: 'You are what you do, not what you say you are.' Our people know enough to ignore our words and instead observe our behavior."

"Children are natural mimics; they act like their parents despite attempts to teach them good manners."

SIGNALING: AN ACTION IS WORTH A THOUSAND WORDS

Confucius said: "The superior man acts before he speaks and afterwards speaks according to his actions." *More than anyone else, cultural leaders must match their words to action.* All eyes are on them and they must respond uniformly to that challenge. Not only must cultural leaders espouse vision, they must reflect the vision and values by personal example.

We call this "signaling." It includes everything from their public statements and speeches (recall Lee Iacocca's repeated references to the "new" Chrysler corporation) to the shine on their shoes or the way they address senior management in the elevator. Don Seibert, retired CEO of J.C. Penney, offers a good example: "I heard that some of our people were quite worried that the company was in some sort of trouble because they had seen me with a worried frown on my face for a couple of . . . days, I realized that I hadn't been thinking about the company or the economy at all. On the first day I was upset because a new reed I had bought for my saxophone had split, and on the second day I was concerned about a decision we were having to make about a family vacation . . . . I hate to think that people may have lost sleep those nights because of what they thought my frowns were indicating."

High Hurdles, a report on executive self-development published by the Center for Creative Leadership quotes a corporate CEO who said: "If I don't smile, people [immediately] think the business is going bad."

Rosabeth Moss Kanter coined a term for organizational leaders who manage to convey to their staff through personal action what they *really* mean: she calls them "prime movers": "Prime movers pushing a new strategy make it clear that they believe, *clear signals, consistently supported, are what it takes to change an organization's culture.*"

"The ultimate measure of a man is not where he stands in moments of comfort and convenience, but where he stands at times of challenge and controversy."
—Martin Luther King, Jr.

Making appropriate responses during a crisis is the acid test of leadership. Playing the part is easy when things are going well. But once the shooting starts, you soon find out how good leaders really are. "Signaling" need not be difficult or subtle, but it must be consistent. David Close, president of Johnson & Johnson—a company that uses techniques like "chunking" and "skunkworks" to signal to its workers that *they* are more important to the organization than size—continually stresses: "Our strategy is growing big by staying small."

David Ogilvy imbues *his* organization with a driving respect for the customer: "Promises are kept no matter what the cost in agony and overtime."

"And the lectures you deliver may be wise and true; but I'd rather get my lesson by observing what you do, for I may misunderstand you and the high advice you give, but there's no misunderstanding how you act and how you live."

—Edgar A. Guest

Show Me!

Of all the tools for cultural change available, the most potent are the trivial, mundane, daily actions of managers:

—"If you don't return phone calls promptly or answer your mail, if you break appointments at the last minute, or have people sitting on their hands because you're late—what kind of message are your sending?"
 —Buck Rodgers,
 former vice-president of marketing, IBM

—"Too many companies are promoting the wrong people and sending conflicting signals through the corporate culture. . . . Promote people who embody key values of the business."
 —Terrence Deal and Allan Kennedy, *Corporate Cultures*

—"Participative management remains a gewgaw bolted on the management machinery by social engineers. It fails often, a victim of backsliding, backbiting, backhanded treatment, and back to business as usual."
—*Fortune*

—At the General Motors plant in Lakewood, Georgia, the decision to stop wearing coats and ties was easily agreed to. However, banning reserved parking was much more contentious. Finally, a labor-management committee decided, "If we work together, we park together."

An industrial magnate once told Mark Twain he would like to climb Mount Sinai and read aloud the Ten Commandments. "Why don't you just stay home and live them," Twain replied.

SIGNALS THAT SHOULD NEVER BE SENT—BUT ARE

ACTION	MAY MEAN
— slow response to phone or mail	— We don't care.
— executive parking spots	— We count; you don't.
— rude behavior	— People don't matter.
— juniors chauffeuring their senior managers around	— My time is more important than yours.
— top-down command flow	— The boss knows best.
— embarrassing employees to make a point	— Self-esteem doesn't matter.
— strong punitive systems	— Employees are screw-ups.
— using "expert" consultants	— Strangers know more than you do.
— allowing low performance	— Standards? what standards?
— promoting for management or technology skills	— People come second here.
— setting incentives without prior consultation	— We know where your chain is—and how to pull it.

SIGNALS THAT SHOULD BE SENT—BUT AREN'T

ACTION	MEANS
— personally delivering training programs	— You matter; we want to grow with you.
— recognizing daily small acts of excellence	— Thank you, we need more.
— group involvement in decision making	— The real experts are the people doing the job.
— visiting customers frequently	— We exist for our customers.
— removing time clocks	— We trust you.
— consulting people when proposing new procedures or systems	— This is a team—we work together.

Sign in a restaurant: "Customers who consider our waitresses uncivil should see the manager."

TOUGHNESS

In discussing cultural leadership, we speak often about the need for "toughness," only to discover that the word has different meanings depending on the listener's mindset. Many equate toughness with the "kick butt and take names" school of management. In that regime, the more employees worry about being noticed, the more effective the manager is deemed to be. (One employee was overheard to describe his job as a "keeper." When asked what he kept, he replied "out of people's way.")

"Tough" to leader-oriented people means dealing with problems in a way that brings about the desired results without tramping over self-esteem. "Tough" means consistency in the signals you send each day regardless of whether you're in a good or bad mood. "Tough" means never losing touch with the shared value system of your organization even though you may be tempted to look for shortcuts or someone to blame. "Tough" means holding people accountable for what they agreed to do. We call this approach "tough" because, compared to the disciplinarian response, it *is* tough to use consistently.

THE CHALLENGE OF CHALLENGE

To managers raised in the "when they say jump, ask how high" era, challenge from a "subordinate" is an attack on their authority. Insecure managers beat their "attackers" into subservience. They overcome resistance by asserting their authority.

"People who make no noise are dangerous."

—Jean de La Fontaine

A sure sign of a decaying organization is a lack of challenge. People behave as mindless drones, doing what they're told. Innovation comes to a standstill.

Effective cultural leaders encourage challenge. *For them, it's a sign of life and energy.* Ron Lippitt asserted, "There is no such thing as resistance, only legitimate concern." We agree! The enemy is apathy. When overly vocal organization members resist or challenge the organization's direction, they are often reflecting the views of the silent majority. They are, in effect, providing an early warning system of potential problems. Effective cultural leaders test these potential signals with the people involved.

James O'Toole provides powerful examples of healthy challenge in open, thriving organizations:

—At Federal Express, a young manager initiated a fierce debate reexamining a decision made by senior management. After a raucous discussion, senior management couldn't defend their decision, so they changed it. Everyone then went out for an amiable lunch.

—Robert Galvin, CEO of Motorola: "Our challenge is to continually evidence a willingness to reach and risk; a willingness to renew. . . . There is no master plan that can anticipate change." (A young middle manager approached Galvin, on another matter, by restating, "Bob, I heard that point you made this morning, and I think you're dead wrong. I am going to prove it!" To which Galvin beamed: *That's how we've overcome Texas Instruments as the world's largest producer of semiconductors."*)

"He that wrestles with us, strengthens our nerves and sharpens our skill. Our antagonist is our helper."

—Edmund Burke

—At an Arco meeting, president Thornton Bradshaw was discussing the company's recent reorganization. He was interrupted by a young employee: "Mr. Bradshaw, either you're lying to us or kidding yourself. We have not experienced any increase in autonomy as a result of the recent reorganization. It has been a name change only. You guys at the top are still making all the decisions." At this point, Bradshaw turned to the other attendees to solicit their opinions. He thanked everyone for their input and, over the next few months, doubled his effort to delegate autonomy.

A skilled cultural leader recognizes a difference between legitimate challengers and those who are disruptive or unduly negative—"the abominable no-man." Effective leaders use coaching-leadership skills to correct this dysfunctional behavior. They never crush resisters but hold them responsible for making a constructive contribution. If that approach fails, the destructive employee is usually relieved of his position.

As change accelerates, as technology advances, as local markets become global, and as organizations flatten by reducing the layers of management to cope better with these stresses — leadership-skilled managers come to appreciate that they can't be all things to all people, that they can't rule by brute force. They become "directors of environment," creating shared vision, trust, and opportunity so that people will pick up the torch and carry on.

The cultural leader understands that when people are afraid, they will often freeze, resist change, and fight progress. But when people see value in their contribution, have fun, and feel like winners, great things are possible. The pathway to higher performance is more easily travelled.

Bert Snider, president of Bourns, a manufacturer of electrical and electronic parts, says: "My mission is to communicate who we are, what our dream is, and why it is going to work for us."

"A very popular error — having the courage of one's convictions: rather it is a matter of having the courage for an attack upon one's convictions."

—Friedrich Wilhelm Nietzsche

CHAPTER ELEVEN

Knowing Isn't Doing

"The great end of life is not knowledge but action."

—Aldous Huxley

So far we've given you a taste of "what" may be missing from your organization and "what" has to be done to increase quality, service, innovation, and productivity in a turbulent world. Many writers at this point, convinced that their job is done, would pack up the typewriter and head for a coffee pot. Many readers, certain that they've got the point, would shelve the book and head for *their* coffee pot, too!

Hold on! None of us deserves a coffee yet. We must put into practice (process) the things we have reviewed (content). Knowing *what* leadership skills are needed to improve performance is a critical starting point. Understanding *how* to develop them, however, is vital. *Without an effective development process (how), you're not much further ahead, no matter how right your content (what) is.*

Failure to give equal attention to *how* leadership skills are developed causes good intentions to fizzle out. It's as if a marketing manager put all his or her focus on *what* message was to be conveyed with no thought to *how* it could best be delivered. Ridiculous? Absolutely. Effective advertising consists of spending as much time selecting the most suitable communication vehicles (*process*) as deciding on the message (*content*). Such is also the case with leadership-skill development.

COMMON SENSE IS RARELY COMMON PRACTICE

Knowing what to do and doing it are two very different things. If there is an oil well on your property and you don't tap it, you won't get a dime in revenue no matter how big the reserves are. Even the brightest concept will fade into obscurity if left undeveloped.

"No amount of travelling on the wrong road will bring you to the right destination."

—Ben Gaye III

Easy to Know; Tough to "Do":
—*To lose weight, exercise more and eat less.*
—*The best way to become rich is to make a lot of money.*
—Playing the market? Easy: *buy low and sell high.*
—To increase market share, *improve service and quality.*
—To increase employee commitment, encourage *teamwork.*
—To improve employee productivity, strengthen *coaching-leadership skills.*
—To build a customer-oriented company, *change the culture.*

 Nobody can argue with *what* needs to be done. The $64,000 dollar question is *how*! Our own industry is rife with examples of development and consulting firms that have trouble following their own advice. A competitor's consultant once came to us for a

	Inspiration
Definitions (*Oxford Dictionary*)	"Thought etc. that is inspired, prompting; sudden brilliant or timely idea."
Key Words	Passion "Aha" Attitude Feelings
How Developed	Vision Inspirational speakers Energized environment
Measurement of Results	Climate survey Energy levels
Effect on Behavior	Short-term enthusiasm Resolution to improve

job. One of the major services his firm offered was performance-appraisal systems, yet after three years he had never had a performance appraisal! In another firm, two partners who sold "conflict resolution" and "team-building" programs eventually came to blows.

To know and not to do is not to know."

—heard on Wall Street

INSPIRATION, KNOWLEDGE, OR SKILL??

Most improvement efforts (quality programs, cultural change, management development, motivating employees, et al.) fall into three categories: inspiration, knowledge and skill.

The following chart clarifies these approaches:

Knowledge	Skill
"Theoretical or practical understanding; the sum of what is known."	"Expertness, practiced ability, facility in an action or in doing or to do something."
Concepts	Actions
Knowledge	Doing
Awareness	Behavior
Understanding	Habits
Books and courses	Outlining key steps
Lectures and case studies	Examples
Study and observation	Practicing real situations
	Feedback and continued practice
Examinations	Behavior change testing
Regurgitation	
Unpredictable	Direct and habit forming
Often low	

"We know better than we do."

—Ralph Waldo Emerson

In comparing the three approaches, we have found that:

—Getting people excited about change or a new approach isn't likely to have a lasting effect on their behavior. (How many well-intended New Year's resolutions are broken by June?)

—Knowledge-oriented approaches are often confused with skill building. When concepts are presented by dynamic speakers, it is assumed that the requisite skills are in place. But ability is seldom improved, no matter how moving the experience was.

—All three elements—inspiration, knowledge, and skills—are needed to sustain any long-term change or improvement. The issue is one of *balance*. Too often, skills are misunderstood, assumed, or just plain ignored.

—Improving skills often increases knowledge and inspires the participant through increased confidence on the job. A hospital client ran pre- and post-knowledge tests on supervisors who had participated in a leadership-skill-building program. The participants' scores on questions relating to management and motivational theories improved after the program even though none of these topics was covered within the program.

—A few (rare) individuals can transfer inspiration and knowledge to the job and so improve their skills. The majority of people, however, cannot bridge that gap on their own.

—Knowledge-based approaches are the route of choice for those with an academic bent. Our school system is based on this approach. But knowledge is to eduction what skills are to training. Most companies think they are buying skills when in fact they are getting education.

—Academic prowess and leadership ability are often considered to be connected. They are not. We've observed with our university clients, for example, that some of the least proficient coaches and team leaders are management professors! They understand the theories but can by no means implement or practice them.

—"Training is training" is no more true than "advertising is advertising." The message (content) is important, but the medium (process) is absolutely critical. The best marketing campaign in the world will fail if poorly executed.

—*Knowledge-centered approaches are content driven. Skill development is primarily concerned with process.*

> That's a Great Idea . . . But
>
> During the Second World War, Pentagon strategists asked war correspondent Ernie Pyle for his advice on the problem of Nazi submarines in the Atlantic Ocean. His solution? "Boil the ocean. Submarines can't operate in boiling water." The reaction was incredulity. "Are you kidding! How can we do that?" asked the military men. *"I've given you the answer,"* retorted Pyle confidently. *"Now it's up to you to work out the details."*

"He not only overflowed with learning, but stood in the slop."

—Sydney Smith

MANAGEMENT CONSULTANTS: CONTENT OR PROCESS?

To help their organizations deal with the chaotic changes swirling about them, many managers hire management consultants. This is where understanding content and process is vital. In some cases, "content" consultants provide key pieces of knowledge or understanding. For example, our exploding technologies make it almost impossible for organizations to stay on top of the latest robotics, office automation, telecommunications, or the myriad of emerging technical specialties. Experts in these fields can provide highly specialized information gleaned from working across industries or organizations. In the management-systems areas, we see a similar need for content consultants to help establish the most useful systems for this age of information overload.

However, as the organizations turn to leadership issues or people problems, a very different kind of help is needed. Now the focus is on gaining employee commitment, capturing customer loyalty, increasing flexibility, improving service, and so on. The problem is seldom one of figuring out *what* needs to be done. Rather, the issue is *how* to do it. It calls for a focus on the process of implementation.

Arthur N. Turner, a professor of organizational behavior at Harvard Business School, has worked in the fields of management education and consulting both at home and abroad.

231

In 1982 he published an insightful article entitled "Consulting Is More Than Giving Advice." In it he says: "Each year management consultants in the United States receive more than $2 billion for their services. Much of this money pays for impractical data and poorly implemented recommendations . . . . Untold numbers of seemingly convincing reports subitted at great expense have no real impact. . . . [They end up] on the client's bookshelf next to other expensive and unimplemented reports . . . . This sort of thing happens more frequently than most management consultants would care to admit."

"If to do were as easy as to know what were good to do, chapels had been churches and poor men's cottages princes' palaces."

—William Shakespeare

Turner created a hierarchy of the various consulting services that are available:
1. provides information to client;
2. solves a client's problem;
3. makes a diagnosis;
4. makes recommendations based on the diagnosis;
5. assists with implementation of recommended solutions;
6. builds consensus and commitment through corrective action;
7. facilitates client learning: that is, teaches clients how to resolve similar problems in the future;
8. permanently improves organizational effectiveness.

He contends, and we heartily concur, that stages 6, 7, and 8 are the most effective ways to improve an organization's long-term performance.

Another way of looking at Turner's hierarchy is that steps 1 to 5 deal with technical or management-systems issues. These steps require an understanding of the content of the problem. For example, if a newly installed automated inventory-control system isn't working, an expert consultant might analyze the equipment and system to come up with a solution. He or she might actually fix the problem for the client, or recommend how best to solve it.

However, steps 6, 7, and 8 describe process consulting. They are concerned with people or leadership issues. In the case of the automated inventory-control system, the process consultant would guide the client organization to solve the problem themselves. This solution would likely entail bringing technical experts (sometimes from outside, but often they can be found or developed within), managers and system users together to solve the problem.

Rarely is a problem purely technical or system related. Almost always the human input, human use, and human expectations are at the heart of the problem—and are key to its solution. Content or expert consultants often ignore the human element and instead focus on the technical or mechanical facts.

Any effort at improvement that bypasses its own internal resources (people!) will run into trouble—for it is the organization's people who will be called upon to make the "outside" recommendation work!

Employees who feel no ownership, no participation in the changes being made are not likely to contribute much effort to make them work. Indeed, many delight in seeing (and perhaps even helping) the expert's plans fail, all the while thinking, "If they had asked *us* in the first place, *we* would have told them what to do!"

Another interesting difference between the two styles of consulting is that content consulting, by its nature, is limited to a specific problem. A mathematical model to increase production on a given line is useful only for that line and only under one particular set of assumptions. Process consulting, since it works with developing people, creates *transferable results*. Once the skills of problem solving are mastered, the skills can be reused for other problems, at other times.

"It is not enough to have great qualities, we must also have the management of them."

—Francois Duc de la Rochefoucauld

SO LET'S DO IT!

The most useful process of all is one that can be administered by the organization itself. Here the consultant becomes a sideline coach helping the organization develop the ability to improve its own leadership skills. Instead of just bringing people together to solve that automated-inventory-control-system problem, the skills-oriented process consultant helps key organization members develop their ability to draw teams together to solve problems, refocus the culture, improve coaching skills, or increase interpersonal effectiveness. These skills can be used across a broad spectrum of the organization's performance issues.

So let's turn our attention to the performance strategy of developing leadership skills throughout an organization. The journey has both troubled and transformed many organizations. We need to pick our way carefully amid the pitfalls, traps, and dead ends. There are a few proven pathways to increased leadership skills, but we need to know where to look for them.

"Everyone of us . . . knows better than he practices, and recognizes a better law than he obeys."

—James A. Froude

CHAPTER TWELVE

Developing an Organization's Leadership Skills

"Not only is there an art in knowing a thing, but also a certain art in teaching it."

—Marcus Tullius Cicero

If everyone could become a brain surgeon, an engineer, or a professional athlete by watching a snappy video, taking a course or reading a book, we'd certainly see some rapid upheaval in our society! It is no different with organizations aspiring to higher performance: if it was that easy, it would be that easy.

Consider the high-wire artist in training: after weeks of work, he is able to walk competently across the wire at a height of about four feet. Then the wire is raised to ten feet. The first time he steps onto the wire at this new height, he loses his balance and falls flat on his face. Weeks later, having mastered ten feet, the wire goes up to twenty feet and again our aspiring circus performer falls off. And so it goes.

The skills of higher performance in these turbulent times are not easy to master. What you can do, however, is choose carefully among the vehicles available to help you in that mastery. There are many programs available, and a great many claims are made for each. In this chapter we have laid out what we have found to be the optimal methods for developing leadership skills. They're the ones that we believe in, because they're well thought out and well researched, but, most of all, because they work.

WHY MOST TRAINING DOESN'T STICK

Much of what passes for leadership-skill development isn't. Part of the reason we've already examined: education is confused with training, and leadership is too often confused with management. Even where the focus is on leadership issues, many development efforts never get the process, or "how," quite right. They provide inspiration or motivation, but lasting habits are seldom developed. Activity is confused with accomplishment. The right content is mixed with the wrong process. These programs turn out executives, managers, supervisors, and employees who know what must be done to improve performance but not how to do it. They become "conscious incompetents," and a state of frustration and ebbing confidence results.

A thoughtful examination of this problem is found in Jack Zenger's article, "The Painful Turnabout in Training." Zenger concluded: "Millions of dollars are spent [on training] with no evidence of on-the-job transfer." He further asserts, "Training, with such a high potential contribution to make, has been missing something. It has fallen short of the task." He attributes this failing to "the fact that training has been operating on shaky assumptions, using inappropriate methodology, relying on untested theories, following fads, ignoring evaluation research, and not defining the behavior change sought."

During our years of work with clients, we've seen the good, the bad, and the useless when it comes to leadership development. Poor programs fall into one (or more) of these five traps:

"Nothing ever becomes real until it is experienced."

—John Keats

1. Dangerous Assumptions and Shaky Foundations
Among the dangerous assumptions are . . .
—*"Fix Their Attitude"* Many managers, and some training directors, believe that if you change the attitude of trainees, you can change their actions on the job. Mel Sorcher, a lesser-known pioneer in the field of modern management development, served as an industrial psychologist at General Electric in the sixties. Sorcher found that supervisors were not changing their behavior through the traditional approach to leadership development. Many would be inspired by the training programs and fervently resolve to look at their staff and jobs in new ways. On Monday

morning, however, the books went back on the shelves, the diploma was hung on the wall, and as the wave of job demands hit them, life carried on pretty much as before. Sorcher's research led him to conclude that trying to change behavior by altering attitude alone was a long and difficult path. He found that attitudes about authority, motivation, and so on were deeply interconnected with social, family, community, and other attitudes. He contended that trying to change a supervisor's attitude was like trying to remove the center cannonball from a pile without disturbing any of the others. He noticed that defense mechanisms automatically spring to the fore whenever a basic attitude or belief is challenged.

Sorcher fought the current of traditional thought by designing a supervisory training program that changed behavior and left attitude alone (we'll discuss this powerful approach shortly). He found that supervisors began to change their attitudes to make them consistent with their new behavior. Where "crusty old Charlie" had defended his "kick butt and take names" approach in traditional training programs, he now embraced a more participative leadership style when behavior became the focus. In effect, Sorcher's approach said, "Believe what you want, Charlie, we're not going to mess with your head. But here are some key actions and basic principles to help you become even more effective on the job." Gradually, as Charlie found that the new behavior worked for him and as he heard about his colleagues' successes, he began to change his own attitudes. This result is consistent with the psychological theory of "cognitive dissonance": we can't continually act without considerable discomfort in a way that is inconsistent with our beliefs, values, and attitudes. The two must be in sync before we feel okay. What Sorcher and many others discovered is that it is easier and more effective to change behavior and not attitude. Or, as Harvard psychologist, Jerome Bruner puts it, "You more likely act yourself into feeling than feel yourself into action."

"What we have to learn to do, we learn by doing."

—Aristotle

—*"If They Know Better, They Would Do Better"* We often refer to this method as the "spray and pray" approach. Here the instructor presents leadership theories, models, situations, cases, examples, "simulations," games, and the like. The problem is a tricky one, because most of these models, examples, stories, and illustrations are well researched and well presented. But the crux of the problem is not just knowing *what* to do, it's *how* to behave in highly effective ways. *How* to get a majority of managers and employees marching in step to a new beat.

–*"Give Them a Case to Study"* J. Sterling Livingston managed hundreds of MBA graduates as president of Management Systems Corporation. When he became professor of business administration at Harvard Business School, he wrote a provocative article entitled, "The Myth of the Well Educated Manager." His comments mesh with our own views on the problems associated with the case study approach: "Lectures, case discussions, or textbooks alone are of limited value in developing ability to find opportunities and problems — what [managers] learn about supervising others is largely second-hand. Their knowledge is derived from the discussion of what someone else should do about the problems of 'paper people' whose emotional reactions, motives, and behavior have been described for them by scholars who may have observed and advised managers, but who usually have never taken responsibility for getting results in a business organization . . . . *Guided practice in real or simulated business situations is the only method that will make managers more skillful.*"

Development efforts that use case studies and role plays educate, inform, sensitize, and increase awareness, but we find that they rarely change behavior. Contrived situations are difficult to transfer back to the job. "My job is different," "Our organization is different," "This industry is different"; these are common responses. Training is best when it is *realistic and practical.*

Training must also relate in real terms to the day-to-day organizational environment. When it does, it provides useful blueprints for the participant to follow.

"Education does not mean teaching people what they do not know. It means teaching them to behave as they do not behave."

—John Ruskin

Knowledge Versus Skills

Failure to improve leadership skills often stems from confusion between education and training, understanding and habits, knowing and doing:

"Many management development programs attempt to alter behavior by imparting knowledge and understanding about particular theories of leadership, motivation, communication. . . . Managers may both understand and agree with the concepts of a program, yet lack the behavioral skills required to translate the concepts into action."
  — Jerry Porras and Brad Anderson, "Improving Managerial Effectiveness through Modeling-Based Training"

"We are still using teaching methodology that has been demonstrated to not really change behavior . . . lecture, film, case discussion, paper and pencil instruments and exercises. Nowhere is there evidence that these techniques really change behavior."
  — Jack Zenger, "The Painful Turnabout in Training"

"Programs designed to teach supervisors how to manage the work and efforts of other people do not necessarily result in trained supervisors . . . . The issues often center about the need for a manager to be a good communicator, to be able to motivate his people, to give recognition, to make constructive criticism. Most managers seek to know *how* to motivate, *how* to communicate, and *how* to carry out the other aspects of leadership."
  — Arnold P. Goldstein and Melvin Sorcher, *Changing Supervisor Behavior*

"Management schools which will begin the serious training of managers when skill training takes a serious place next to cognitive learning . . . [which] is detached and informational like reading a book or listening to a lecture . . . . Cognitive learning makes no more managers than it does swimmers. . . . They will drown the first time they jump in the water if their coach never . . . gets them wet and gives them feedback on their performance."
  — Henry Mintzberg, "The Manager's Job: Fact and Folklore"

2. Lack of Managerial Reinforcement

In early 1986, the American Society for Training and Development commissioned a study that addressed, among other things, the question of why some training fails. Of the eight most common reasons given by training-and-development executives, five related to poor support by management:

–"No on-the-job rewards for behaviors and skills learned in training."

–"Insufficient time to execute training programs."

–"Work environment does not support new behaviors learned in training."

–"Management does not support training."

–"Insufficient funding of training program."

Several studies conducted by the Xerox Corporation showed that *"in the absence of follow-up coaching 87 percent of the skill change brought about by the program was lost within two months."*

As we discussed in Chapter 10, managers send signals whether they intend to or not. When leadership-skill development is an isolated effort aimed at "them" (usually middle and lower-level managers, supervisors, and employees), the message is strong. When that is, in turn, coupled with senior managers' inconsistent attention to the skills being taught, the message is unmistakable: put in your time, be a good student, hang your certificate on the wall, and then get back to real business. Training directors operating under these conditions do so with permission but seldom with any real support from senior management. They are often as much to blame for not building sorely needed management support and reinforcement processes into their development effort.

"For what his wisdom planned, and power enforced, more potent still his great example showed."

—James Thomson

3. Aspirins and Band-Aids

Imagine going to a doctor with little sores all over your body, a nauseous stomach, and headaches. Imagine your response if he or she responded to your complaints by prescribing salve and Band-Aids for your sores, antacid for your stomach, and aspirins for your headache. Are you cured? Has he or she treated you or just relieved symptoms? Did he or she deal with the root cause of your discomfort?

We are continually amazed by the number of organizations that treat the symptoms of poor leadership skills rather than the root cause. A glaring example is time-management techniques. Faced with ever-increasing demands to be "everything to everyone," "fight fires," and solve problems, technomanagers are understandably stretched very thin. *But learning how to "diarize," "priorize," plan, record, and "chunk" their days often only applies Band-Aids and aspirins.* Useful, but they don't treat the underlying problem.

Our position is supported by Charles Garfield's extensive research on peak performers: "Based on simplistic concepts about the nature of managerial work, these [time management] programs instruct managers to stop allowing people to 'interrupt' their daily work. They tell potential executives that short and disjointed conversations are ineffective . . . . They advise people to behave differently from the effective executives in this study."

The real issue is how managers are using their time. And that depends on their skills. Following are some common managerial time eaters and their likely skills-deficiency cause:

Time-Management Symptom	Possible Leadership-Skill Problems
—Constant interruptions	—People are unclear about accountability and responsibility or lack people skills.
	—"Heroic Management."
—Crisis management	—Early warnings are suppressed by "closed" system.
	—Innovation is infrequent.
—Conflict management	—Employees are unskilled at resolving conflicts.
—Quality and service problems	—Vision and values are not lived.
	—Team skills are weak.

- Disciplinary actions

- Union actions
  (strikes, grievances, etc.)

- Performance coaching is poor.
- Recognition/reward system is weak.
- "We/they" gap is large.
- Culture is adversarial and autocratic.

4. Bits and Pieces Approach

Some organizations offer a "cafeteria approach" to training and development. They produce a catalogue of courses, workshops, and seminars for the participant's choosing. Usually this is combined with a centralized facility.

This not-very-effective (and fortunately declining) approach is generally a reflection of the organization's laissez-faire culture. Development efforts are seldom linked to organizational strategies. Leadership skills are spotty and inconsistent.

"Knowledge is a treasure, but practice is the key to it."

—Thomas Fuller

One- or two-week learning sessions, or "data dumps," held at a central facility are also, fortunately, on the decline. Organizations that want to build practical, job-specific skills, as well as trim travel and delivery costs, are moving training out to the operating locations. IBM, a world leader in training and development, has saved millions by closing education centers and eliminating burdensome traveling and living expenses. According to the Work in America Institute, "decentralization [of training] is the wave of the future."

5. "Happy Sheets"

Another aspect of training that is susceptible to confusion and misinformation is evaluation research. Until recently there wasn't much hard data to compare the results of skill training to seminars, audio-visual slide shows, encounter sessions, "edutainers," and other colorful activities that pass themselves off as leadership development.

The typical method of judging the effect of a training process was to pass out questionnaires to the participants after the session was over while the experience was fresh in their minds.

We call these questionnaires "happy sheets" because they tend to provoke positive responses. The way the questions are phrased, the point at which they are given out, and the mood of the people to whom they are given all reflect a common value: pleasure and good intentions. Pleased to meet you, hope we all

---

The Woo-Woo Factor

It's a jungle out there. The training-and-development field is rife with witch doctors and snake-oil salesmen. *Training* magazine editor Jack Gordon developed a "woo-woo scale" to assess the effectiveness of a training effort. A "1" is highly effective, a "5" is moderately effective, and a "10" is highly suspect. As the woo-woo level increases toward "10":

—goals or expected outcomes of the training become more subjective;

—the training goals move from producing some demonstrable skill (a "1") to having trainees affirm that the experience was meaningful to them;

—the real point of any activity, comment, or exercise resembles less and less its tangible or surface meaning ("What were we learning about ourselves when we allowed our partners to draw on our foreheads with those crayons?");

—programs tend to focus on making the simple complex, rather than vice versa. Twenty minutes' worth of information becomes a three-day workshop, a bromide becomes a book, and two pedestrian (and often shopworn) insights into a dramatic "system";

—the training is driven by "gurus" who abuse English with such phrases as "transpersonal organizationalism." Subsidiary gurus, licensed to deliver high woo-woo programs, will remind you of TV weathermen;

—the subject matter becomes more conceptual and less procedural;

—the only proofs of effectiveness offered are endorsements from satisfied users.

---

had fun, where's my cinnamon jelly roll, coffee double sugar no milk, and thank you very much for your trouble!

Later on, when the after-glow begins to fade and participants begin to realize that they have to catch up with missed work and convince their bosses the session was time well spent, positive first impressions often change. When managers try to figure out what real gains were achieved for the dollars paid out, a new set of conclusions may be reached.

"In teaching, it is the method and not the content that is the message . . . the drawing out, not the pumping in."

—Ashley Montagu

BUILDING LEADERSHIP SKILLS IN THE CLASSROOM

Almost a decade ago, we began looking for a leadership-development process to help clients strengthen their managerial ranks. Our search led us to a budding management-development firm in California. Examination of their programs, discussions with their clients, and a study of the research supporting and validating their training design led us to conclude that Zenger-Miller, Inc. had a powerful and effective process.

The first leadership-skill-development program, "Supervision," designed by Zenger-Miller was based on the pioneering work by Dr. Mel Sorcher at General Electric. Mel had helped Jack Zenger and Dale Miller design a supervisory development program at Syntex, a pharmaceutical firm. The results were so positive that, when Zenger-Miller was formed, Jack and Dale immediately set out (with Mel Sorcher's blessing) to design an "off-the-shelf" program for other organizations to use. Achieve assisted in the development of a "Facilitator's Manual" and the design of the three-and-a-half-day "train the trainer" workshops, which allowed organizations to deliver the program internally through training professionals or selected line managers.

Over the next few years, Zenger-Miller and Achieve's growth sky-rocketed. Sales climbed at a rate unparalleled in the training and development industry. *Yet the program content was not unique.* Hundreds of competing firms offered similar topics. *The key difference was the development process.* The "Supervision"

The Verdict Is In

—"The data is overwhelming: Programs that use behavior-modeling technology in their design have a better success rate with respect to transfer of skills to the workplace."
   —Ron Zemke and John Gunkler, "28 Techniques for Transforming Training into Performance"

—"In the eyes of their subordinates, supervisors did significantly change their behavior . . . . The changes reported immediately after the workshops were essentially maintained. . . . This result is particularly significant since most related research tends to report an erosion of change . . . . The six-month-running average of total monthly production per labor worker increased 17 percent from its original level . . . . The trends toward lower turnover and absenteeism were significant."
   —Jerry I. Porras of Stanford University and Brad Anderson of Hewlett-Packard, "Improving Managerial Effectiveness through Modeling-Based Training"

—"During the past seven years, we have encouraged the conduct of research and evaluation studies of behavior modeling training systems. Forty-one separate research projects were completed by client organizations or external researchers. . . . All 41 studies showed positive improvements from before training to after training, and 37 of the studies showed statistically significant improvements . . . . These reports provide convincing evidence of the effectiveness of a behavior modeling training program . . . . Behavior modeling [also] produces positive changes in participants' attitudes about the organization, about management and the climate of the organization. Certainly no other training methodology has come close to producing the broadly based research evidence of behavior modeling."
   —Jack Zenger and Darlene Russ-Eft, "Research on Behavior Modeling: The last Five Years"

program used the approach pioneered by Mel Sorcher called "Behavior Modeling."

Behavior modeling was so simple that many initially dismissed it as simplistic. It works by first breaking broad topics into specific skill sets. For example, "Communications" is divided into sessions on giving information, listening, and setting job expections. Once a "bite-sized" topic is isolated, skills were practiced in a three-hour session with twelve to fifteen people attending. During the session, four steps are followed to develop skills:

1. introduction and discussion of specific "Key actions" for that skill unit;
2. observation and discussion of the "Key Actions" that were used in video model and class demonstration;
3. practice in groups of three using the "Key Actions" in one of the participant's own real situations;
4. feedback on effective use of "Key Actions" and suggestions for improvement.

"I hear and I forget, I see and I remember, I do and I understand."

—Chinese Proverb

Since the introduction of "Supervision" in 1979, more than a thousand North American organizations have trained hundreds of thousands of supervisors and managers. During that time, graduate students from Stanford University and dozens of clients have had the opportunity to evaluate the impact of this pioneering behavior-modeling approach. Consistently, results such as significant behavior change on the job, improvements in productivity, diminishing union grievances, and lower turnover and absenteeism have been thoroughly documented.

As behavior modeling and our strong position on training evaluation caught on, researchers began comparing this new approach to traditional methods. A study by Michael Burke of New York University's department of management and Russel Day of the Illinois Institute of Chicago and North Western Transportation Company typified the findings: working independently of Zenger-Miller or Achieve, they compared results of the following types of programs: (1) lecture plus group discussion; (2) lecture and role playing; (3) self-paced workbooks; (4) behavior modeling; (5) multiple techniques. They found the least amount of on-the-job behavior change resulted from methods 1 and 2. Self-paced workbooks were marginally more effective. Multiple methods were slightly more effective than the lectures or self-paced workbooks. *Behavior modeling, however, was substantially more effective in changing on-the-job behavior than any of the other methods.*

"Example is the school of mankind, and they will learn at no other."
—Edmund Burke

Cue Sensitivity and Pro-action

The four steps of behavior modeling deal with only the "how to" aspect. A second component commonly overlooked in skill development efforts is "when to." J. Sterling Livingston asserts: "Managers need to be able not only to analyze data in financial statements and written reports, but also scan the business environment for less concrete cues that a problem exists."

Important though they are, we often miss cues because:
1. they are too familiar;
2. automatic (thought-free) responses;
3. one thought blots out all others;
4. we are too self-absorbed;
5. our brains are overloaded;
6. we have reached satiation (no new input sought);
7. we have insufficient knowledge to identify cues.

Pro-active (initiating rather than reacting) management and cue spotting (identifying signs that action may be needed) are no more than different sides of the same coin. Far-sighted organizations tend to see problems and predicaments as solutions and results to be acted upon quickly. In our tumultuous world, this skill is now mandatory at all levels to build a flexible responsive organization. It is no longer just a "nice to do."

Reactive	Preventive	Proactive
—Wait for problems to flare and respond once they appear.	—Nip 'em in the bud.	—Anticipate, don't wait.
	—Use an ounce of prevention.	—Take positive steps.
	—Stay one step ahead.	—Have a plan.

Getting Better with Experience

In the last decade, thousands of companies have developed their employees' leadership skills using a four-step process called behavior modeling. (Note: This is not B.F. Skinner's controversial method called "behavior modification.") From this rich base of experience have emerged clear guidelines for designing powerful development programs. Whether you want to develop your personal skills or to strengthen your organization's leadership skills, here are some of the problems you may encounter with this potentially effective process. Also shown are some of the keys to successful application.

Learning Step	Common Misapplications	Most Effective
Key Actions	– lengthy and complex	– short and simple
	– loosely associated with other steps	– behavioral descriptions
	– lots of theory and "styles awareness"	– videos, workbooks, reminder cards, posters, etc.
Models or Examples	– overemphasis on "negative" (how *not* to do it) examples	– short "positive" models showing successful applications
	– long complex situations to model various skills	– television-quality acting, settings, and production

	– organizational setting distracts viewers	– participants document key actions used and suggest changes
	– actors who are too slick	– at least 2-3 video models per set of key actions
Practice	– artificial role plays with contrived situations	– using participants' real situations
	– discussion of applications rather than practice	– small groups — pairs, trios, or foursomes
	– lack of key actions and/or models to follow	– following 2-3 video or live classroom demonstrations
Feedback	– general and superficial	– modeled and practiced as a skill of its own
	– coming from "expert" instructor rather than peers	– underlying values/philosophies base (e.g. basic principles)
	– stressing "body language or minor "sub-skills"	– built around Key Actions being practiced

Once again, Zemke and Gunkler's views are consistent with ours: "Any good training is aimed at imparting not only knowledge and skills, but the conditions under which specific skills are to be used back on the job." Video is a particularly effective tool here. Participants are shown brief video clips of a situation where a problem is emerging. A discussion of which "Key Actions" might have been used, or how the situation could have been headed off then follows. Participants thus become more pro-active — and better time managers!

"Practice is the best of all instructors."

—Publilius Syrus

Action Planning

This final component is also vital to effective skill building in the classroom. If within fifteen to thirty days of a training (or a planning) session specific actions are not taken, the chances that anything will come of the training are almost nil. Skills developed in the classroom and not used in the job quickly will, like any muscle, atrophy and weaken.

Here are the elements of effective action planning for proper utilization of those newly acquired leadership skills:
—The participants' manager must be aware of the plans, and must support, reinforce and encourage them.
—Accountability should be built in and should include the participants' manager. Another effective approach is to set up "coaching pairs." Here, participants end each session by telling a peer or "buddy" what they plan to do. The following session then begins with an accounting to that fellow participant.
—Planning questions should be used to guide participants through the following: (a) objectives in using that skill, (b) potential problems to anticipate, (c) personal pitfalls and traps to avoid, and (d) the likely response of key figures or groups in their job situation.

"People seldom improve when they have no model but themselves to copy after."

—Oliver Goldsmith

BRINGING IT ALL TOGETHER: IMPLEMENTING A LEADERSHIP-DEVELOPMENT PROGRAM

Having worked with hundreds of organizations to implement leadership-development programs, we see a clear pattern of the key components to success emerging. Like a powerful computer or well-designed accounting system, the best training program in the world is useless if it's used improperly. Covering the following bases is critical to the success of a concerted leadership-skill-development effort.

1. Management Must Be Involved

This logical and straightforward message gets lots of agreement but painfully little action, so let's spin the broken record one more time: *leadership-skill development is a cultural change effort. A culture truly changes only when the behavior of its cultural leaders clearly signals every day the new skills to be practiced.* Actions really do speak louder than words.

In the extensive research conducted by Zenger and Russ-Eft, management support and involvement emerged as a critical factor determining the success of the leadership-development effort: "One study in which two plants with the same technology both underwent supervisory training showed dramatically different results for each plant. The only discernible difference [in implementation] was management support . . . . In a series of hospitals, one of which produced behavioral change far in excess of the others, the only difference [in implementation] appeared to be the degree of line management involvement."

Management professor Donald L. Kirkpatrick of the University of Wisconsin reached similar conclusions: "If the climate is 'preventative' or 'discouraging,' there is almost a 100 percent chance that no change in behavior will take place; if the climate is 'neutral' or better, there is a 50—50 chance that something will happen. If the climate is 'encouraging' there is about a 75 percent chance the desired behavior will take place. And, if the climate is 'requiring,' there is almost a 100 percent chance it [change] will happen."

When you ask most training directors if they have management support, they say yes ("After all, management gave me a job and a budget"). When you ask most managers if they support training, they say, "Absolutely." Yet there's support and there's support. We find it ranges across a continuum:

Permission	Ceremonial	Encourage-ment	Reinforcement	Leading by Example
—Sets budgets	—Attends kick-offs and gradua-tions	—Sets training objectives	—Recognizes use of skills	—Builds skills (not just for overview)
—"Blesses" an action plan	—Gets an overview	—Follows up	—Arranges for regular coaching	—Teaches the program

Our experience shows that the closer senior management is to the right side of the continuum, the faster and more lasting the development effort. In fact, simple permission usually leads to spotty behavioral change and little overall shift in the culture.

2. The Trainers Need Effective Training

There are two main reasons organizations are equipping their own people to deliver leadership-development programs inside the organization. First, it is a more cost-effective way to train a

---

Two Top Managers on Management Involvement

. . . "You should train your senior managers and not just those people down in the organization . . . . The CEO, Bob Galvin, and I participate. We go through training ourselves to set an example—we audit the performance of our business organizations to see who is using training and how effective it is . . . . The top executives of Motorola act as instructors. . . . We participate, we challenge, we question."
—William Weisz, Chief Operating Officer, Motorola Inc.

—"Management development requires the full support of the CEO, or it will not be taken seriously . . . . It should rank on par with profit and loss responsibility."
—Sir Austin Pearce, Chairman, British Aerospace

---

large group of people. Second, it allows the organization to tailor development to its own needs and to become self-sufficient. This contributes to a culture of pride and increases training's relevance and effectiveness.

When we began training instructors in 1980, the vast majority of them were professional trainers or human-resource/personnel people. In the past few years, we've seen a significant shift: now, line supervisors, managers, and executives are becoming certified trainers in order to deliver leadership-development programs to people in their organization. The benefits of this approach are substantial:

— It further develops a manager's leadership skills. Helping others learn requires an even higher level of personal mastery.

"To teach is to learn twice."

—Japanese Proverb

— A skilled instructor becomes especially good at coaching others through constructive feedback. This is a critical leadership skill that most managers perform dismally, if at all.

— It is an excellent development for "fast-track" managers slated for greater responsibility. One of our large utility clients delivers the company's coaching-leadership program exclusively this way. A few "fast-track" instructors have already been promoted and are now top-performing managers.

— It strengthens and deepens the leadership base of the organization. "A single manager who can foster the development of many others during his or her career helps us in two significant ways," says Foss Boyle, vice-president for human resources at Honeywell Corporation, "by providing us with the people we need to make Honeywell's strategies succeed and by making Honeywell an exciting, rewarding place for all of us to work."

— An army of managers as trainers leads to a learning organization. This is critical to creating an innovative adaptive organization. Studies by the Work in America Institute conclude: "If learning is to be truly continuous, the organization must look to its own resources for more and more of the teaching."

— It sends a resoundingly clear signal to the organization: leadership-skill development is something that *must* be done, not something that is merely nice to do. General Foods president Philip L. Smith has personally led seminars on business leadership. Kathy Hanson, organization development associate, observes: "[He] clearly favors the notion of 'managers as trainers' and believes this should be a major managerial responsibility. And his actions speak louder than his words."

—When managers become the prime mode of delivering leadership development programs, human-resource professionals are freed to plan development strategies and share their training-*process* expertise with the managers. Many of our clients accomplish this by training a human-resources professional to become a "master trainer." He or she then trains internal trainers and acts as coach and resource to the manager-trainers.

—Manager-trainers give the leadership-development program extra credibility. When Will Barrett, president of AVCO Financial Services, together with his vice-presidents, personally delivered a team-leadership-skills program, there were few attendance problems! And rarely did participants complain, "My boss should be taking this," or ask "Is this organization really committed to these new approaches?"

—A manager delivering skills training feels extra pressure to practice what he preaches. This leads to even higher skills and better role models.

Not just any manager can deliver a program in leadership skills. When working with clients to select potential manager-trainers, we suggest that the best candidates should: (1) have credibility in the organization, (2) be in step with the leadership skills to be taught, (3) practice the basic principles (see Chapter 7), (4) have good listening skills, (5) be able to conceptualize comments from others and "give up the floor," (6) be good coaches, (7) respond nondefensively to challenge, and (8) be skilled at giving constructive feedback.

Of course, few managers are as "perfect" as this list suggests.

"Never has a man who has bent himself been able to make others straight."

—Mencius

Don't Treat 'Em Like Kids

Consider the chart below. On the left side (P column) are teaching methods that following what the Greeks called pedagogy, or the teaching of a child. The teacher is clearly established as superdominant to the student. Communication is a one-way experience. Learners and students are arranged in groups (grades or forms) to assist the teacher, and the knowledge imparted is hoary with age, having been passed along from teacher to teacher.

In sharp contrast, andragogy (see: A column on the right) deals with adult-to-adult learning. The principals in the relationship are on an equal footing. Communication is multichannelled and shared by all. Learners group themselves by subject so they can learn in the way that is best for them, not the teacher. And the group probes questions related directly to the matters at hand: *problems of the present and solutions of the present.*

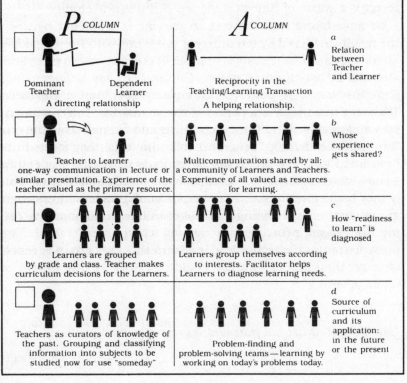

P COLUMN

Dominant Teacher — Dependent Learner
A directing relationship

A COLUMN

Reciprocity in the Teaching/Learning Transaction
A helping relationship.

a Relation between Teacher and Learner

Teacher to Learner one-way communication in lecture or similar presentation. Experience of the teacher valued as the primary resource.

Multicommunication shared by all: a community of Learners and Teachers. Experience of all valued as resources for learning.

b Whose experience gets shared?

Learners are grouped by grade and class. Teacher makes curriculum decisions for the Learners.

Learners group themselves according to interests. Facilitator helps Learners to diagnose learning needs.

c How "readiness to learn" is diagnosed

Teachers as curators of knowledge of the past. Grouping and classifying information into subjects to be studied now for use "someday"

Problem-finding and problem-solving teams—learning by working on today's problems today.

d Source of curriculum and its application: in the future or the present

3. "Critical Mass" Must Be Reached

Peter Drucker feels that an organization must train at least 30 percent of any group in order to affect the whole in any way. Our experience suggests his figure is too conservative. Changing an individual's behavior is dependent on three interconnected factors: (1) the *content* and *process* of the training; (2) the rewards or punishments for using the skills emanating from his or her manager; and (3) the examples and experiences of peers.

Since we've already looked at 1 and 2, let's examine peer pressure. We know that a peer group exerts enormous pressure to conform. Only loners or exceptionally strong individuals escape this powerful social pressure. In leadership development, peer pressure will either defeat the effort or boost it to even higher levels.

That's where critical mass comes in. If a leadership-skills program is given haphazardly to only a few people, the group norm will not shift significantly. If the skill program is of poor quality or accompanied by little management involvement, the result is a waste of time and money. Nothing will change.

We have found that there is an enormous difference between the results achieved by ten different programs with twenty people attending each one (cafeteria approach) and one or two programs attended by two hundred people. *Cultural change happens only with the latter.* A powerful example comes from a Northern Telecom division. Over a period of twelve months, thirty supervisors and managers built their coaching and team skills using our "Frontline Leadership" program. Following this, they formed the Frontline Club. The group meets regularly to discuss leadership issues, share experiences, solve problems, and so on. Occasionally they invite guest speakers or senior managers to address their group. Just imagine being a manager in this division and violating the basic principles or not practicing leadership! The pressure to be an effective leader within this peer group is much stronger than that anyone else could ever bring to bear on any of its members!

"Mr. Morgan buys his partners; I grow my own."

—Andrew Carnegie

4. There Must Be Spaced Repetition

The move away from five-day marathon meetings along with the growing decentralization of training provides another important benefit: spaced repetition of development sessions. These extend the leadership-skills program over a longer period of time, perhaps one session a week for ten, fifteen or even twenty weeks. Participants are thus able to work at a new skill *on the job* and come back to report on their experience and to get further help and ideas from others.

This approach shows yet another benefit of developing manager-trainers. Trainers are then available in larger numbers and at regional or divisional levels to deliver sessions over a period of time. These sessions cause only minimal disruption to the manager-trainer's regular management job.

Zenger and Russ-Eft found that spaced repetition is more effective than "massed training": "Research confirms the general superiority of spacing the sessions of behavior modeling out over time." They did find, however, that variations of grouped, but spaced, one or two-day sessions work well. This finding is consistent with our experience.

CHAPTER THIRTEEN

World of Change, World of Learning

"Leadership and learning are indispensable to each other."

—John F. Kennedy

The fact that you have read this far indicates that you have at least some belief in leadership development. This chapter is designed to remove any doubts you may have that an *effective* leadership-skills-development strategy can pay enormous performance dividends. All pathways to improved quality, service, innovation, and productivity begin with leadership development. The tools and techniques—your organization's technology and management systems—are only as good as the people using them.

Today's managers must improve their personal-, coaching-, team-, and cultural-leadership skills if they hope to adapt themselves or their organizations to our strange and changing new world. Today's employees must enlarge their responsibilities, involvement, and leadership skills if they are to be innovative and productive and to provide improved quality and service. So how do we adapt? Obviously, through heavy amounts of training, retraining, and organization development.

But once again, obviously, the obvious isn't so obvious. Flying in the face of this "obvious" logic are an alarming number of near-sighted technomanagers, concerned mainly with "next quarter's earnings." They don't see development as a "must do" investment, but as a "nice to do" cost.

Tom Peters is emphatic: training and development forms the cornerstone of an organization that can stand up to the chaotic changes swirling about us. He finds that training is both "a national disgrace [and] an epic opportunity." He quotes the highly successful Ross Perot, founder of Electronic Data Systems:

"Brains and wits will beat capital spending ten times out of ten." Peters gives another example of an industry giant with a long history of growth through training that is again using training and development to reshape its company: "Today, IBM is facing major problems in many of its markets. It is doing many things to turn the tide, but none more important than massive retraining aimed at equipping the work force for the new challenge . . . . Only constant training will provide the basis for constant adaptation."

"The secret of success in life is for a man to be ready for his opportunity when it comes."

—Benjamin Disraeli

Here Comes the Training Wave

"We are about to go into the training and retraining business on a tremendous scale . . . more than simple occupational skills. The new industries operate in, or create, a new culture as well—they bring new values: they reward new attitudes and lifestyles . . . . It's a cultural jump as well as merely a change in job skills . . . . Unless we help them enter the new cultures as well as the new economy, we are going to tear society apart."
—Alvin Toffler, Futurist

"Whereas in former years an organization could expect reasonable periods of technological stability between waves of change, today, in more and more industries, one change rapidly follows another. The purpose of training is to help people develop skills, not only for today's technology, but for tomorrow's and the day after's . . . . Learning has to be continuous because organizations face continual change of products, services, processes, markets, and competition, as well as technology. *Since everyone is caught up in change, everyone should be involved in learning.*"
—The Work in America Institute report, "Training for New Technology"

"I am still learning."

—Michelangelo's motto

LEADERSHIP: A LIFELONG JOURNEY

Leadership-skill building is not just a sometime thing; it is a lifetime thing. Like muscles, the skills, information, and abilities you had *last* week need exercising *this* week or they will soften from lack of use. Training and development must be ongoing, not something you did once during your school days. Simply flashing your diploma as "proof of innoculation" may have done the trick

---

Pay Now or Later

Many organizations proclaim their desire to improve, but find the cost in time and money too great. If training is expensive, what then is the cost of weak leadership skills (Cost of Skills)?

—Promotion from within becomes difficult. Failure rates and turnover skyrocket. According to a 1980 survey of sixty-four companies, replacing first and second levels of supervision costs an organization $57,000. If outside managers and executives are parachuted in, there is a hidden cost for the initial decline in morale and the deflation of the company's internal pride.

—Poorly skilled supervisors and managers severely curb the productivity of employees and professionals while at the same time stunting management potential.

—Without constant creative stimulus and experimentation, innovation suffocates.

—Poor team and coaching skills result in mediocre customer service and poor quality.

—Employees and managers who haven't learned how to serve their "internal" customers won't do much better with "external" ones.

—Union grievances increase in the absence of leadership skills. (A transit company client saw a 40 percent decline in labor problems shortly after implementation of a coaching-leadership program.)

---

yesterday, but it won't do so today or tomorrow. Learning? Skill building? "I did all that stuff. I live in the real world!" is an all-too-familiar refrain. *The "real world" of today swallows whole those who know what they are doing but don't do what they know.* We have a name for individuals who understand that development *and* application continue long after one leaves the hallowed halls of academe, and that the road to high performance is accessible only to those who keep renewing these skills while traveling it. It's a name we have used before: *leaders.*

"In life it is training rather than birth which counts."

—Ihara Saikaku

THE GOOD NEWS: LEADERS ARE MADE, NOT BORN

One of the more subtle ironies of our approach to performance is that debating where leadership comes from, although interesting, plays a distant second fiddle to *becoming a leader.*

Would a starving individual stay home and grumble that the only ones who know where to find food are fat people? Of course not—he would go out and find something to eat! Find it, buy it, hunt it—it makes no difference: you can't satisfy a churning stomach with theories about who gets to eat and who doesn't.

To get to the top of an oak tree, you can climb it branch by branch, or sit on an acorn and wait for it to sprout! Looking for "born leaders" is as foolhardy as sitting on an acorn. Developing leadership, on the other hand, is a reliable and direct route—one that produces measurable results.

"The intellect, character and skill possessed by any man are the product of certain original tendencies and the training which they received." —Edward Lee Thorndike

There is a growing body of evidence to show that leaders are made, not born. Bennis and Nanus, after sifting through the results of their five-year research project on leadership, discovered that: "When we asked ninety leaders about the personal qualities they needed to run their organizations, they never mentioned charisma, or dressing for success, or time management, or any glib formula . . . . Above all, they talked about *Learning* . . . the major capacities and competencies of leadership can be learned. Nurture is as important as nature in determining who can become a successful leader."

Donald Seibert, retired J.C. Penney chairman, argues that leaders are made, not born: "An upper level executive doesn't appear in his job out of nowhere. He's usually been in his field—and often in the same company—for decades." What sets such a person apart from his peers, he concludes, is the extra care taken to master the skills of his craft.

One of her coaches once said of Nadia Comaneci, the young gymnast who stunned the sports world with a "perfect 10" performance at the Montreal Olympics: "We almost cut her from the team when she was eight years old. There were so many other eight-year-olds better than she was. But she had such fire in her eyes! *Sometimes people that determined can fool you!*" (In a similar vein, golf superstar Arnold Palmer is reported to have observed: "The more I practice and work at my game, the luckier I get.")

"If I had eight hours to chop down a tree, I'd spend six sharpening my axe."

—Abraham Lincoln

Roads to success and accomplishment *are* accessible to those who have the drive and self-determination to choose them. The hallmark of virtually all great leaders, speakers, athletes, and

---

"Rainy Days and Chopping Trees"

The "leaky roof" dilemma: when times are good, many organizations don't feel the need for training. When times are bad they can't afford the time or the money.

The "woodcutter's" dilemma: when tree-chopping production drops, it's time to sharpen the axe. "But I don't have time to stop and sharpen it," puffs the woodcutter. *"I am too busy chopping trees!"*

"I shall prepare myself and my opportunity must come."

—Abraham Lincoln

"But I Am Not a Born Leader!"

It is easy to dismiss strong leadership as the product of auspicious genes or luck; but throwing up our hands and making excuses is a cop-out:

"Developing into an upper level executive is a lot like developing a top-flight professional athlete . . . . It may seem that certain star athletes burst onto the scene out of nowwhere [but] a closer study of their background and training usually shows years of perspiration and hard work."
  —Donald Seibert, former J.C. Penney chairman

"Biographies of great leaders sometimes read as if they had entered the world with an extraordinary genetic endowment. . . . Don't believe it!"
  —Warren Bennis and Burt Nanus (after completing their study of ninety top leaders in various fields)

"I don't think anyone is a born leader. A person who aspires to a high managerial position can develop the necessary skills if he or she is ambitious and dedicated enough."
  —Buck Rodgers, retired vice-president, marketing, IBM

"Peak performers are made, not born . . . . Every one of the peak performers we studied confirms that the gap can be spanned. People can learn how to be peak performers . . . . Pavarotti was an average singer in the boys' choir when he was a teenager. The only reason they let him stay was because his father ran it . . . . He studied and practiced and trained."
  —Charles Garfield (after a nineteen-year study of 450 outstanding individuals)

Education specialist Benjamin Bloom of the University of Chicago spent four years studying highly successful athletes, artists, and scholars. He found that none had been child prodigies. Each had spent more than fifteen years perfecting his or her craft.

other outstanding individuals is an overpowering willingness to take what they have and make it better.

Organizations desiring the fruits of performance — productivity, quality, innovation, and service — must examine their commitment to the process of leadership-skill building within their only unlimited asset — people.

SKILL DEVELOPMENT: PATHWAY TO HIGHER ORGANIZATION PERFORMANCE

"In the information society, education is no mere amenity; it is the prime tool for growing people . . . and profits"
—John Naisbitt and Patricia Aburdene, *Re-Inventing the Corporation*

Alvin Toffler observed that the illiterates of this age of information will not be just those who cannot read or write, but also those who cannot learn or relearn.

Ron Zemke notes: "In the 1890s John Patterson, founder of National Cash Register, became so determined to communicate his vision of the organization he was building that he created the first sales-training manual and started the world's first company-sponsored sales-training school to ensure that his message got across to the troops. In 1922, when Patterson died, NCR held 90 percent of the U.S. cash-register business and was dominant in the industry."

Skill-Development Pays

The Manpower Services Commission NEDO report on skill-development programs in the U.K. states: "The link between corporate performance and training investment has been proved . . . . [Data showed] that whereas high performance companies had 8.9 days training per employee per year, low performers showed only 2.8 days. High performers showed nearly a 25 percent increase in training activity over the past five years, but low performers reported a 20 percent decline."

"Men are anxious to improve their circumstances, but unwilling to improve themselves; therefore they remain bound."

—James Allen

Why Aren't Leadership Skills Developed??

In our experience, the following are reasons (or excuses) that explain why leadership skills are often underdeveloped:

—The training process used doesn't work.

—The notions of "management" and "leadership" are muddled or confused.

—"I know all that stuff," or "I took a course once," become the stock responses.

—The pride hurdle. Management trainer Rebecca Morgan comments: "To participate [train] is to make oneself vulnerable. Some managers feel they must appear flawless to the staff; if they show shortcomings, areas of weakness, they believe they will lose their staff's respect . . . . Instead we must reinforce the positive side of vulnerability: Vulnerability is weakness only when coupled with passivity; vulnerability plus strength equals power. It takes a big person to admit areas of him or herself that need improvement."

—Most training and development programs simply don't work!

—"You can't teach an old dog new tricks." Well, you aren't a dog and these aren't tricks! Many veterans have dramatically improved their skills late in life.

—Basic leadership skills are confused with "subskills," such as body language. These are fun exercises, but useless. Develop leadership skills and the rest will follow.

—Senior management remains detached. Lip service isn't commitment, nor is throwing money at the problem. If this item describes your organization, don't use it as an excuse. Many organizations have found ways to develop in spite of senior management.

Tom Watson, Sr., IBM's founder, believed that the company's annual investment in education, training, and internal communication should increase at a rate greater than the company's internal financial rate of growth. Each year, every IBM manager is given forty hours of training—even customers are routinely invited to participate in training sessions! Buck Rodgers says: "It's estimated that an experienced IBM marketing rep will spend fifteen days each year in the classroom." The company's Ray Zayyad, president of the "general products" division, comments: "That's like having two of our entire fifteen divisions in class—every day!"

The Motorola company requires each division to set aside a minimum of 1.5 percent of each employee's salary to be used for training. Company spokesperson Ed Bales commented: "This is not a negotiable item . . . . The funds come out of profits. *This is never seen as an expense.*" The company boasts that it provides more than three million days of training a year to more than 90,000 employees worldwide. According to the company, the trackable payoff from the program is in the "multimillions" of dollars.

In stark contrast are companies that routinely spend 1 to 10 percent of their revenue on advertising, sales, and marketing, while relegating training to the "miscellaneous" column along with charitable donations.

Charles Garfield says bluntly, "Top performers do not leave training to chance." He continues: "A rule of thumb . . . is that when times get tough and companies look for ways to reduce budgets, the marginal ones—which have seen training all along as a fringe benefit—often cut their training programs. By contrast, *peak-performing companies often increase theirs.*"

"My degree was a kind of innoculation. I got just enough of it to make me immune for the rest of my life."

—Alan Bennett

THAT "OTHER" EFFECT OF SKILL DEVELOPMENT

Beyond its impact on the organization's bottom line, skill development conveys a message that the organization thinks its employees are partners in success. People instinctively react in a positive way to indications from others that they matter. It puts trainees into "larger fish tanks." Tom Peters found this factor at the heart of grocery-store entrepreneur Stew Leonard's phenomenal success. "Leonard focuses on courtesy and communication skills; the shoddy training of most retail clerks focuses on how to run the cash register—and what a message that sends!"

Training is synergistic: changing behavior frequently improves or upgrades the group's standards and culture. Effective training enhances team communication and byplay; this, in turn, benefits other groups and teams throughout the organization. Training has many messages, but if one had to be selected to take precedence over the others, it would be this: *People count here. We intend to give you every opportunity to develop your potential and improve your contributions.*

FINALLY: A LESSON FROM THE CHINESE BAMBOO

Myopic "this-quarter's-earnings" technomanagers want to see an immediate payoff from training. High-performing organizations demand that development programs quickly and measureably change behavior, but know that the effect on service, quality, innovation, and productivity is cumulative. Consider the Chinese bamboo: the seed is planted. It is watered. It is fertilized. But the first year nothing happens. The second year it is watered and fertilized again, but again nothing happens. The same process is repeated during the third and fourth years, still nothing happens. Yet during the fifth year, in a period lasting no more than six weeks, the bamboo grows ninety feet.

Did the bamboo grow ninety feet in six weeks, or ninety feet in five years? The answer is five years because, at any time during that interval, had fertilizing and watering *not* been maintained, the plant would have died.

Shifts in leadership skills (and subsequently in culture) take time, effort, and persistence. They also require effective development processes. But once the effects take hold, results often measure double-digit percentage increases. The return on *effective* training-and-development investments is proving to be enormous.

EVALUATING SKILL-DEVELOPMENT EFFORTS

In "Assessing Training Results: It's Time to Take the Plunge!", Jack Zenger and Kenneth Hargis outline five ways to evaluate the payback of any leadership-development effort:

1. Assess participants' reactions to a program (happy sheets).
2. Collect anecdotes, incidents, or testimonials.
3. Measure knowledge gains.
4. Assess behavior change.
5. Collect data about organizational performance.

As we've discussed, Happy Sheets may give some useful information if something is causing participants to resist the training. *However, these give no indication of whether anything has changed on the job.*

Anecdotes and testimonials help spread enthusiasm, but they offer no objective assessment of changes in the real world.

Like school exams, knowledge testing will tell you whether participants have learned anything. But once again — knowing isn't doing. "How to motivate" programs that teach Maslow's Hierarchy of Human Needs don't help participants get Mary to work on time.

Measuring organizational performance is obviously the clearest way to assess whether improved leadership skills have improved organizational performance. Some of our clients have zealously measured quality levels, service, innovation, productivity, absenteeism, grievances, safety records, and even turnover. While many are convinced that the leadership-skills program was the cause of substantial improvement, there's no decisive way to establish that fact. Other variables like the economy, prior technology, management systems, political climate, competition — all these will have played a role.

So how to assess behavior change? Zenger-Miller has developed its considerable reputation for effective training systems by measuring behavior change on the job. They give questionnaires to the employees and managers of those attending the training as well as the participants themselves. Questionnaires are administered before and after training to measure the change over time. Experimental groups (those who were trained) and control groups (those not trained) are used to guarantee that observed changes are the result of training and not some other factor.

This process was recently refined further by Tom Janz, assistant professor at the University of Calgary. Working with Achieve, Tom developed "clusters" of leadership skills and organizational elements using our Vision Integrated Performance model as well as data collected by Zenger-Miller from dozens of studies conducted for their clients. From that data base, Tom was able to determine how much groups who scored average or below before training would improve if they followed our behavior-modeling process. The "skill-improvement-potential" gap allows an organization to assess in advance the impact of developing the four leadership skills. This approach also allows an organization to assess not only the impact of a leadership-development program on a particular skill cluster (eg. coaching leadership) but also to assess the broader impact on vision, values, culture, and the other three leadership skills. Tom also added a section to assess perceptions of potential and actual effectiveness in improving quality, service, innovation, and productivity. The audit not only measures the impact before and after training, but also is a useful tool for assessing leadership and culture needs.

NOTES

CHAPTER 1
Page 5
Naisbitt, John, *Megatrends*, Warner, New York, 1984.

Page 6 (box)
"Time's Man of Year": Frank Clement, "New Technologies and Instruction," *NSPI Journal*, February 1983. Page 35.

"Information more important than gold": Tim Smart, Orlando Sentinel as reported by Toronto Star, June 23, 1985.

"50% of published research": Cited by Terrence E. Deal and Allan A. Kennedy, *Corporate Cultures: The Rites and Rituals of Corporate Life*, Addison-Wesley Reading, 1982. Page 178.

"90% of scientists alive now": Cited by Charles Garfield, *Peak Performers: The New Heroes of American Business*, Morrow, New York, 1986. Page 236.

Page 6
"48% of workforce": David N. Campbell, R.L. Fleming and Richard C. Grote, "Discipline Without Punishment—At Last," *Harvard Business Review*, July–August 1985. Page 163.

"1957 AT & T study": David Miller, "Not-me Generation Shuns Job Ambition," Toronto Star, January 23, 1983.

"1980 study": ibid.

Page 7
"half the electorate by 1988": Thomas Moore, "The New Libertarians Make Waves," *Fortune*, August 5, 1985. Page 74.

"63% of entrepreneurs under 65": ibid.

Page 7 (box)
"Yankelovitch survey": Cited by Perry Pascarella, *The New Achievers*, Free Press, New York, 1984. Page 21.

"Public Agenda Foundation studies": Cited by Warren Bennis and Burt Nanus, *Leaders: Strategies for Taking Charge*, Harper and Row, New York, 1985. Page 7.

"U.S. Chamber of Commerce": Pascarella, page 38.

"Connecticut Mutual Life Insurance Co. study": Ibid. Page 38.

Page 8
"2/3 decline Kraft transfers": Miller.

Toffler, Alvin, *Previews and Premises*, Bantam, New York, 1985. Pages 59–60.

"white collar outnumbering blue collar": Ronald Anderson, "Technology Forces Managers to Rethink Work Traditions," *Globe and Mail*, June 16, 1983.

"plight of farmers": Cited by Peter Drucker, *The Changing World of the Executive*, Random House, New York, 1982. Page xiv.

"wages and sales 80–90% of national income": Ibid., page 146.

"Cogniculture": Garfield, page 254.

Page 9
"gold-collar workers": Kelley, Robert E., *The Gold-Collar Worker*, Addison-Wesley, Reading, 1985.

Page 10
Toffler, page 76.

Ibid., page 15.

Page 11
"75% of machined parts": Gene Bylinsky, "The Race to the Automatic Factory," *Fortune*, February 21, 1983. Page 53.

"Flexible manufacturing": Ibid.

"*Fortune* suggests": Ibid., page 58.

Page 13 (box)
Bolles, Dick, *The Three Boxes of Life; And How to Get Out of Them*, Ten Speed Press, Berkeley, 1978. Page 33.

Page 14
O'Toole, James, *Vanguard Management: Redesigning the Corporate Future*, Doubleday, New York, 1985. Page 151.

"Mennen Company": O'Toole, page 151.

Page 15 (box)
Peters, pages xi, 3, 10, 11, 35, 45.

Page 16
"Strategic Planning Institute Studies": Peters, page 67.

Peters, Thomas J. and Waterman, Jr., Robert H., *In Search of Excellence: Lessons From America's Best-Run Companies*, Harper and Row, New York, 1982.

"Dunkin' Donuts": From *The Winning Performance: How America's High-Growth Midsize Companies Succeed*, by Donald K. Clifford Jr. and Richard E. Cavanagh, Bantam, New York, 1985. Page 66.

Page 17
"why people leave car dealers": Tom Peters cites a survey he found in Fay Borbour's book, *Deals on Wheels*, "Deliver What you Demand," *Success*, September 1985. Page 14.

"reasons for not complaining": TARP's White House Study. Cited in "Customer/Service Complaint Handling Management," produced by Technical Assistance Research Programs, Washington, D.C.

Albrecht, Karl, and Zemke, Ron, *Service America: Doing Business in the New Economy*, Dow Jones-Irwin, Homewood, 1985. Page 81.

Page 18
Ibid., page 98.

"Theodore Levitt": ibid., page 4.

Page 19
"Proctor and Gamble's 800 number": Ibid., pages 7 and 13.

Ibid., page 13.

Kanter, Rosabeth Moss, *The Change Masters: Innovation and Productivity in the American Corporation*, Simon and Schuster, New York, 1983. Page 20.

Page 20
Moss, page 39.

Page 20 (box)
"Xerox 9900 copier": Hirotaka Takeuchi and Ikujiro Nonaka, "The New Product Development Game," *Harvard Business Review*, January–February 1986. Page 144.

"John Sculley at Apple": Ibid.

"Yamaha threatens Honda": Ibid.

"Compaq's product development": Bro Uttal, "Speeding New Ideas to Market": *Fortune*, March 2, 1987. Page 63.

"Philips V2000 video disc player": Ibid., page 64.

Page 21 (box)
"American Business Centre study": Clifford and Cavanaugh.

Page 22
Drucker, Peter, *Innovation and Entrepreneurship: Practice and Principles*, Harper and Row, New York, 1985. Page 34.

Page 23
"Gord Forward of Chapparal Steel": Alan M. Kantrow, "Wide Open Management at Chaparal Steel," *Harvard Business Review*, May–June 1986. Page 99.

Ranftl, Robert, "Training Managers for High Productivity," paper presented at NASA National Productivity Conference, September 1985.

Page 24
Skinner, Wickham, "The Productivity Paradox," *Harvard Business Review*, July–August 1986. Page 56.

"American Society for Quality Control": from "Easy as Apple Pie," a booklet produced by the American Society for Quality Control, Milwaukee, WI. Page 2.

Page 25 (box)
Goodman, John, "The Dark Side of Productivity Improvement," *Mobius*, October 1982. Pages 12 and 13.

CHAPTER 2
Page 28
"field of science": From *Speaker's Lifetime Library* by Leonard and Thelma Spinrad, Parker, New York, 1979. Pages 218 and 219.

Page 29
Curley, Kathleen and Pyburn, Philip, "'Intellectual' Technologies: The Key to Improving White-Collar Productivity," *Sloan Management Review*, Fall 1982. Page 33.

Levitt, Theodore, "Management and the Post Industrial Society," *The Public Interest*, Summer 1976. Page 73.

Page 30
Lippitt, Ron, "Leadership: A Performing Art in a Complex Society," *Training and Development Journal*, March 1983. Page 72.

Prentice, William, "Understanding Leadership," *Executive Success: Making It In Management*. Edited by Eliza G.C. Collins, Wiley, New York, 1983. Page 140.

Page 34
Cole, Robert E., "Target Information for Competitive Performance," *Harvard Business Review*, May–June 1985. Page 100.

Page 35
Peters, Tom and Austin, Nancy, *A Passion for Excellence: The Leadership Difference*, Random House, 1985. Page xvii.

Page 36 (box)
"dark side of cost efficiency": From *The Official Explanations* by Paul Dickson, Delacorte, New York, 1980. Pages 54–55.

Page 37
"Fortune magazine": From "Corporate Strategists Under Fire", Walter Kiechel III, *Fortune*, December 27, 1982. Page 36.

Page 38
"Senator Lawton Chiles": Dickson, page 24.

Page 43
Fromm, Erich, *The Revolution of Hope: Toward a Humanized Society*, Harper and Row, New York, 1968. Page 44.

Page 44 (box)
"Stephen Roach": Quoted by William Bowen, "The Puny Payoff from Office Computers," *Fortune*, May 26, 1986. Page 20.

"MIT study": Cited by Joel Dreyfuss, "Toyota Takes Off the Gloves," *Fortune*, December 22, 1986. Page 78.

"International Data Systems": Cited by Robert E. Cole in "Target Information for Competitive Performance," page 103.

"flexible manufacturing systems": Reported by Ramchandran Jaikumar, "Postindustrial Manufacturing," *Harvard Business Review*, November–December 1986. Pages 69–70.

Peters, page 31.

Page 46
Levinson, Harry, "Asinine Attitudes Toward Motivation," *Harvard Business Review*, January–February 1973. Page 74.

Page 46 (box)
"Alfred Sloan": O'Toole, page 56.

Page 47
Janz, Tom, "On the Compelling Link Between Motivational Culture and the Causes of Unionization," Unpublished bulletin, Human Performance Systems, Inc., Calgary, Alberta.

Page 48 (box)
Quinn, Brian, "Managing Innovation: Controlled Chaos," *Harvard Business Review*, May–June 1985. Page 82.

Pascarella, page 47.

"Mary Cunningham": Pascarella, page 159.

Albrecht and Zemke, page 78.

Page 49 (box)
Schrank, Robert, *Ten Thousand Working Days*, MIT Press, Cambridge, 1978. Page 141.

Page 50
Cole, Robert, "Target Information for Competitive Performance," pages 100–109.

Page 53
Barnes, Louis, "The Paradox of Organizational Trust," *Executive Success: Making It In Management*. Edited by Eliza G.C. Collins, Wiley, New York, 1983. Page 371.

Page 54
Von Oech, Roger, *A Whack on the Side of the Head*, Warner, New York, 1983. Page 32.

Page 55 (box)
"Walter C. Minnick": From a letter to the editors of *Harvard Business Review*, November–December 1986.

"George Klemp": Quoted in an item entitled, "Shuttle Disaster Linked to Experts' Lack of 'Influence Skills,'" *Training and Development Journal*, September 1986. Page 8.

Cound, Dana M., "A Call For Leadership," *Quality Progress*, March 1987. Page 12.

Page 56
Skinner, Wickham and Sasser, Earl, "Managers with Impact: Versatile and Inconsistent," *Harvard Business Review*, November–December 1977. Page 144.

Page 57 (box)
"Carnegie Foundation study": Cited by Jim Cathcart, "Voices of Experience," audio cassette, National Speaker's Association, June 1985.

CHAPTER 3
Page 61
Peters, page 400.

Page 62
Ohmann, O.A., "Skyhooks," *Executive Success: Making It in Management*. Edited by Eliza G.C. Collins, Wiley, New York, 1983. Page 199.

Collins, page 199.

Page 64 (box)
Garfield, Charles, *Peak Performance: Mental Training Techniques of the World's Greatest Athletes*, Torcher, Los Angeles, 1984. Page 66.

Page 65
"Karl Wallenda," Bennis and Nanus, page 70.

Fromm, page 23.

Kanter, page 304.

"Robert Haas": Quoted by David Freudberg, *The Corporate Conscience: Money, Power and Responsible Business*, Amacom, New York, 1986. Page 209.

"Tom Watson": Garfield, *Peak Performers*, pages 81 and 222.

"Peter Drucker": *Peak Performers*, page 81.

O'Toole, page 266.

Page 69 (box)
"William O'Brien": Quoted by John Naisbitt and Patricia Aburdene, *Reinventing the Corporation*, Warner, New York, 1985. Page 21.

"McBer and Company": From "American Work Force Underused by Management," *Training and Development Journal*, October 1985.

Page 70
"Jean Ribaud": Cited by Jack Zenger, "Leadership: Management's Better Half," *Training*, December 1985.

Page 71
Garfield, *Peak Performers*, page 87.

Page 71 (box)
Bennis and Nanus, pages 28, 30, 39, 89, 90, 91, 101.

Page 72 (box)
Quinn, Brian, "Managing Innovation: Controlled Chaos," *Harvard Business Review*, May–June 1985. Page 78.

"William Bricker": Quoted by Robert H. Hayes, "Strategic Planning—Forward in Reverse," *Harvard Business Review*, November–December 1985. Page 114.

Page 73
"gas company survey": An item entitled "Pay's Role" in *Success*, April 1985.

Page 74
Naisbitt and Aburdene, page 21.

CHAPTER 4
Page 76
"James Cash Penney": O'Toole, page 391.

Page 77
"Michael McCaskey": Quoted by David March of the Boston *Globe*, *Toronto Star*, "Who's Behind the Refrigerator," *Toronto Star*, December 1, 1985. Page B-4.

Page 78 (box)
"Jean Coyle": Cited by Chris Lee, "Raiders of the Corporate Culture," *Training*, February 1984. Page 32.

Page 79
Rodgers, Buck, *The IBM Way: Insights Into the World's Most Successful Marketing Organization*, Harper and Row, 1986. Pages 10, 19.

"James Burke": Quoted by Richard S. Ruch and Ronald Goodman, *Image at the Top: Crisis and Renaissance in Corporate Leadership*, Free Press, New York, 1983. Page 38.

Page 80
McNeil, Art, *The "I" of the Hurricane: Creating Corporate Energy*, Stoddard, Toronto, 1987.

Page 80 (box)
Tulega, Tad, *Beyond the Bottom Line: How Business Leaders are Turning Principles into Profits*, 1985. Soundview Executive Book Summaries, Briston, VT. Page 3.

Page 82 (box)
Pascale, Richard, "Fitting New Employees into the Corporate Culture," *Fortune*, May 28, 1984. Page 38.

McCoy, Bowen H., "The Parable of the Sadhu," *Harvard Business Review*, September–October 1983. Page 106.

Page 83
"Charlie Sporck": Cited by Jack Zenger, "Leadership: Management's Better Half," *Training*, December 1985.

Pages 84–85
"Atari manager": From "Fitting New Employees into the Corporate Culture," by Richard Pascale, page 39.

Page 85 (box)
"Levi Strauss executive": O'Toole, page 154.

Page 86 (box)
"Values Challenge Maslow?": Drawn from *Beyond Self-Actualization: The Persuasion of Pygmalion*, by Gerald D. Baxter and John K. Bowers, *Training and Development Journal*, August 1985. Page 70.

Page 87 (box)
Pascarella, pages 101, 102, 105, 175, 176.

Page 88
O'Toole, page 53.

Page 89 (box)
"Irving Kristol": Ruch and Goodman.

Page 90
"Boston College study": Garfield, *Peak Performers*, page 103.

Freudberg, page 5.

CHAPTER 5
Page 92
"Martin Bower": Deal and Kennedy, page 4.

Peters and Waterman, page 77.

Clifford and Cavanaugh, page 14.

"Bob Waterman": Quoted in *Success*, April 1983. Page 41.

Pascale.

Page 98 (box)
"Noland Archibald": In a letter to the editors of *Harvard Business Review*, November–December 1986.

Page 100 (box)
"U.S. Department of Agriculture study": From "Beyond the Myth of Leadership-Style Training—Planned Organizational Change," by Craig Dreilinger, Richard McElheny, Bruce Robinson and Dan Rice, *Training & Development Journal*, October 1982. Page 71.

Page 101
"Eliza Doolittle": From "Beyond Self-Actualization by Gerald D. Baxter and John K. Bowers, page 69.

Pages 101–102
"Goodfellow, Matthew": "Why You Should Train Now to Prevent Strikes Later," *Training/HRD*, June 1982. Page 38.

Pages 102–103
Bennis, Warren, *The Unconscious Conspiracy: Why Leaders Can't Lead*, Amacom, New York, 1976. Page 174.

Page 103 (box)
Livingston, Sterling J., "Pygmalion in Management," *Harvard Business Review*, July–August 1969.

Pages 103–104
Townsend, Robert, *Further Up the Organization: How to Stop Management from Stifling People and Strangling Productivity*, Knopf, New York, 1984. Page 140.

Page 105
O'Toole, pages 97–98.

Pages 106–107
"Thornton Bradshaw": Ibid., page 46.

Page 107
Kanter, pages 75 and 228.

Page 107 (box)
Goodfellow, Matthew, "Why You Should Train Now to Prevent Strikes Later," *Training/HRD*, June 1982. Pages 34–38.

"A.H. Whyte": Ibid., page 35.

Bennis and Nanus, page 224.

Ibid., page 56.

Pages 113–114
"Peter Drucker": Quoted by Donna Shaw, "In Search of Leadership," *Canadian Associations Canadiennes*, June 1985. Page 3.

Page 114 (box)
"Marilyn Kennedy": Quoted by *Boardroom Reports*, May 15, 1986.

"Olle Stiwenius": Albrecht and Zemke, page 190.

Naisbitt and Aburdene, pages 52–54.

Kanter, page 397.

Page 116
Kotter, John, "Why Business Has So Few Leaders," *New York Times*, October 20, 1985.

Page 118
"theories of Frederick Herzberg": Pascarella, pages 116–117.

Page 119
Levinson, Harry, "Asinine Attitudes Toward Motivation," *Harvard Business Review*, January–February 1973. Pages 73–74.

Page 120
Fonvielle, William, "Behaviour vs. Attitude: Which Comes First in Organizational Change?," *Management Review*. Page 14.

Page 122 (box)
Livingston, J. Sterling, "Myth of the Well Educated Manager," *Harvard Business Review*, January–February 1971. Page 69.

"J. Williard Marriot, Jr.": Albrecht and Zemke, page 108.

Page 123 (box)
"Kennedy said of Churchill": Quoted by Jim Rohn on audio cassette album, "Take Charge of Your Life," Nightingale-Conant, Chicago, Ill.

Page 128
Collins, pages 397–398.

CHAPTER 6
Page 111 (box)
Peter, Laurence J., *Why Things Go Wrong*, Morrow, New York, 1985. Pages 192–193.

Page 112 (box)
"GM and Toyota joint venture": From *Car & Driver*, July 1986. Page 9.

Page 112
"Wall Street Journal": Cited by Jack Zenger, "Leadership: Management's Better Half," *Training*, December 1985.

CHAPTER 7
Page 131 (box)
Peters, page 39.

Page 132 (box)
Pascarella, page 117.

Page 135 (box)
Ibid., page 148.

"Service Master": From "Lessons in the Service Sector," by James Heskett, *Harvard Business Review*, March–April 1987. Page 121.

Pages 137–140
"Basic Principles": From the management development system, FRONTLINE LEADERSHIP™. Developed by Zenger-Miller, Inc., Cupertino, California. Distributed in Canada by The Achieve Group, Mississauga, Ontario.

Page 139 (box)
Albrecht and Zemke, pages vi–vii.

Pages 140–147
"how to's of Interactive Leadership": From the employee and professional development system, WORKING™. Developed by Zenger-Miller Inc., Cupertino, California. Distributed in Canada by The Achieve Group, Mississauga, Ontario.

Pages 147–148
"Ogilvy and Mather": Peters and Austin, page 352.

CHAPTER 8
Page 151
"Robert Half": Cited by Calvin Lawrence, Jr., "Goofing Off Costs Billions: Survey," *Toronto Star*, January 2, 1983. Page B-6.

Page 152 (box)
"Red Auerbauch": From "Red Auerbauch on Management." An interview by Alan M. Webber, *Harvard Business Review*, March–April 1987, Page 86.

Page 153
"Maryann Keller": From *Car & Driver*, November 1986. Page 36.
"Time magazine": Ibid.

Page 156 (box)
Hurst, David, "Of Boxes, Bubbles, and Effective Management," *Harvard Business Review*, May–June 1984. Page 84.

Townsend, page 161.

Zemke, Ron, "Is Performance Appraisal a Paper Tiger?," *Training*, December 1985. Page 24.

"Honeywell study": Ibid., page 25.

"Dean Spitzer": Ibid.

Page 158 (box)
Blanchard, Ken, "When Should You Fire?," *Success*, September 1985. Page 20.

Pages 159–160
"Donald Petersen": Quoted by Steve Fishman in "New Age Management," *Success*, December 1985. Page 49.

Pages 160–161 (box)
"Taking Corrective Action": FRONTLINE LEADERSHIP™.

Page 161
"Kotter, John P., *Power and Influence: Beyond Formal Authority*, Free Press, New York, 1985. Page 88.

Page 162
"John Robinson": Bennis and Nanus, page 64.

Pages 162–163 (box)
"Novations": Research and programme described in *Novations: Strategies for Career Management*, by Gene W. Dalton and Paul H. Thompson, Scott, Foresman and Company, Glenview, Ill., 1986.

Page 164
"Cohen, Stephen and Jaffee, Cabot": "Managing Human Performance for Productivity," *Training and Development Journal*, December 1982.

Pages 164–165
"Frontline Leadership": Excerpt from "Coaching for Optimal Performance." Page 5. Developed by Zenger-Miller, Inc., Cupertino, California. Distributed in Canada by The Achieve Group, Mississauga, Ontario.

Page 166
Walton, Richard, "From Control to Commitment in the Workplace," *Harvard Business Review*, March–April 1985.

Pages 166–167
Townsend, page 224.

Page 167
Leboeuf, Michael, *The Greatest Management Principal in the World*, Berkley, New York, 1985. Pages 96–97.

Page 168 (box)
"Recognition skill steps": from "Recognizing Positive Results": FRONTLINE LEADERSHIP™.

Page 169
Blanchard, Ken, "Jelly Bean Motivation," *Success*, February 1986. Page 8.

Pages 169–170
"Tom Watson, Sr.": Rodgers, pages 11, 13, 194.

Pages 171–172 (box)
"developing employee skills": from "Developing Job Skills": FRONTLINE LEADERSHIP™.

Pages 172–173
Campbell, David N., Fleming, R.L., and Grote, Richard C., "Discipline Without Punishment—At Last," *Harvard Business Review*, July–August 1985.

Page 174 (box)
"Performance Coaching": from "Coaching for Optimal Performance": FRONTLINE LEADERSHIP™.

Page 175
Leonard, Joseph, "Why MBO Fails So Often," *Training and Development Journal*, June 1986. Page 38.

CHAPTER 9
Page 176
"Franklin Murphy": Bennis and Nanus, page 211.

"William Dyer": Garfield, *Peak Performers*, page 181.

Peters and Waterman, page 155.

Page 178
Kanter, page 401.

"William Ouchi": From "An Interview with William Ouchi," Soundview Summaries, Darien, CT.

Page 180
"Ford Ranger": From "Ford's Drive for Quality," by Jeremy Main, *Fortune*, April 18, 1983. Page 64.

"David Ober": From "How a Textile Firm Expanded Its Business," by Mark Gill, *Success*, May 1986.

Pages 180–182
Kanter, page 167.

"Stew Leonard": Cited by Tom Peters in "Let the Crew Sail the Ship," *Success*, December 1985. Page 12.

"Rockwell's Gene Little": From "The Renaissance of American Quality," *Fortune* supplement, October 14, 1985.

"Management Discovers the Human Side of Automation": *Business Week*, September 29, 1986. Page 74.

Page 181 (box)
"Mellon Bank": From "The Quality Imperative," supplement in *Fortune*, September 29, 1986.

"Gaines Foods": From "Management Discovers the Human Side of Automation," *Business Week*, September 29, 1986. Page 75.

"Honeywell in Arizona": Kanter, page 201.

"General Electric": From "The Revolt Against Working Smarter," by Bill Saporito, *Fortune*, July 21, 1986. Page 59.

"Kubota tractor": Pascarella, page 122.

Page 183
"Business Week cover story": Ibid., page 72.

Pages 184–185
Grove, Andy, "How (And Why) To Run a Meeting," *Fortune*, July 11, 1983.

"Robert Half study": An item entitled "Meeting of the Minds," *Success*, December 1986.

Page 187
Kanter, page 244.

Page 188 (box)
Bradford, David and Cohen, Allan, *Managing for Excellence: The Guide to Developing High Performance in Contemporary Organizations*, Wiley, New York, 1984.

Houghton, James R., "The Old Way of Doing Things is Gone," *Quality Progress*, September 1986.

Page 189
Maier, Norman F., *Problem-Solving Discussions and Conferences*, McGraw-Hill, New York, 1963.

Page 189 (box)
"Tao of Team Leadership": From *The Tao of Leadership: Strategies for a New Age*, by John Heider, Bantam, New York, 1986.

Page 190
"William Weisz": Quoted in "The Renaissance of American Quality," *Fortune* supplement, October 14, 1985.

Pages 191–192
"Group Problem Solving Skills" taken from groupAction™. Developed by Zenger-Miller, Inc., Cupertino, California. Distributed in Canada by The Achieve Group, Mississauga, Ontario.

Page 193
Garvin, David, "Quality on the Line," *Harvard Business Review*, January–February 1987.

"effective meeting skills": from "Conducting Information Exchange Meetings": FRONTLINE LEADERSHIP™.

Pages 193–194
"presenting ideas": from "Presenting Your Ideas": groupAction™.

Page 194
"pulling team together": from "Clarifying Team Roles and Responsibilities": FRONTLINE LEADERSHIP™.

"when trouble comes up": From "Managing Diversity": groupAction™.

Page 196 (box)
"Calvin Coolidge": O'Toole, page 273.

"Alfred Sloan": Von Oech, pages 113–114.

"General Douglas McArthur": Cited by Peter Drucker in an interview by *Boardroom Reports*, "Encourage Dissent at the Top," September 1, 1986.

CHAPTER 10
Page 200 (box)
Kanter, pages 100–101.

Page 201
Ibid., page 278.

Ibid., page 150.

Page 206
Deal and Kennedy, page 167.

Page 208–209 (box)
"Excuses, Excuses, Excuses": From "Reasons Why Not," *The Official Explanations*, Delacorte, 1980. Pages 168–169.

Page 210
Pascarella, page 195.

"James Olson": Quoted in "On a Silver Platter." Booklet from The American Society for Quality Control, Milwaukee, Wisconsin. Page 9.

Pages 210–211
Albrecht and Zemke, page 46.

Page 211
"American Society for Quality Control": From a booklet entitled "Quality First", Milwaukee, Wisconsin.

"Thomas Melohn": Quoted in April 10, 1978 (Vol. 6, #10) issue of *The Productivity Letter*, page 4. From The American Productivity Center, Houston, Texas.

Page 211 (box)
"Vision at General Foods": From "Tailor Executive Development to Strategy", James F. Bolt, *Harvard Business Review*, November–December 1985. Page 173.

Page 214
"Opinion Research Corporation", Ruch and Goodman, page 17.

Kiechel, Walter III, "No Word From On High," *Fortune*, January 6, 1986. Pages 125–126.

Page 215
O'Toole, page 276.

"Bill Hewitt": Ibid., pages 337–338.

Page 217
"Jack Welch": Deal and Kennedy, page 41.

"Holiday Inn manager": From "Accentuate the Positive" by Ken Blanchard, *Success*, November 1986. Page 8.

"bragging at Transco Energy": Ibid.

Page 218
"North American Tool and Die": From "How to Build Employee Trust and Productivity," by Thomas A. Melohn, *Harvard Business Review*, January–February 1983. Page 56.

Page 218 (box)
Argyris, Chris, "Skilled Incompetence," *Harvard Business Review*, September–October 1986. Page 76.

Page 220
O'Toole, page 275.

Page 221
Seibert, Donald, *The Ethical Executive*, by Donald V. Seibert and William Proctor, Cornerstone (Simon and Schuster), New York, 1984. Page 37.

"High Hurdles": Quoted by Robert Bove, "Is This The Dawn of the Non-Information Age?," *Training and Development Journal*, April 1986. Page 45.

Kanter, page 298.

"David Close": From TOWARD EXCELLENCE™ by Zenger-Miller Inc., Cupertino, California. Distributed in Canada by The Achieve Group, Mississauga, Ontario.

Page 222 (box)
Rodgers, page 145.

Deal and Kennedy, page 49.

"Fortune": From "The Revolt Against Working Smarter" by Bill Saporito, *Fortune*, July 21, 1986. Page 58.

"Lakewood GM plant": From "New Age Management" by Steve Fishman, *Success*, December 1985. Page 48.

Page 225
O'Toole, pages 290, 292, 293.

Page 226
"Bert Snider": Clifford and Cavanaugh, page 95.

CHAPTER 11
Page 231 (box)
"Ernie Pyle's advice": From "Performance Appraisal: When Two Jobs are Too Many," *Training*, March 1986. Page 69.

Page 232
Turner, Arthur N., Consulting is More than Giving Advice," *Harvard Business Review*, September–October 1982. Pages 120 and 121.

CHAPTER 12
Page 236
Zenger, Jack, "The Painful Turnabout in Training," *Training and Development Journal*, December 1980.

"Mel Sorcher": Arnold P. Goldstein and Melvin Sorcher, *Changing Supervisor Behaviour*, Pergamon Press, New York, 1974.

Page 237
"Bruner, Jerome S.": *On Knowing: Essays for the Left Hand*, Atheneum, New York, 1973. Page 24.

Page 238
Livingston, Sterling J., "The Myth of the Well Educated Manager," *Harvard Business Review*, January–February 1971. Page 67.

Page 239 (box)
Porras, Jerry and Anderson, Brad, "Improving Managerial Effectiveness Through Modeling-Based Training," *Organizational Dynamics*, Spring 1981. Pages 60–61.

Zenger, Jack, "The Painful Turnabout in Training," *Training and Development Journal*, December 1980.

Goldstein and Sorcher, page 17.

Collins, pages 430–431.

Page 240
"Why Training Fails": From "Employee Training in America," *Training and Development Journal*, July 1986. Page 37, Table 9.

"Xerox studies": Cited by Neil Rackham in "The Coaching Controversy," *Training and Development Journal*, November 1979.

Page 241
Garfield, *Peak Performers*, page 137.

Page 242
"Work in America Institute": From "Training for New Technology, (Part III) Cost-Effective Design and Delivery of Training Programs," Jerome M. Rosow and Robert Zager, Work in America Institute, Scarsdale, N.Y. Page 13.

Page 243 (box)
Gordon, Jack, "The Woo-Woo Factor," *Training*, May 1985. Pages 26–42.

Page 245 (box)
Gunkler, John and Zemke, Ron, "28 Techniques for Transforming Training into Performance," *Training*, April 1985. Page 54.

Porras, Jerry and Anderson, Brad, "Improving Managerial Effectiveness Through Modeling-Based Training," *Organizational Dynamics*, Spring 1981. Pages 71–74.

Zenger, Jack and Russ-Eft, Darlene, "Research on Behaviour Modeling: The Last Five Years," Unpublished paper, Zenger-Miller, Inc., Cupertino, California.

Pages 246–247
Burke, Michael and Day, Russell: Cited by Michael Godkewitsch in "The Dollars and Sense of Corporate Training," *Training*, May 1987. Page 80.

Page 247
Livingston, page 67.

Page 250
Gunkler, John, and Zemke, Ron, "28 Techniques for Transforming Training Into Performance," *Training*, April 1985. Page 57.

Page 251
Zenger and Russ-Eft.

Kirkpatrick, Donald L., "Advice to Trainers: Keep One Eye on the Classroom and One on the Job," *Training and Development Journal*, July 1982. Page 83.

Page 252 (box)
"William Weisz": From "Show This to Your CEO," *Training and Development Journal*, May 1986. Page 47.

"Sir Austin Pearce": Quoted in *Boardroom Reports*, September 15, 1986.

Page 253
"Foss Boyle": Quoted in item entitled "Managers Rewarded for Mentoring," *Training*, July 1986. Page 55.

"Work in America Institute": From "Training for New Technology, (Part II) Toward Continuous Learning," Jerome M. Rosow and Robert Zager, Work In America Institute, Scarsdale, N.Y. Page 14.

Page 254
"Kathy Hanson": Ibid., page 69.

Page 255 (box)
Adapted from: "The 3 Boxes of Life": by Richard Bolles, Ten Speed Press, Berkeley, 1981. Pages 92–93.

Page 256
"Peter Drucker feels": From "Training for Organizational Excellence," a booklet produced by Zenger-Miller, Inc., Cupertino, California.

Page 257
Zenger and Russ-Eft.